Professional Obligations and Approaches to The Aged

Edited by

ARTHUR N. SCHWARTZ, Ph.D.

Ethel Percy Andrus Gerontology Center
University of Southern California
Los Angeles, California

and

IVAN N. MENSH, Ph.D.

Professor and Head
Department of Psychiatry
School of Medicine
University of California
Los Angeles, California

CHARLES C THOMAS • PUBLISHER
Springfield • Illinois • USA

Published and Distributed Throughout the World by

CHARLES C THOMAS • PUBLISHER

BANNERSTONE HOUSE

301-327 East Lawrence Avenue, Springfield, Illinois, U.S.A.

© *1974, by* CHARLES C THOMAS • PUBLISHER

ISBN 0-398-02922-9

Library of Congress Catalog Card Number: 73-10019

With THOMAS BOOKS *careful attention is given to all details of manufacturing and design. It is the Publisher's desire to present books that are satisfactory as to their physical qualities and artistic possibilities and appropriate for their particular use.* THOMAS BOOKS *will be true to those laws of quality that assure a good name and good will.*

Printed in the United States of America

HH-11

Library of Congress Cataloging in Publication Data

Schwartz, Arthur N
   Professional obligations and approaches to the aged.

   1. Aged—United States—Addresses, essays, lectures.
   2. Aging—Addresses, essays, lectures. I. Mensh, Ivan N., joint author.
II. Title. [DNLM: 1. Aged. WT100 S399p 1973]
HV1461.S3   362.6'0973   73-10019
ISBN 0-398-02922-9

To Frances, Betty and Jonathan; to Our Older Citizens, and to Professionals Who Care.

CONTRIBUTORS

JAMES E. BIRREN, Ph.D., Director
Ethel Percy Andrus Gerontology Center
University of Southern California
Los Angeles, California

FRANCES M. CARP, Ph.D.
Research Psychologist
Institute of Urban and Regional Development
University of California
Berkeley, California

YUNG-PING CHEN, Ph.D., Professor
Department of Economics
University of California
Los Angeles, California

DONNA COHEN
Ethel Percy Andrus Gerontology Center
University of Southern California
Psychogenetics Unit
Brentwood VA Hospital
Los Angeles, California

ALBERT G. FELDMAN, Ph.D.
Associate Director for Community Projects
Ethel Percy Andrus Gerontology Center
University of Southern California
Los Angeles, California

FRANCES L. FELDMAN, M.S.W.
Professor of Social Work
University of Southern California
Los Angeles, California

LISSY F. JARVIK, M.D., Ph.D.
Professor of Psychiatry, University of
California at Los Angeles, School of Medicine
Chief, Psychogenetics Unit
Brentwood VA Hospital
Los Angeles, California

OSCAR J. KAPLAN, Ph.D.
Professor of Psychology
California State University
San Diego, California

M. POWELL LAWTON, Ph.D.
Director, Behavioral Research
Philadelphia Geriatric Center
Philadelphia, Pennsylvania

MARION G. MARSHALL, M.A.
Specialist in Gerontology
Los Angeles Unified School District
Division of Continuing Education
Los Angeles, California

ROBERT ONTELL, D.S.W.
Professor of Social Work
California State University
San Diego, California

JAMES A. PETERSON, Ph.D.
Director of Liaison, Professor of Sociology
Ethel Percy Andrus Gerontology Center
University of Southern California
Los Angeles, California

ARTHUR N. SCHWARTZ, Ph.D.
Project Director, Adjunct Professor
Ethel Percy Andrys Gerontology Center
University of Southern California
Los Angeles, California

FRANCES G. SCOTT, Ph.D., Director
Oregon Center for Gerontology
University of Oregon
Eugene, Oregon

ALEXANDER SIMON, M.D.
Professor and Chairman
Department of Psychiatry
University of California School of Medicine
Director, Langley Porter Neuropsychiatric Institute
San Francisco, California

SAUL TOOBERT, Ph.D.,
Professor and Associate Director
University Counseling Center
University of Oregon
Eugene, Oregon

DIANA S. WOODRUFF, Ph.D.
Department of Psychology
University of California
Los Angeles, California

FOREWORD

A few weeks before *Professional Obligations and Approaches to the Aged* was committed to the printer, the Organization for Economic Co-operation and Development issued the first report from its Social Indicator Development Programme. The small booklet, entitled *List of Social Concerns,* identifies twenty-four areas of human aspiration on which there was nearly total consensus among the representatives of the twenty-three American, European and Pacific member nations. The concerns identified by the Organization's Manpower and Social Affairs Committee include: health through all stages of the life cycle; maintenance of participation by the impaired and handicapped; opportunity for self-development, for development of skills and assurance of gainful employment if desired and for choice among modes of utilization of free time; accessibility of goods and services, including suitable housing; control of environmental pollution; personal safety; and opportunity for lifelong community participation. The pervasive awareness of their older populations among the member states is revealed by several direct references to older, aged and retired persons and by recognition that there is no place for an age-associated cutoff in the allocation of national resources. The ultimate objective of the OECD social indicators project is to develop techniques for measuring the extent of dysfunction and progress in achieving aspirations.

In the United States, national attention was directed toward the older population when it became apparent that the dramatic increase in average life expectancy and in the absolute numbers of older people was giving rise to widespread need for maintenance of income during the post-work years and to sharp increases in the prevalence of long-term illness and impairment among the growing numbers surviving into the seventh decade of life and beyond. National conferences on aging in 1950 and in 1961, together with the publication of reports and studies on the circumstances of older people, soon revealed that the range of their problems and needs was much broader than had been supposed and stimulated a good deal of social action.

By the time planning began for the 1971 White House Conference on Aging, the rapidly emerging area of national concern was commanding the attention of legislators, of administrators and practitioners in the wide-ranging welfare, health and social fields and of significant numbers of researchers, teachers and students. Documentation for the conference was able to draw on a relatively large amount of recorded experience and scientific knowledge.

Reflecting the growing sophistification of the field, the Congress, in enacting the legislation for the conference, called for the formulation of proposals designed to provide the basis for a comprehensive national policy for aging. During the fifteen-month preconference period, literally thousands of older people, professional workers, lay leaders and representatives of labor and business worked in older American forums, organization meetings, task forces and community and state conferences to resolve critical policy issues and to prepare recommendations for the guidance of national conference delegates. The large scale involvement of persons of all ages representing urban and rural America, all ethnic groups and all income levels clearly denoted a deepening of national concern for the present and future generations of older people.

The final report of the conference with its considered, far-reaching policy recommendations is an impressive document. Today, more than a dozen federal departments and agencies, every state and territory, scores of communities and voluntary organizations, numerous educational institutions and important elements of the private sector have some type of planned effort responsive to the requirements of older people. Organizations of increasingly articulate older people lobbying for measures to improve their circumstances are able to substantiate their claims for upward of ten million members fifty years of age and over. New federal and state legislative initiatives and enactments—notably in the areas of income security, improved nutritional status and in the intensification of effort to provide comprehensive, coordinated services at the community level—give promise of maintaining the momentum provided by the 1971 White House Conference on Aging.

Professional Obligations and Approaches to the Aged is a product of this rising interest. The underlying philosophy of the book, frankly stated by the Editors, is that human aging is primarily a succession of interrelated losses generated by natural, internal processes and by external environmental and/or cultural factors which operate to deprive older people of positive stimuli and supports which sustained them during the developmental and earlier adult years. The cumulative losses result in reduced competency and opportunity for self-expression, hence weakening personal control over the environment and threatening or destroying the self-esteem essential to well-being and life satisfaction. The challenge issued to the professional community by the editors is to create conditions that enable older people to compensate for losses, to prolong the period of effective functioning and, thus, to enhance, or at least maintain, the quality of living over the second half of the life span.

Specifically, the aim of this book is to provide planners, decision-makers and practitioners with scientific knowledge that will guide their efforts into imaginative productivity, to better equip teachers and students involved in preparation for careers in aging and to stimulate researchers to further pursuit of knowledge about older people and the effectiveness of varied approaches to the design of total societal and community environments suited to their needs. In order to achieve their objectives, the editors recruited fifteen experienced behavioral and social scientists all of whom have committed themselves to careers in the discovery, communication and application of gerontological knowledge.

Fortunately, the compilation of essays becomes available at a time when literally hundreds of person are assuming important responsibilities in planning, advocating and seeking to coordinate comprehensive programming on behalf of older people at community, state and national levels. It is unlikely that many such persons will have had systematic training in social gerontology and its applications; hence, they, along with students and others to whom the book is addressed, should find it valuable in orienting themselves to tested knowledge and creative possibilities in the field.

CLARK TIBBITTS
Administration on Aging
U. S. Department of
Health, Education and Welfare

INTRODUCTION

D URING THE PAST SEVERAL years the concept of "quality of life"
increasingly has been receiving attention. Meaningful as it is,
the phrase lacks definition, even an imprecise one. Yet, our selection of this term has not been accidental or faddish, rather we wish
to convey that the goal of this volume is to maximize the quality of
life of older individuals in our society, through a focus upon the
concepts and methods which gerontologists in many disciplines
can and do use, or propose to do so in the relatively near future,
in upgrading the quality of life of those with and for whom they
work.

Three general areas will be examined. The first involves the
current relationships between the gerontologic professions and
the aged in today's society. The second area concerns the kinds of
training and the requisite emphases required for professional
responsibilities in the field of gerontology. The third focus bears
upon new approaches by gerontologists for enhancing the effectiveness of their work with the aged.

To accomplish the task which we have set for ourselves, we
have enlisted the aid and cooperation of a number of colleagues,
all highly specialized in the respective areas in which they write
and each sharing our goals for the aged and for the professionals
dedicated to work with them.

The ideas of this volume were developed by the senior author
(A.N.S.) and shared with the second editor (I.N.M.). Their
timeliness relates to the then-in-planning sessions of the 1971
White House Conference on Aging, the active and involved commitment of A.N.S. in community-based committees of older citizens under his chairmanship and in his participation in the
conferences of the California State Commission On Aging, and the
participation of I.N.M. on the Task Force on Aging, American
Psychological Association, as a Delegate to the White House
Conference and including preparation of a position paper on

Community Mental Health and other Health Services for the Aged.

The 14 Sections and 17 Special Concerns Sessions of the White House Conference illustrate the range of gerontology. The sections included education; employment and retirement; physical and mental health; housing; income; nutrition; retirement roles and activities; spiritual well-being; transportation; facilities, programs and services; government and non-government organization; planning; research and demonstration; and training. The special concerns included aging and blindness; aging and aged blacks; Asian American elderly; the elderly consumer; mental health care strategies and aging; the older family; homemaker-home health aide services; the elderly Indian; legal aid and the urban aged; long-term care or older people; the poor elderly; rural older people; Spanish speaking elderly; the religious community and the aged; physical and vocational rehabilitation; volunteer roles for older people; and youth and age.

The editors recognize the value of the score and more of areas just listed, but selected from among them the topics of this text, because of the expertise of our colleagues and in order to produce a volume of manageable size.

CONTENTS

Part IV

MULTIDISCIPLINARY STRATEGIES

PROFESSIONAL OBLIGATIONS AND APPROACHES TO THE AGED

PART I

FRAME OF REFERENCE

Chapter I

A TRANSACTIONAL VIEW OF THE AGING PROCESS

Arthur N. Schwartz

STATEMENT OF THE PROBLEM

Iɴ A Rᴇᴄᴇɴᴛ interview published in Life Magazine, Dr. Edwin Land, inventor of the polaroid process and camera, is quoted, "If you are able to state a problem it can be solved." This assertion appears to be a corollary of the ancient dictum attributed to Galton, "If something exists it can be measured." Those who devote their energies to aging research are not long in discovering that the complex dimensions and parameters of the aging process do not readily lend themselves to such summary characterization. Aging indeed exists but is not easily measured. Those who routinely address themselves to the many problems confronting the aged are even more persistently faced with the nagging dilemma of how to state these problems in ways which will elicit society's sustained response and facilitate creative solutions. For gerontological practitioners as well as researchers, this appears to be a matter of no small significance. Obviously, we still have a long and difficult road to travel. To be sure, as many have pointed out, we have even yet to come to terms with an adequate definition of aging.

The anamoly seems to be that today's generation of elderly people is able to articulate its problems readily enough, often with succinctness and precision, at times even with eloquence. In whatever way the professional gerontologist chooses to define the problems of aging and however he chooses to address himself to them (and this is usually more contingent upon the training provided by his professional discipline than upon any other single factor), he surely cannot avoid that singular and overriding concern of the old which intertwines and permeates all other concerns, increasingly so in the later decades of life. This is a concern for a quality of life which translates daily experience into a framework of self-esteem (Schwartz and Proppe, 1970). As evident as the wrinkles on the faces and the gray in the hair of the aged is the fact that the repeated and well-catalogued needs and problems of the old—the need for adequate and appropriately-designed housing and furnishings, adequate diet and medical care, economic security, appropriate stimulation and opportunities for new learning, options for privacy and socializing, meaningful roles for work and play, mobility via affordable and accessible transportation—all of these and others provide the soil in which the self-respect and competence of the old will either continue to flourish or will wither and die away.

The chapters of this book, deriving as they do from a diversity of backgrounds and proposing a variety of approaches to the study of and service to the old, all may rightly be read in the context of the foregoing assertion. For these chapters all converge ultimately upon this one point that, in whatever ways professional gerontologists may elect to collaborate in helping us better to understand the aging process or better to serve the needs of the old, in the end it is surely the competence and self-esteem of the old which are at stake. What remains then for professional gerontologists is, at least, to respond to this underlying need appropriately, effectively, and in concert. It is to just these objectives that the chapters in this book severally and collectively address themselves.

The present state of the art from both a scientific and professional point of view strongly suggests at best a fragmented accumulation of diverse bits of information about aging; at worst one might be tempted to characterize it as a vast disarray, which is to say that we are still searching for a unifying theory of human aging or even a way of, as Neugarten (1968) puts it, ". . . describing a meaningful context against which to view psychological change over the life cycle." When it comes to solving the problems of and providing services to the aged, we become even more acutely aware of the distressing gap between our good intentions toward the aged and a common frame of reference leading to mutually agreed-upon goals and programs.

It is becoming increasingly evident, however, that at least two basic concepts are agreed upon by both the elderly themselves and professional workers in the field. One such principle is that the process of aging is inextricably linked to change and that many, if indeed not most, such changes may be placed into the matrix of loss. The second widely-held premise is that the old are significantly affected by their environment which, in turn, is shaped by the aged themselves. How can one define aging apart from the environmental context (which includes societal expectations) in which the event occurs? That is, can aging be defined or even described in idiopathic, physical terms alone? Can one clinical observation or another about aging be "good" or "bad" except with reference to the context? The parameters of such person/environment transactions are explored at length by Proshansky, Ittelson, Rivlin *et al.* (1970) and with special reference to the aged by Schwartz and Proppe (1970, 1969).

The relevance of both principles to the present discussion lies in the fact that they promise to provide a perspective from which many novel as well as more traditional problem-solving techniques can flow all the while they maintain complementarity with each other. The problem may be stated in this way: If the many changes experienced across time are closely associated with loss, and if losses do in fact affect well-being, delimit competence, and ultimately diminish self-esteem of the old, how do we attempt to reverse what Birren (1964) has referred to as this "degradative spiral?" The answer, though not simplistic appears straightforward enough: by compensating for such losses to the greatest degree possible.

THE NATURE OF CHANGE AND LOSS

Many of the losses associated with change may in one sense be characterized as "natural" losses in so far as they appear to be genetically and physiologically determined and occur for all practical purposes universally, although at varying rates and in varying degrees. The elevation of threshholds in the several sense modalities, such as hearing and vision, loss of CNS function at the cellular level, reduction in efficiency of the cardio-vascular system and degeneration of collagen tissue, might be cited as examples of such "natural" losses. These can be contrasted to what may be called culturally-determined and circumstantial losses, such as the break-up of one's social network, economic loss, loss of assigned roles, and loss of options and/or privacy.

The several aspects of these losses are important to specify clearly and to understand thoroughly if we are to develop an adequate appreciation of their profound psychological consequences. For one thing, many of these changes (losses) begin to occur much earlier than we become cognitively aware of them and they occur very gradually, often subtly. In this sense, one is not being wholly whimsical in observing that we begin to age from the day we are born. Another feature of such losses is that they often overlap, that is, occur concomitantly, and do not necessarily occur in a sequential manner. Again, individual differences must be taken into account here as well, in that losses occur neither at uniform rates nor to the same degree. Especially is this true with respect to the so-called "natural" losses. Rate and degree clearly are influenced strongly by such individual factors as genetic input, maintainence (nutrition, weight, exercise factors), and exposure to disease and other intrusions from the outside (smoking, accidents).

Also, we must see that these losses tend to be cumulative. Illnesses incurred during the course of a lifetime are bound to have residual effects, some more severe than others, depending upon the nature of the disease. In some instances, the residual effects are pronounced and blatant (as in the case of rheumatic fever); in other instances the residual effects may be so mild as to be only inferred. In either event, it would seem a safe assumption that the baseline with respect to the physiological substrate changes across the years and, thus, the subjective perception and assessment of what functional state constitutes "health" for the individual may be at variance with other, more "objective," judgments of health. Indeed, Shanas' findings (1962) with regard to how people subjectively rate their own health, irrespective of a physician's findings,

indicate that old persons make a functional rather than a pathological assessment of health, and that such judgments are associated
with level of activity rather than with medical diagnoses.

What appears to happen is that the routine accomodation to
one's perception of unchanged circumstances is suddenly over-
whelmed by the accumulated weight of a series of rather small,
gradual, often imperceptible losses, precipitating the self-revealing
acknowledgement, at some point in time, that things indeed *have*
changed. In that moment of truth, one is acutely aware of loss and
of the process of aging as never before, a moment of truth often
provoking depression. Simone de Beauvoir in her recent book
(1972) spotlights this "moment of truth" in dramatic fashion, "the
aged . . . brood upon dangers that they have no means of averting.
Even if no particular threat hangs over them, it is enough for them
to know that they are defenseless to be filled with anxiety: the
peace they enjoy seems to them precarious; and since they are
no longer masters of it, the future is heavy with frightening
possibilities."

To complete this picture of gradually accumulating loss it is
necessary to include, along with "natural" changes, those culturally-determined and circumstantial changes which also mark
the passage of time. The gradual disintegration of one's social and
interpersonal network is one of the hallmarks of the passage of
time. Undeniably, a high price one pays for survival into the latter
decades of life is that most (eventually all) those persons with
whom one grows up are eliminated from the network—parents,
siblings, friends, co-workers. Much of this is accounted for in terms
of a mobile society and as a function of the loss of physical proximity, activities in common and thus common interests, and innumerable other distractions. Certainly, if one survives long
enough, the attrition rate is increased because of death. Retirement is another factor which adds to the disruption of the social and
interpersonal network, as is divorce which, while not necessarily
a function of aging, does bear upon this disruption vis-à-vis the
aging process. The disruption of this network induces significant
changes in one's social status and roles, reflecting the usually decre-
mental nature of such changes, especially within our own society.
This is a point we shall come back to shortly.

Economic losses also have enormous impact upon the aging process, especially in such instances where economic loss turns upon the factor of chronological age. The most obvious example, again, is that rite of passage known as retirement. It is at this point in time that a large number of persons, previously managing to support at least an adequate or tolerable standard of living, now find themselves abruptly demoted to the level of poverty through no fault of their own other than having survived to a ripe age. In addition to its all-too-frequent impoverishing effect, retirement has in many instances effectively produced a permanent vocational loss. The enormous obstacle encountered by enforced retirees (by reason of age) in attempting to compete in the open job market are too well documented and too familiar to require elaboration here. Thus, retirement is the vehicle of multiple loss; not only economic and vocational, but also social loss. Many persons, upon retirement, lose not only a job with its attendant source of income but, at the same time, lose status as a co-worker or colleague with its attendant source of close contact and friendship. They also lose opportunities to participate in a number of valued activities such as membership in company bowling leagues, organizational picnics, and union meetings.

All of the gradually cumulating losses over time—and the ones touched on here are meant to be indicative and illustrative rather than an exhaustive survey—have important psychological consequences which exert enormous impact upon the process of aging as we experience it in our culture. Left untouched and unmodified, these accumulating losses signal an increasing loss of control over one's environment and with it an increasing subjective sense of loss of impact upon and effectiveness within the environment. It is easy enough to see here a parallel to the early developmental pattern, but in reverse fashion. This reversal of the early developmental pattern seems to be not only a critical factor in understanding what in large measure happens from the viewpoint of personality and behavior in the later decades of life, but also is most important in formulating any attempt to respond appropriately and effectively to the problems of the aged. In a sense, then, there is here proposed an underlying rationale for the chapters which follow.

In so doing I emphasize the phrase "control of the environment"; some clarification, therefore, would be in order. First, environment is to be understood in a broad sense as encompassing both the total environment external to the individual as well as the internal environment, that is, the environment which exists within the boundaries of the skin. I refer to any and all external factors ranging from temperature and light through designed space and objects to other human and sub-human organisms that impinge in some way upon the individual. In similar fashion, the internal environment covers the phenomenological field, ranging from the sense modalities through proprioception to habit patterns and memory. Whatever, then, impinges upon or potentially can influence or affect the individual, in much the same way Lewin described "life space," comes under the rubric of "environment" for purposes of the present discussion. The concept of control is here to be understood with reference to a continuum, a matter of degree, and connotes impact, or effect upon. When referring to one's control of his environment I mean to describe his impact upon (or sense of effectiveness within) his life space. Thus "control" is always considered to be limited rather than absolute, with the parameters of control defined by the capacities, opportunities, and motivations of the individual.

When considering old age we need to remind ourselves of the truism that the human infant enters life as possibly the most impotent, helpless of animals. The neonate's initial impact upon its environment derives largely from its reflexive activity. With its first awareness of temperature changes, discomfort from hunger pangs, wet diapers or a sticking pin, it wriggles and cries and thus help is solicited. Gradually but steadily, of course, as the maturational process takes place, the early random movements begin to take on a more purposeful, coordinated form. Toilet training can be instituted, once the necessary maturational sequential events have taken place, and with it another crucial step in the chain of mastery over the internal environment occurs. This entire developmental sequence is studded with like instances of control of and impact upon the environment (life space). The child learns his cultural symbols for verbal and non-verbal communication and in so doing learns to manipulate his circumstances. He learns to say "mommy" and elicits smiles; learns to play off mother against father; learns to trade toys with playmates; learns to smile and chatter and to be chosen as a playmate; learns to work his way up the ladder of school grades; and learns the strategies of socializing, of high school achievement, of college and/or specialized training, of courtship, of job hunting and finding, of career advancement, and so on, in an increasingly upward spiral of sophistication in exercising control of his environment.

Throughout this process, all things being equal, this process of increasing control is reinforced in multiple ways via transactions with others in his environment. And when these rewarding responses, ranging from the response "I like you" to being selected chairman of a committee or receiving an increase in pay, the essential message to the individual is "You are effective; you are making an impact; you count; you are important, useful, and needed." To describe this process is at the same time to describe the onset and growth of self-esteem. However much the specific details, patterns of circumstances, and quality of behaviors may vary from individual to individual, the essential process remains the same.

Ordinarily, we expect this increasing control of and impact upon the environment with its concomitant increase in self-esteem to proceed somewhat as described above from the period of infancy up to and through the middle years. For many this period of the life cycle connotes the "prime" or "peak" years, the "apex of a man's career." For most people, the years beyond those called "prime," the sixth, seventh, eighth, and succeding decades of life, unhappily denote the period of decline, the downward "degradative spiral" referred to earlier. In certain respects this is a realistic perception of events because changes are indeed taking place, many if not most of which are associated with loss. These gradual, cumulative, multi-dimensional losses tend to confront the individual, plagued as he is with diminishing reservoirs of energy and with physical, social, economic vocational losses, with the realization of his diminishing control of the environment, lessened effectiveness, and lessened impact. In many overt as well as covert ways the individual gets the message that less and less is he needed, does he count, or is he important. And whenever and wherever this occurs without mitigation, the probability increases that self-esteem also is highly likely to decline, in extreme instances even to crumble.

Were we, then, to generate a curve representing across time (horizontal axis) the foregoing events, with the vertical A axis calibrated as a measure of control of the environment and the B axis calibrated to measure self-esteem, it would seem a reasonable assumption that we would get something very nearly approximating the "normal" curve, as indicated in the illustration. Heuristically, such an assumption, based upon more than a modicum of anecdotal and "common sense" evidence, is certainly amenable to systematic testing and empirical validation.

Such a conceptualization of the aging process leads us inescapably to certain pragmatic conclusions. For one, we might derive the principle that, if the diminution of self-esteem is closely associated with increasing loss of control of the environment in the

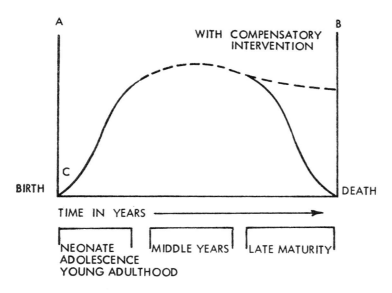

A AXIS: DEGREE OF CONTROL OF (IMPACT ON) ENVIRONMENT

B AXIS: DEGREE OF SELF ESTEEM

C CURVE: LEVEL OF COMPETENCE

Figure I-1.   Control of Environment Across the Life Span.

later decades of life, and if self-esteem is closely allied with competence, as is so cogently and persuasively argued by Kuypers and Bengston (1969), then a basic intervention strategy in helping maintain competence in the later decades (or at least to stabilize the downward spiral) must be to compensate for these gradually accumulating losses. Kuypers and Bengston concur that, in this context, self-esteem is a central factor and they cite, for example, M. Brewster Smith (1968), "For Smith, the base on which competence is defined [rests] on feelings the person has of himself in regard to ability to influence one's environment."

A most eloquent statement of this fundamental need has been provided by Helen Harris Perlman (1968)

> . . . each man, in order to feel whole, must feel that someone cares for him as himself, that to love and be loved becomes a powerful drive (p. 17) . . . observations of how people act . . . show that the maximal use of innate powers, for exploration beyond what is customary and routine, a desire for further engagement with things and people and . . . a drive to be a "cause" or to master new experience is an impelling motivation . . . [We see] a drive to re-achieve a once-held level of stability or to recoup losses and sometimes, of course, we have seen a hopeless relinquishment of drive in those persons who have known only defeat and frustrations for all these efforts . . . environmental opportunities for people's growth and stretch must be present and open (p. 27 ff).

In this regard Kuypers and Bengston raise another very real but also a very troubling issue. They state,

> In the Gladwin, Murphy, and Haan tradition, competence is characterized by a flexible, adaptable, and personally rewarding response to environmental demands, *whatever they may be.* (Ed. note: Italics added.)

A tradition such as this inevitably places most, if not the entire onus, at least by implication, upon the indivdual as responder. Stainbrook (1967), on the other hand, suggests the inequity and ineffectiveness of such a stance. He cites as a case in point the example of a young black living in ghetto circumstances, faced with what he perceives (not entirely unrealistically) as poor prospects for adequate training opportunities; facing what he believes to be a bleak, grim, even hopeless future vocationally and economically. Certainly, his view of his present circumstances are in sharp contrast to the style and quality of life he sees represented on TV and through other media. And so he begins to experience a profound sense of depression. Were this to be observed by some well-meaning friend or agency worker and were he to be referred in the traditional procedure for "therapy" for his depression syndrome, we would not be surprised to know that the therapist was engaged in "getting the patient out of his depression." To the extent that the therapist is successful in eliciting a cheery, hopeful disposition on the part of that young black, *even in the face of unchanged circumstances,* Stainbrook asserts, to that extent the therapist has entered into a collective delusion. For whatever may be argued on the other side, it still remains that depression in the face of a hopeless future is not altogether an inappropriate behavioral response; the real trick of the game, Stainbrook suggests, would be to mitigate or change those bleak and grim circumstances which originally elicit the undesirable behavioral response.

In similar fashion, I submit that this point of view can and should be applied to the often esteem-lowering circumstances of the aged in our society. Compensating for the multifaceted and multi-dimensional losses experienced by the elderly as an intervention strategy may sound simple, but it is not simplistic, nor is this a novel notion. In point of fact, we really have no trouble with this concept when it comes to things we "attach to the body," because we have so many models and precedents in that regard.

The dictionary defines "prosthetics" rather coldly as a 'medical and dental procedure for artificially replacing missing parts." However we define them, prosthetic devices are a means of compensating for losses and thus to reduce a given physical deficit in a physical function. When visual acuity begins to fail, eyeglasses in most cases compensate for the loss and restore the sufferer to a level of adequate visual functioning. So it is with a myriad of other kinds of physical losses; when a limb is lost an artificial one can be attached and the individual can learn to function satisfactorily once again. In sum, we are accustomed now to compensating for physical losses with devices ranging from hearing aids to heart-pacers and so the possibility of continued competence is enhanced. This means, of course, that an accumulation of deficits and "chronic" diseases may be reduced as far as the individual's functioning is concerned, whenever he is restored to satisfactory function by means of compensatory devices.

We need to learn more and to think more imaginatively about the modes and techniques of compensating when it comes to social, economic, vocational, and psychological losses than we have heretofore. We need much more research in this area of concern; to that end we need a greater focus of attention upon the necessity and appropriateness of special design for the aged. For one thing, it is necessary and appropriate because we have the overwhelming evidence of models and precedents, not only with respect to physical losses but also with regard to design for children and other special classes and groups of persons in our society, as well as for special events and/or activities. In this day and age it goes without saying that a nursery school, for example, must be specially designed to meet the particular requirements of little children (the special chairs, tables, blackboards, doorknobs, water fountains, etc.). Why, then, should we assume that furniture which is appropriate for young and middle-aged adults can and should adequately serve the needs of the old? We do not design housing for persons living in temperate zones in the same way we design for those living in an arctic or tropical region. In truth there is nothing new under the sun; when it comes to our response to the old we need to learn from our own experience.

Much discussion has been generated in the past few years among professionals relating to so-called "barrier-free" living arrangements for the elderly. This discussion fits nicely with the notion that appropriate design for the old should be (at the minimum) based upon the principle that the old should not be penalized vis-a-vis the deficits associated with old age. The point of view advanced by this and the ensuing chapters is that the environment which we of necessity are called upon to envision and design for the old, as well as the "practice" to go with it, must go beyond this minimum principle of "barrier-free" living. Avoiding a barrier-ridden environment on the one hand may help the aged escape the implicit "penalties" but may, on the other hand, leave such persons still functioning at a relatively low level of competence and/or capacity. We must go beyond, that is to say, we must compensate the old—must "make-up" for—to the greatest extent possible, the effects of accumulated losses.

The broad strategy for such compensating intervention is already indicated by the modes of intervention in cases of physical deficit; things we attach to or put into the body. There is no presumption here that what is being advocated must necessarily always be on a grand scale and dramatic in nature. The response to this need is presumed to be most appropriate and effective when multifaceted and multi-dimensional. Sometimes the response will be narrowly focused and even subtle but with critically important consequences. Marion Marshall's chapter, for example, suggests that we can effectively challenge the age-old myth that "you can't teach an old dog new tricks" by following such principles as providing appropriate learning opportunities and incentives and opportunity for "pacing."

ENVIRONMENTAL DESIGN

As physical deficits cumulate and thresholds of the sense modalities rise in the later years the influence of environmental stimulation becomes of ever increasing importance. The rich and varied research on sensory deprivation points to the noxious effects upon subjective experience and behavior, a circumstance which is enormously exacerbated in the case of the aged person whose environment already is becoming increasingly filtered through a series of natural events. Those with diminishing visual acuity require increased levels of light, for example, for reading and safety, as well as a maximum use of light, color, and texture for stimulation. Large-print books, periodicals, magazines, and newspapers provide additional compensating modes for failing vision in a great many instances.

Fiske and Maddi (1961) have challenged the notion of homeostasis or equilibrium as the overriding need in human experience. They have pointed out that human beings need a sense of "adventure" and often will behave in ways that disrupt the equilibrium of the status quo, seeking out circumstances that may even involve an element of danger in order to achieve variety and novelty in experience.

Robert W. White (1961), in a review of animal psychology, suggests that the traditional conceptualization of "motivation" based upon drive reduction principles is inadequate. He proposes motivation in the sense of a feeling of effectance or efficacy as a motivational source in its own right. Again, Perlman addresses herself to this issue in a cogent and eloquent way:

> So we are driven and spurred and drawn forward by multiple needs and motivations . . . we drive to relieve ourselves of frustration and tension; we push out to escape stalemate and boredom; we are drawn by hope to reach for satisfactions and pleasures beyond those we have; and we are both pushed and pulled when we encounter life circumstances that threaten our well-being or that throw us off our customary trackage. [Thus we are moved] . . . in small ways to accomodate ourselves, to adapt, to manipulate circumstances (p. 33).

Need for Options

Such a concept, of course, is directly antithetical to the usual tendancy to protect the elderly from situations and circumstances which are likely to involve risks to the old. Such considerations alert us, then, to the alternative risks of over-protecting the old, in such a way as to literally "infantilize" them. The very fine line which separates such an over-response from a needed and desired service is best identified in the light of individual requirements, capabilities, and preferences. Quite apart from one's willingness to do so, the opportunity for making such a determination may simply not be available in every instance. In designing the space to be used in congregate living, for example, those who will eventually be living there may not be available for interview or consultation. Furthermore, where some degree of turnover is anticipated, tailoring the environment to suit a specific group of residents, i.e., those who will first occupy the space, would seem to be ill-advised on the part of those who must make long-range decisions. Ultimately we are led to conclude that the key to this dilemma must be to provide the maximum number of options possible in any given situation. And, while recognizing that certain constraints inevitably must be considered (economic, for instance), the whole principle of compensating for loss implies that, in dealing with an on-going process of attenuation of options, "compensation," by definition, mandates that we not exacerbate but rather reverse the process of option-loss.

Nutritional Patterns

Let us take a look at some of the circumstances involving diminishing options which, when modified, hold promise for reversing the degradative spiral with its undermining of self-esteem and at the same time help maintain competence. One such familiar circumstance has to do with nutritional factors and the dietary habits of the old. Commonly, the response of professions to this set of problems targets on the desire to inform and train the aged to understand and utilize the principles of a well-balanced diet. This is usually aimed at the poor aged who must fend for themselves and are viewed as particularly susceptible to "poor eating habits." Unquestionably, many older people can make use of additional information about the constituents of optimal nutritional patterns. Nonetheless, it is still a moot question as to whether mere lack of factual information is certifiably the primary cause of malnutrition and associated ailments among the aged.

An inspection of alternative explanations suggests that the loss of the social component can and often does have a seriously deleterious effect upon eating habits and nutritional patterns. For many people, socializing is one of the great pleasureable factors in eating. Eating alone constantly (except for those relatively few whose life-style demands it) can, for the most part, turn eating into a dreary event and dampen the appetite. It can also effectively eliminate most incentive for preparing not only "elaborate" but even "well-balanced" meals. Those who must eat alone know full well how much easier, quicker, and convenient it is to just open a can. And, of course, ill-fitting dentures can exacerabate the whole process just described. When dentures are ill-fitting and uncomfortable, even painful, to wear, one can tentatively predict a regular diet of milk-soaked bread or coffee and crackers. For those circumstances with little hope of compensatory change (as with the poor aged), our prediction of an inadequate diet becomes almost a near-certainty. In such circumstances, mere information is not a sufficient vehicle for change.

HEARING LOSS

In parallel fashion we can see the ever-widening circle of discomfort, distrust, and disruption which so often accompanies the diminution—sometimes even small decrements—of hearing. This appears to instigate more social dissonance than losses in any other sense modality, a disruption all the more insidious when the hearing loss is gradual and barely noticeable than when the onset of loss is dramatically abrupt and marked; and for an easily apparent reason. A word or two or a phrase here and there not heard is easily rationalized away by an individual. But the longer the deficit persists the more likely the sufferer is to emit inappropriate responses and thus something of a vicious circle is generated, embarrassing and confusing to the sufferer, annoying to others, utterly devastating to satisfactory social intercourse. As the individual with a hearing deficit becomes aware of conversations garbled and confused because of missed words he asks for a repetition, but this can easily make a person self-conscious and he begins to make guesses at what is going on. Others not infrequently presume the individual either to be cantankerous, inattentive, or else downright bizarre, no doubt the victim of senility. At times others will converse as if the individual with a hearing deficit is simply not present. The natural consequence is for those with a hearing deficit not to respond to conversations at all, eventually to avoid social situations as much as possible, a move usually welcomed and encouraged covertly and sometimes overtly by others. And so the cycle leading to disengagement is complete, a process that can be avoided altogether or at least ameliorated (depending upon the nature of the hearing deficit) by appropriate compensation.

LIVING PATTERNS

The multiple problems of neighboring, friendship-formation, social contact, and mobility of the old need to be examined further in the light of the principle of compensation for loss. These horrendously demoralizing problems require much more imaginative and inventive solutions than the more traditional responses of the past have produced. Irving Rosow's investigations (1967) of congregate living arrangements of the elderly should make it abundantly clear that the social integration of the elderly is not assured by an either-or approach to housing; either an age-segregated ghetto away from the mainstream of life (often far away from the city or in a depreciated portion of "central city" where land or house values are lowest) or embedded in an age-mixed, tenement-like complex where the activity and noise level often proves almost intolerable for the old. Certainly, no logical solution lies in shunting the old together simply on the basis of chronological age. It is encouraging that designers are beginning to communicate and talk in collaboration with social scientists and social planners (cf. Kaplan's chapter on "Social Indicators") with the result that imaginative, non-traditional solutions to the dilemma are being proposed: congregate living for the old, for example, sharing the "old neighborhoods" with younger families and providing "buffer zones" (life parks and green belts) where young and old can meet and enjoy each other's company. Long-term care facilities (e.g. nursing and convalescent homes) are just beginning to think about and, in a few instances, to explore the possibilities of nursery schools and kindergartens built adjacent to such LTC facilities, with the potential enriching of life for both age groups. Chen's proposal (cf. chapter VI), which will in fact provide the option of continuing to live in one's own home and neighborhood following retirement without worry, is an important and imaginative proposal which breaks in many respects with the traditional solution to the problems of housing following retirement.

Mobility of Aged

The other side of this same coin is the matter of mobility of the aged, particularly as it involves transportation. The extent to which the aged are victimized in terms of the lack of cheap, accessible, convenient and fast transportation, and the extent to which their plight is buried beneath the morass of official rhetoric and public debate over the mess of "mass transportation" beggars description. Private transportation (primarily the automobile) becomes so costly as to be prohibitive for many older Americans living on fixed and extremely limited incomes, to say nothing of the additional hazards in negotiating crowded streets and freeways which includes elderly drivers with much slower reflexes. In Los Angeles County alone, for example, approximately 1,200 persons over 90 years of age are licensed to drive. By what logic should such an older person be expected to maintain a two or three thousand dollar automobile in his garage or car-port, pay the annual licensing tax, the enormously inflated costs of repair and maintenance, and the cost of gasoline, in order to play a game of cards once or twice a week, or to attend a club meeting, or to visit a friend living four miles away, or just to spend the afternoon in a park on the other side of the city.

Within the past decade, communities in a number of areas such as New York and Los Angeles have begun to pay at least nominal attention to this need of the old. The customary arrangement is to provide a 10¢ or 15¢ "discount" on public transportation for individuals who can identify themselves as "Senior Citizens"; usually this is done with a special ID card or by showing a Medi-care or Medi-cal card. Although a desirable first approximation, such a "solution" not only tends again to limit options for the old but patently begs the entire question. Such "discount rides" are limited (usually to certain hours of the day, the non-rush hours). But, more importantly, what advantage is it to an elderly person to know he can ride the subway in New York City at a lower fare if to do so means he must walk down two or three flights of stairs from his apartment, walk three or four more blocks, then descend the equivalent of another two blocks below street level in order to use the subway? How useful are cheap bus fares in Los Angeles if it means four blocks to a bus line, a 20-minute wait at the corner, then two or three transfers on bus lines which still take the rider no closer than a half-mile from his destination? For transportation to be truly useful to the old it must be not only affordable but fast, convenient, and above all accessible. If a man is washed overboard at sea and you want to help, it does no good to throw him a sandwich.

Clearly what are called for here, in terms of compensating for loss, are our most innovative, imaginative efforts. For instance, it is not entirely fantasy to envision a large geographical area like greater Los Angeles divided up into a number of districts, each consisting of approximately two or three square miles and served by a fleet of six or eight passenger mini-busses or trams. Largely funded by federal funds, such a system might charge the elderly a nominal annual subscription of $10 for the service. When called, a mini-tram could be expected to appear at the door within minutes and for a small fee, say ten cents, take the elderly subscriber to visit or market quickly and conveniently. Should the oldster require transportation to a more distant part of the city, he would have the opportunity of riding the mini-tram to his area's borders and immediately transfer to a mini-tram in the adjoining area, and so on until he reaches his destination. Such a service system eliminates (for city travel and thus for most purposes) the need for an auto and meets, at the same time, the mobility criteria for the old mentioned above. It is worth noting that the basics of such a system have justification and application not only for the elderly but also for many other classes of citizens in the population.

A transportation service modelled along similar lines as that described, but limited to a few neighborhoods of older people in the San Fernando Valley of Los Angeles was tried as a demonstration project in 1971. The primary objective of the project was to demonstrate its feasibility and utility as a service for "marketing" on the part of the old; that is, subscribers called, made an appointment, were picked up at their door, taken to a desired market and were called for at an agreed-upon time. The older person was then assisted with his groceries up the stairs and into his home or apartment. It is unfortunate that federal contract money ran out and the project was discontinued, in view of the fact that it was judged most feasible by the service-provider and responded to enthusiastically by elderly subscribers. Nonetheless, this project is an example of the kind of creative solutions to this pressing need of the old which remains to be realized. If compensating for loss is indeed a viable principle then both extensive research and imaginative action with respect to mobility must be considered a matter of considerable importance and urgency.

Affectional Needs

Another important and highly sensitive area of concern with respect to compensating is the need for attention, love, affection, particularly as this involves sexual activity. As indicated earlier, the price one pays for survival into the later decades of life is the gradual loss of family, friends, even spouse. And, not surprisingly, one of the most pervasive hazards of old age is loneliness. The need for affection is universal (again, individual differences operate here); most especially in the late years, when many of the self-esteem supporting factors diminish, does the need for affection, for love, for "stroking," become more, not less, intense (cf. Peterson's chapter). Such an assertion is hardly controversial. Indeed, such needs evoke widespread empathy as well as endorsement in our society.

Paradoxically, however, two factors primarily appear to confound the full satisfaction of this need in the old. One factor is the broadly-based attitude bias and the stereotype held by many regarding physical intimacy and sexual behavior in the old. The second factor is the all-too-prevalent lack of opportunity for such behavior on the part of elderly people. Although our society's mores and norms are clearly changing in this respect, nonetheless we recognize the unmistakable tendency to view physical intimacy, when exhibited by the old, not merely as irrelevant but even inappropriate (when we respond to physical intimacy, courting behavior, or sexual behavior on the part of the older person with the injunction "act your age" we strongly imply inappropriateness).

The degree and intensity of show of affection, of course, seems to be at issue. In general we can look with tolerance, even bemusement, upon hand-holding, hugging, even gentle kissing by older persons. When manifestations of affection become passionate and/or meld into overt sexual activity the indications of uneasiness on the part of others frequently emerge, ranging from surprise, shock and apprehension all the way to distaste, horror, and even outrage. Much of the quality of this kind of response is frequently masked by snide "jokes," the content of which invariably demean sexuality in old age. The research findings which show the continuity of sexual response into the seventh and eighth decade of life, and even beyond, point up the burdensome dilemma placed upon the elderly in the expression and manifestation of a most necessary and natural human need. Masters and Johnson (1968) particularly have made a major research contribution in reporting that in general the major reasons for diminished sexual activity in old age are ill-health and/or lack of available, willing partners (reasons which, interestingly, apply at any age).

The modes for compensating for loss in this area are apparent, but must surely stem from and begin with a bias and stereotype-free attitude toward passionate behavior and sexual activity in old age. As the proportional and absolute number of aged increase in our society and with it the increasing utilization of congregate living and long-term care facilities, it becomes increasingly urgent that such living arrangements not penalize the older person with respect to sexual behavior, as is often the case now. Far too many institutional facilities now, either on the basis of administrative policy, or because of objections by next-of-kin, or because of regulatory "requirements," simply do not provide the endorsement nor the privacy options which would allow, even facilitate, sexual behavior on the part of their older residents. Many a sixty-odd-year-old individual entering such a facility must in effect face the dismal prospect of abjuring further sexual contact until he or she dies, excepting only an occasional furtive excursion. Such a loss seems too bitter to tolerate, especially when the opportunity for compensation appears so easy to provide.

Productivity of the Old

Among the many and varied elements of loss associated with later years not the least to be considered and attended to is that of economic loss. As a matter of fact, the all-pervasive character of economic loss tends to exacerbate many of the other losses experienced in the later years. Housing, nutrition, medicare, even friendship formations and "neighboring" behavior, often become "problems" for the old simply because of severely diminished economic power and resources.

To illustrate, we might refer to the kind of data characteristically used to support the theory of disengagement. Typically, a researcher interviewing a "little old lady" living alone in a one-room apartment on $96 a month is likely to discover and document an elderly individual whose social "contacts" have been dramatically reduced. She seldom leaves her apartment, rarely visits acquaintances or friends, plays cards, or goes to movies; in a word, she fits into the disengagement theory matrix. An alternative explanation, however, based upon more situation-specific evidence, is possible. The disengagement of our hypothetical lady may turn out to be something of an artifact. Her minimal income no doubt contributes heavily to her inadequate diet which in turn affects an already considerable loss of energy. Perhaps her loss of social contact is largely a function of diminished energy level added to the simple fact that she's "broke;" she has no car and no money for taxi or even bus fare.

The reader doubtless will agree that it would be redundant to attempt to document in detail the full extent of economic loss associated in large measure with old age. The literature, both scientific and popular, is replete with stories and statistics that underscore this phenomenon, pensions (and social security) which are grossly inadequate as well as hopes for pensions which often are not realized. This appears to be a major reason why, for too many aged, the dream of "the golden years" turns to dross.

To repeat, the economic loss that plagues the old is an all-too-familiar fact which we need not belabor. But, equally important in this connection, are the psychological consequences which flow from this distressing circumstance. What is often overlooked or underestimated, even by social scientists, is the hard fact that, in our society, money represents in a substantial way the modality through which we exercise control over our environment. Money has become, in some ways, the index of our effectiveness and impact upon the "world"; in a colloquial sense, money is frequently seen even as a measure of one's value and worth to society.

Although patently not true of all elderly, it is still difficult to deny the tendency we have of associating "being old" with "being poor." Through a kind of twisted syllogistic logic, our society has moved from perceiving the old as no longer producing children, no longer producing goods, no longer producing income, to applying the simple label "unproductive." One wonders, then, is such labelling of the old fair and is it accurate?

The answer, in large part, depends upon how we define "productivity." Weisskopf (1967) neatly captures that aspect of the economic philosophy of our culture which seems to contribute so

deleteriously to the economic position of many of our elderly when
he states,

> Our world is dominated by a utilitarianism and functionalism
> in which everything, man, nature, society, is evaluated according
> to their economic and technical usefulness and not according to
> the essential qualities of their being.

Historically, economists have provided a gross index of our nation's
overall productivity in terms of what is called the gross national
product, the GNP consisting of measurable goods and services. In
the earlier days of our nation's industrialization, "goods" contributed by far the largest proportion to the GNP. In recent times we
are told that "services" contribute the larger component of the
GNP, and these services are therefore enormously important to
our nation's economy and productivity. It is no surprise to knowledgeable gerontologists that an amazingly large number of those
in the later years continue to provide a rich variety of "services"
ranging from RSVP programs to "Foster Grandparents" and
"Friendly Visitors." And the numbers of such elderly providers of
services continue to grow.

Unfortunately, we seem not only to continue to avoid including
such tangible services in our assessments of productivity but, what
is worse, we continue to ignore our economic obligation to the providers of such indispensible services, i.e., fair payment for services
rendered. And we do it by the same neat trick which we have traditionally used to short-change patients in our so-called "mental
hospitals" which provide equally indispensable services (maintenance, clerical, etc.) In this latter instance, payment for services
is avoided by the simple device of defining the work as "therapy"
(one doesn't *pay* people for therapy, does one?). In much the same
way, we urge our older people to join volunteer groups and
volunteer their time and energies for a vast array of critically important community enterprises and programs. All the while, we
avoid (except for the recent movement to provide such "out-of-
pocket" expenses as car fare and "lunch money") the rightful
remuneration for their services—as we are obliged to do for the
attorney, the physician, the social worker, the politician—by the
simple rationalization that we are encouraging and helping the

old to keep active, to "stay in the mainstream," to "keep happy by participating."

If we mean to compensate for economic loss, too, in as creative a manner as possible, an important task confronting us is the necessary re-evaluation of our traditional definitions of productivity, especially as relating to the later decades of life. Perhaps in maintaining the rite of retirement we are clinging to what is already an anachronism. The relationship of competence and productivity and their meaning for the early and middle years must be redefined for those later years when, although less energy is available, productivity need not necessarily diminish; it can, rather, assume different dimensions, different proportions, different manifestations.

One of the important tasks, then, of the gerontologist-researcher is to study, to measure, and to disseminate data relative to the dimensions and parameters of the productivity of the old. Similarly, it follows that one important instrumental task of the gerontologist-practitioner is to utilize such data in potentiating the productive capacities of the elderly within the mainstream of our society. This kind of compensating response augers well for a reversal of the present negative image of old age.

In summary, the aim of this chapter has been to suggest a point of view with respect to the aging process which will provide a frame of reference for a diversity of approaches to the old. To undertake the compilation of an exhaustive inventory of all possible compensatory devices, designs and programs, a "cookbook" of compensation for loss would not only be an interminable task but one which may ultimately be self-defeating. If the accumulating losses of the years tend to diminish self-esteem and competence, then compensating for such losses must produce a better quality of life. This simple proposition in reality ought to provoke in professional gerontologists more imaginative thinking and creative solutions to "age's dilemma." For the gerontologist, be he researcher or practitioner, no small satisfaction lies in the anticipation that he will be instrumental in turning the years of loss into years of promise.

BIBLIOGRAPHY

Bates, A.: Privacy—a useful concept. *Social Forces, 42*:429, 1964.

Birren, James: *The Psychology of Aging.* Englewood Cliffs, N. J., Prentice-Hall, 1964.

de Beauvoir, Simone: *The Coming of Age.* New York, G. P. Putnam Sons, 1972.

Fiske, D., and Maddi, S. (Eds.): *Functions of Varied Experience.* Home wood, Ill., Dorsey Press, 1961.

Kuypers, J. A., and Bengston, Vern.: Competence, Social Breakdown, and Humanism. In Feldman, A. (Ed.): *Community Mental Health and Aging: An Overview.* University of Southern California Press, Los Angeles 1960.

Lawton, M. P., and Simon, B.: The ecology of social relationships in housing for the elderly. *Gerontologist, 8*(2), 1968.

Masters, William and Johnson, V.: Human Sexual Response: The Aging Female and the Aging Male. In B. Neugarten, (Ed.): *Middle Age and Aging.* Chicago, University of Chicago Press, 1968.

Neugarten, Bernice L. (Ed.): *Middle Age and Aging,* Chicago, University of Chicago Press, 1968.

Perlman, Helen H.: *Persona: Social Role and Personality.* Chicago, University of Chicago Press, 1968, pp. 17, 27.

Pincus, A.: The definition and measurement of the institutional environment in homes for the aged. *Gerontologist, 8* (3):207, 1968.

Proshansky, Harold M., Ittleson, W., Rivlin, L. (Eds.): *Environmental Psychology: Man and His Physical Setting.* New York, Holt, Rinehart, and Winston, Inc., 1970.

Rosow, Irving: *Social Integration of the Aged.* New York, Free Press of Glencoe, 1967.

Schwartz, Arthur N., and Proppe, H.: Toward Person/Environment Transactional Research in Aging. *Gerontologist, 10*:3, 1970.

————: Perception of Privacy Among Institutionalized Aged, *Proceedings,* 77th Annual Meeting, American Psychological Association, 1969.

Shanas, Ethel: *The Health of Older People: A Social Survey.* Cambridge, Mass., Harvard University Press, 1962.

Sommer, R.: *Personal Space.* Englewood Cliffs, Prentice-Hall, 1969.

Stainbrook, Edward, public address, mimeo, 1967.

Weisskopf, W. A.: Existential Crisis and the Unconscious, *J Humanistic Psychol,* Spring, 1967.

White, Robert W.: The Concept of Competence. In Fiske, D., and Maddi, S. (Eds.): *Functions of Varied Experience.* Homewood, Ill., Dorsey Press, 1961.

Wolpert, J.: Migration as an adjustment to environmental stress. *J Social Issues, 22*(4):92, 1966.

Chapter II

SOCIAL INDICATORS AND THE AGING

Oscar J. Kaplan and Robert Ontell

THE TIDES OF HISTORY are carrying the aging to a more central place in our national life. The aging are increasing rapidly in number, the nation now is sufficiently affluent to permit allocation of more of its resources to their needs, and a sense of obligation has developed toward them. Vast sums now are being spent on the aging in the United States and even larger amounts almost certainly will be devoted to their welfare in the future. This chapter mainly is concerned with measuring the consequences of investments in time and money in programs for the aging.

Even a nation as wealthy as the United States cannot do all that it would like to do for its elderly citizens. It must pick and choose, and establish a hierarchy of goals. It must seek the largest possible social returns for its expenditures. Although government programs do not live or die on the basis of the bottom line of a profit-and-loss statement, there is growing interest in what is called social accounting. Social indicators are destined to play a major role in social accounting.

What Is A Social Indicator

The term social indicator has achieved a vogue and a popularity unexampled in the recent history of social science, yet there is very little agreement about what the term means. Among those concerned with operationalizing this concept, there is general agreement that a social indicator is a special kind of social statistic. Differences arise over what kind of social statistic it is. Emmanuel Kant is cited by Gross as having once very aptly said that concepts without precepts are empty and that precepts without concepts are blind (Gross 1969).

What are some of the referents to which this concept has been applied in the social indicators literature? There are at least three: (1) descriptions of social conditions, (2) specification of social goals, and (3) indices of program evaluation. Used as descriptive statistics, they answer questions about the current state of particular social conditions. Social indicators are distinguished from other statistics by the requirement that the social indicator also answers the question whether the particular social condition is getting 'worse' or 'better'. Thus, a statistic like the infant mortality rate for a given place and time would not be a social indicator if it stood alone. This statistic becomes a social indicator when it is embedded within a time series or when it is used to compare the condition in a particular locality with a comparable condition in other localities or with various subgroups within a specified population.

Others have suggested that social indicators differ from other descriptive statistics in that they furnish interpreted information about social conditions. These interpretations are subject to the judgment that, if the change in the condition is in the ". . . 'right' direction, while other things remain equal, things have gotten better, or people are 'better off' " (OHEW, 1969).

Social indicators also have been used to specify social goals. Wilbur Cohen, in testimony before the U. S. Senate Special Subcommittee for Evaluation and Planning of Social Programs, gives examples of the employment of social indicators for purposes of goal setting (GPC, 1970). For example, Cohen, in discussing life expectancy, noted that average life expectancy in 1966 was 70.2 years. He recommended that the national policy goal should be to raise life expectancy to 72 years by the year 1976. In setting this goal, Cohen did not say how the goal was to be obtained; but implicit in his presentation was the suggestion that public social policy should be concerned with developing programs which would lead to this desirable result.

Finally, a third use for social indicators which has been discussed in the literature relates to questions about the effectiveness of programs designed to achieve desirable goals. When used in this fashion, social indicators become evaluative statistics. Presumably, the evaluation has been preceded by the collection of baseline social data and the setting of goals. Given a description of the social conditions at time one (T_1) and a goal specified for time two (T_2), measurements taken between these two points $(T_1 + n)$ would then constitute a measure of progress at that particular junction.

These multiple usages of the term social indicator have caused Dial to recommend its discontinuance, since it is "defeatingly vague, and imprecise". He recommended that it be replaced by a set of terms such as Quality of Life Indicator; Goal(s) Indicator(s); Social Change Indicator; and Social Statistics" (Dial, 1972). This is a useful suggestion, but it is doubtful whether the generic term will disappear from the vocabulary in the foreseeable future. Since all of the uses to which the term has been put are interrelated, there is really no reason for abandoning the collective noun "social indicators" to include the variety of distinctive meanings.

There are a number of problems related to each of the uses for which social indicator statistics are recommended. For example, there is the problem of making social judgments about specified social conditions. Who is to determine whether a social condition is good or bad? Similarly, who is to specify the goals for change and who is to decide what the priorities should be in designing social programs for current social needs? These issues have been discussed elsewhere but there is little unanimity among the discussants concerning the answers to these questions (Harland, 1971; Ontell, 1972; Proceedings, 1972). The discussion is too involved to review in this brief paper. Of more immediate concern is another issue. To what areas of the social arena are social indicators to be addressed? Douglas Harland, for methodological as well as analytical reasons, proposes that social indicators be developed in at least twelve areas of the social arena or what he terms "organizational groupings of welfare commodities". Harland (1971), following the lead of others, lists the following domains:

Culture	Environment	Public Safety
Economics	Health	Recreation
Education	Housing	Social Security
Employment	Legal Justice	Transportation

This list is not exhaustive and is, in some cases, redundant. For example, the categories "Employment" and "Social Security" could be subsumed under a comprehensive designation called "Income Maintenance," which in turn could be subsumed under Harland's "Economics" domain. The list is nevertheless exemplary of some of the current fashions used to designate areas in which social indicators may be applied.

In conceptualizing this paper, it occurred to the authors that the people who inhabit these domains can be differentiated by age, income, education, ethnic status, etc. Each such social grouping could, then, be regarded separately with respect to the entire domain system. Thus, the aged could be considered as a distinctive social entity. A social indicators report on the aged would include a description of how the aged population fares in each of the social domains. On the descriptive level, this would involve generating statistics about the social condition of the aged with respect to health, housing, education, etc., at any given point in time.

We have noted that a social indicator is more than a descriptive statistic so that an additional requirement would be to view the present status in terms of the past within each domain and to make cross-cultural and cross geographical and cross-age comparisons. We have also noted that a complete set of social indicators would require specification of social goals and the evaluation of any current programs which specify such goals. What would emerge from such an analysis would be a specialized social report on the aged population who reside in a designated geographical or political entity. On the national level, the requirement might be to issue an annual social report on the social conditions of the aged in the United States. Such a document could conceivably have counterparts localized to smaller units of political or geographical jurisdiction. Indeed, the current, most active thrust in the development of social reports is at the local, mostly large city, level.[1]

The Administration on Aging has sponsored the development of a questionnaire designed to obtain information about the aged in the domains of housing, health, economic well-being, social relations and activities, etc. (OHEW, 1970). Aside from this survey-type approach, there are the usual statistics available from the Federal agencies on the social composition, health, and economic situation of the aged population. As far as the authors are aware, there is no comprehensive social report devoted to the aged as a special group.

Most social reports in process or in prospect tend to be comprehensive in their presentation but give unsystematic information about various subgroups in the population. As a result, only partial overviews of special populations are available. Krieger has recommended that social scientists consider the possibility of assuming an advocacy role with respect to developing social reports for disenfranchised groups (Krieger, 1971). The H.E.W. document, *Toward A Social Report* (DHEW, 1969), deplores the general paucity of social information available in the United States and declares that if the nation is

> . . . to do better social reporting in the future . . . it will need . . . information on different groups of Americans. It will need more data on the aged, on youth, and on women as well as on ethnic minorities. It will need information not only on objective conditions but also on how different groups of Americans perceive the conditions in which they find themselves. (DHEW, 1969).

As employed in this chapter, the term "social indicator" will not only include objective and subjective measures of the quality of life in various categories, but also statistical information relating to delivery of services, allocation of resources, and demographic variables. The authors believe that a wide range of measures are

[1] The Urban Observatory Project, funded by the National League of Cities, currently involves the development of local social reports in seven United States cities (Albuquerque, Atlanta, Denver, Kansas City, Milwaukee, Nashville, San Diego). The U.S. Bureau of the Census is developing indicators for Los Angeles, Chicago, Phoenix, Providence, and Mound Bayou, Mississippi. Other cities which are developing indicators programs are Washington, D. C., Wichita, Baltimore, and South Bend.

needed to adequately represent complex sectors of later life, such as those of housing or recreation or health.

Social Indicators and the Aging

Social indicators may deal with more than "hard data", such as nose counts or building inspection findings. Above all, they are concerned with quality of life, which is very hard to define and even harder to measure. Some of the special problems in developing social indicators in the field of aging are illustrated by examples from the fields of housing, income maintenance and employment, and health.

HOUSING. Most housing data have to do with physical structure and facilities. Some of the most important aspects of housing of the elderly are socio-psychological. For example, the location of housing has important implications for friendship relationships, for access to recreational facilities, and for opportunities for interaction with other persons in shopping and other activities. There are many instances where older individuals have been involuntarily moved from inferior housing to adequate housing in the course of urban renewal and with severe disruptive consequences to the lives of those involved. Older people in the central city living in dilapidated quarters often have long-term friendship and dependency relationships which are very supportive and which are lost when there is transplantation to new housing which physically may be more desirable. The quality of life actually may suffer even in the face of a gain in the physical quality of housing.

INCOME MAINTENANCE AND EMPLOYMENT. Perception of income adequacy is a function of basic needs, previous income, income of friends and associates, total assets, and other factors. The cost of living may differ substantially from one area to another. A person with a high income may feel more deprived than one with a lower one. Income maintenance is achieved through employment, social security benefits, private pension plans, systematic savings, and in other ways. It should be possible to monitor these components of income maintenance through review of continuing data releases by government agencies and private oganizations, and through sample survey research. However, we must be prepared to find discrepancies between subjective reports of income adequacy and objective data. It also is unlikely that there will be a one-to-one relationship between gains in income and perception of income adequacy, particularly as the aged as a class rise above the poverty line.

It may be possible to develop continuing reports on employment and unemployment of older persons on a regular basis by systematic analysis of data in the possession of government agencies concerned with employment. For example, in San Diego, the State Department of Human Resources has all applicants for employment complete a form which inquires into work experience; the form also seeks information on age, sex, place of residence, type of work sought, etc. This information could be put on punch cards and tabulated and cross-tabulated, yielding a continuing series of measures of employment level of older persons. This kind of information could be tied into campaigns to secure higher employment of older persons.

It is not always easy to properly interpret the significance of social indicator data. Is a high employment level among persons over age 65 good? Possession of a job by one 70-year-old may represent personal and social gain, but it may be hastening the death of another or impairing the efficiency of the organization with which he is connected. In many instances, there is a trade-off between personal gain and social gain. In other words, it may be necessary to look at each case individually to determine if a net social gain has been accomplished as a result of employment after age 65. This is impractical under present circumstances, pointing up the difficulty of obtaining meaningful social indicators in the field of employment.

HEALTH. Numerous problems exist in developing social indicators in the field of health. Mortality and morbidity data represent very crude measures of the effectiveness of health programs. There is lack of agreement within the medical profession as to what is pathological. For example, is there reason for concern if the blood pressure of an 84-year-old man is 140/90? How are we to judge the quality of the medical care given older people? How much weight should be given to subjective measures of the adequacy of medical care? What are the ingredients of a medical program which is highly acceptable to older people? These are but a few of the questions which need attention if valid social indicators are to be developed in the field of health.

There is need to probe the efficiency of the nation's health care programs for persons over age 65. Such persons now constitute 9.9 percent of the population but account for 27.4 percent of the nation's health spending. This is due largely to the greater medical needs of this segment of the population, but there may be opportunities to reduce costs without substantial loss in service. Indicators related to cost-benefit analysis are very much needed in the geriatric health field.

As we approach the time when there is comprehensive health care in the United States, particularly for the aged, it may be possible to develop a continuing flow of medical data which will make it possible to chart the progress of older age groups using computer-generated findings.

A major problem in the development of mental health indicators, a significant area of health, is the absence of measuring tools that are fully satisfactory. The etiology of many of the major psychiatric complaints still is very obscure and this makes diagnosis difficulty, particularly with regard to many of the mental disorders of the aged. It might be better to gain information on the extent of mental disabilities of old age by developing behavioral indices rather than by using diagnostic labels. Sometimes, intake statistics are misleading with regard to the level of service being made available to older persons by community mental health clinics. For example, alcoholism and drug addiction are rare among persons of 65, but these are among the leading reasons for referral in the young age group. Moreover, some of the major psychiatric difficulties of older persons are chronic and irreversible, such as senile brain disease. Those afflicted cannot look for assistance with such disorders from community agencies, such as the church.

Local Social Indicators

Although there will always be interest in national social indicators, and measurements of progress toward national goals, it is likely that local social indicators will prove more useful in implementing and evaluating programs for the aging. The good life for older people must be tailor-made in the communities in which they live, and those who are its architects must build upon existing services and institutions. Problems of housing, recreation, transportation, and health exist everywhere, but their manifestations and management will vary from city to city. For example, the problem of public transportation is very different in New York City as compared with San Diego, California or Pocatello, Idaho.

Communities differ in geography, climate, recreational facilities and programs for the aging. They differ in terms of income and educational attainments of their older residents. Well-designed social indicator studies in dozens of communities of different types may force us to reconsider some of our present conceptions of the needs of the aging. For example, it may be that the more successful we are in integrating older people into programs in which there is no segregation by age, the happier they will be. We are almost certain to find that the aging are so heterogeneous that multiple solutions will be required in each problem category. Analyses of data no doubt will show that not all elements of the aging population are sharing equally in the overall gains that are being reported. Perhaps Mexican-Americans or males over age 80 or those who reside in the southeastern part of the city are not participating in the gains as fully as others. Such findings will provide a basis for reexamination of existing programs and for the establishment of new ones. Students of social gerontology may find that reading the literature on local social indicators and aging will be very profitable.

Notwithstanding the uniqueness of cities, it may be that social indicators research will point the way to solutions which will be applicable to cities of the same general type. For example, cities with low population density share problems of transportation and of optimum location of senior citizen facilities.

Social indicators data, along with other kinds of data, may provide the inputs needed for building theoretical models about aging. Such models may eventually generate prognostications on the number of older persons who will seek a particular recreational or medical service, the number who may be admitted to nursing home care, etc.

In deciding which series to establish and maintain, thought should be given not only to the intrinsic importance of the series but to the extent of its interrelationships with other series. For example, transportation of older people not only is of major importance in and of itself, but it has implications for access to medical care, recreation, and education. Studies of this kind eventually may demonstrate that, if more money is invested in increasing the mobility of the elderly, there will be compensating savings in cost of new recreational buildings, in lowered welfare costs as a result of increased employment, etc. In other words, it may be possible to superimpose cost-benefit studies upon social indicator investigations, though this may still be a long way off.

Changes in social indicators at the local level may be affected by events over which local authorities have no control. For example, a sharp increase in Social Security retirement benefits may profoundly affect housing and recreation patterns. A large influx of affluent aged into a community may boost the overall position of older persons in areas such as income and health. Local programs sometimes credited with such improvements may have made no contribution in bringing about the change.

Broad social indicators, such as mortality and morbidity statistics, rarely are sufficiently specific to provide a basis for evaluating special projects. They will not eliminate the need for evaluation studies tied to specific projects.

For example, a drop in the tuberculosis death rate in persons over age 65 may be due to a discovery program linked to chest x-rays, to improved nutrition among the elderly, to a more efficacious treatment program, etc.

Sources of Information

Collection, organization, and interpretation of age-related information are among the most important tasks of social gerontology. Immense amounts of data of all kinds are obtained from the American public and much of it can be processed so that it will enhance our understanding of the aging. Unfortunately, only a small amount of available information is being used. Every city of substantial size should develop a data bank on aging; such a bank could be tapped for many different purposes.

One of the richest and most respected sources of information about the aging is the decennial census. Unfortunately, the pace of change is so rapid that it soon becomes out of date. Moreover, even after the census is taken, several additional years may elapse before detailed analysis by age is completed. Pressure is growing for a full census every five years; the work of social gerontology would be aided by such an innovation. The census made at the beginning of each decade often is supplemented by special censuses made for particular purposes, frequently sponsored by State or local governments. These usually include a question about age. The Federal government, which undertakes or supports more survey research than any other body in the world, is a gold mine of data about the aging. Some of the samples are large enough to make local analyses meaningful.

Indeed, the available amount of so-called "secondary data" about the aging is staggering; it can be scooped up quickly by resourceful investigators, particularly if government agencies are cooperative. Examples of such data include age-related reports on adult school and college enrollments, by field or subject; library book borrowing; hospital admissions, by cause of illness and length of stay; marriage and divorce; mental hospital commitments and incompetency proceedings; arrests, by type of offense; convictions and sentences, by type of offense; crime victims, by type of crime; automobile accidents, drivers and pedestrians; licensed automobile drivers; welfare beneficiaries, income and property tax returns; Social Security recipients; veterans; and health and vital statistics. As more and more information is put on punch cards and analyzed by computers, the possibilities for characterizing an aging population expand sharply.

The collectors of information must be persuaded to include age as an item, and either cross-tabulate other data against age themselves or make their cards or tapes available to those who are interested in doing so. It is also important to be able to disaggregate or reaggregate information on a geographical basis. The Census Tract is the preferred basic unit for most gerontological studies and much would be gained if all collectors of information would systematically record the Census Tract in which it was obtained.

Non-government organizations are another rich source of information about the aging. Utilities, such as those that provide electricity and telephone service, could supply information on movements of the aging within their area of operation. How much in-migration and out-migration is there? How much moving by older persons is taking place within the area? Where are older persons coming from and where are they going?

Market research activities generate hugh amounts of data about the behavior and preferences of older consumers. Much of this material is potentially valuable to social scientists. Since it is proprietary, and often used for competitive purposes, some of it may not be immediately available for public use. However, some of the item runs—particularly those included for cross-tabulation purposes—may be available on request. For example, it may be possible to get an age breakdown of a newspaper's subscribers or of a bank's savings and demand account holders. Radio and television program rating services often publish age breakdowns of audience composition.

Many political and social surveys are made, both locally and nationally. Usually, these are not repeated. The discerning scholar, however, can pick up age trends even if the questions are not identical at different time periods. A question about age is included routinely in most surveys of this kind.

Up to this point, attention has been focused on information collected primarily for non-gerontological purposes and which is available at little or no cost. The primary source of gerontological information must be the sample survey addressed to the aging, since the quality of their lives can best be judged by them. A social indicators questionnaire places heavy emphasis on subjective as well as objective data. Since the items in such a questionnaire will be repeated year after year in order to establish trends, they must be carefully constructed. Since such a questionnaire usually deals with many topics—such as housing, free time, transportation, health, employment, and education—it is possible to work out interrelationships and trends in interrelationships. The chief problem with the repeated administration of a social indicators questionnaire is the cost. On the other hand, the cost of a survey is trivial in comparison with the sums that are being blindly invested in facilities and services for the aging.

Data-gathering on the position of the aging presents problems of timing, cost, and changes in the phenomena that are being measured. Ideally, it would be desirable to have continuous reporting on at least some of the measures of importance to the aging. For example, it would be useful to have a monthly report in each locality on the number of persons age 65 or over seeking work, the number placed during the previous month, the characteristics of those who obtained employment, the characteristics of those who did not obtain employment, etc. Similarly, it would be helpful to have continuous reporting in the health area, such as the number and characteristics of those who have had tests for diabetes or glaucoma, or immunization against flu. It is conceivable that the adoption of a comprehensive national health program may make it possible to gather immense amounts of information which can be tapped as needed in the service of the aging and which would yield progress reports at short intervals. Although it has become traditional to issue annual reports, in many action programs it is important to have information on a more frequent basis.

Gerontologists have pioneered in the development of longitudinal studies and much of their experience is applicable to the social indicators field. Time and money invested in the perfection of instruments which will be used repeatedly over a long period of time is worthwhile. Anticipation of areas of information which will become important in the future can be rewarding. The following of individual lives through time may provide insights which may be lost if only gross statistical summaries are prepared, particularly in the interrelationships of the variables under analysis.

The social indicator movement cannot escape the problem of establishing priorities and of consciously identifying some areas as more important than others. These priorities will be reordered as changes occur and as basic problems are solved. Existing data series will be curtailed or eliminated and new series will be started within such broad categories as health, employment, recreation and housing.

As a result of government intervention, by placing a floor

under income, the aging probably will be first major group in this country to be lifted en bloc above the poverty line. Substantial percentages of the aging already are in the middle or upper income categories. It is predictable that the private sector will become increasingly interested in the aging as their disposable income and discretionary spending rises. Private enterprise has demonstrated its ability to produce attractive new facilities, goods, and services when the market is able to support them. The development of data banks of the type proposed in this chapter would aid private enterprise in more effectively serving the aging.

As activities in behalf of the elderly increase, and as information of the kinds described in this chapter become available, it will be possible for local governments or agencies to prepare an annual local social report on the aging. Such a report would present all significant statistics on the aging that are available, particularly those that exist in series form so that changes may be noted. The collected information would be analyzed and evaluated. Unmet needs would be identified and proposals for meeting these needs would be spelled out.

Increasingly, the community will be the place "where the action is" in the development of programs for the aging. Much of the money may come from Washington, D.C., but planning and implementation can best be accomplished by those who are familiar with local conditions. Moreover, local government has the ability to exercise a controlling influence through its powers of taxation, zoning, and allocation of public services and facilities. A continuing study of social indicators will enable local government to do a better job for the aging.

BIBLIOGRAPHY

Dial, O. E.: *Some Ambiquities of Social Indication.* Greenvale, N. Y., Long Island University Press, August 1972, p. 10. (Paper prepared for the Panel on Social Indicators, 1972 Conference of the Urban Regional Information Systems Association, San Francisco, August 29-September 2, 1972.)

Full Opportunity Act, Hearings Before the Special Subcommittee for Evaluation and Planning of Social Programs of the Committee on Labor and Public Welfare, U.S. Senate, 91st Congress, First and Second Sessions, on S. 5 to Promote the Public Welfare, July 7, 8,

10, 18; December 8, 1969, and March 13, 1970. Washington, U.S. Government Printing Office, 1970, p. 63.

Gross, Bertram M.: The State of the Nation: Social Systems Accounting. In Bauer, Raymond A., (Ed.): *Social Indicators*. Cambridge, Massachusetts Institute of Technology Press, 1969, pp. 255-256.

Harland, Douglas G.: Social Indicators in a Futures Context, an unpublished paper presented to the Ottawa, Canada, Futures Society, November 25, 1971.

Krieger, Martin H.: *Social Reporting for a City: A Perspective and Some Problems*. Berkeley, University of California Center for Planning and Development Research, 1971.

Ontell, Robert: *Toward A Social Report for the City of San Diego*. San Diego, Urban Observatory of San Diego, 1972, ch. 1 and 2.

U.S. Department of Health, Education and Welfare, Administration on Aging: *Social Indicators for the Aged*. Minneapolis, Institute for Interdisciplinary Studies, American Rehabilitation Foundation, 1970.

U.S. Department of Health, Education and Welfare: *Toward A Social Report*. Washington, D.C., U.S. Government Printing Office, 1969.

Walters, Dorothy and Stewart, Gail: Unpublished papers presented at the Canadian Council Seminar, Ottawa, Canada, April 1972.

PART II

MODELS AND
THEIR APPLICATIONS

Chapter III

A MODEL FOR COMPREHENSIVE MENTAL HEALTH CARE FOR THE AGED

Alexander Simon

THERE WERE MORE than twenty million persons aged sixty-five and older in the United States in 1970—10 percent of the population. This age group has increased much faster than the rest of the population and is today six and a half times as large as in 1900, while the population under age sixty-five is only two and a half times as large. About 5 percent of the aged live in institutions of various kinds, fewer than 1 percent in mental hospitals and the remainder in nursing homes, boarding homes, old age homes, and other types of residential care facilities, where it is estimated that from 50 to 80 percent of the residents suffer from some degree of psychiatric impairment (Goldfarb, 1962; Stotsky, 1967). About 26 per cent of the aged live alone or with nonrelatives, depending upon community resources and services for survival. A significant segment of the aged population is concentrated in urban ghettos, in substandard housing in broken-down rooming houses and hotels. Many are lonely, apathetic, depressed, isolated, and poverty-stricken, living in fear of being robbed or attacked and restricting their movements outside their rooms to the minimum. It is estimated that from 15 to 25 percent of the elderly who live in the community suffer from mental impairment of moderate to severe degree, with a minimum of 8 percent being as severely impaired as elderly patients who have been hospitalized (Lowenthal *et al.*, 1967).

The increase in the elderly population and growing interest in the health problems of the aged have led to the development of the field of geriatrics. Questions about this field are widely debated: Is geriatrics a branch of medicine in its own right? Is it a medical specialty, and if so, how is it defined? Is there such a thing as a "geriatric patient?" Is it true that every internist and general practitioner is, in a sense, a "geriatrician?" Are special units needed for the care of old people, or is this merely a way to siphon off aged patients from the acute medical wards of general hospitals? Whatever the answers to such questions, it is clear that the aged population presents a major health problem for society and especially for those professionals on whom the primary responsibility has fallen for providing care not only for the "hard core" of old, deprived, dependent, and seriously ill but also for the much larger group of aged for whom preventive and supportive services are needed in order to avoid or postpone as long as possible any future illness and disability and, just as important, to encourage the maintenance of a full and satisfying life (Isaacs *et al.,* 1972).

The group we call the "aged" like all age groups is made up of individuals. They do not constitute a homogeneous group, and the existence of individual differences as well as differences such as those between ethnic groups, varying socioeconomic levels, circumstances, needs, and desires, must be recognized when services are planned for them. Programs of all kinds, including those for physical and mental health, must have as their aim the preservation of the older person's personal dignity, the treatment of individuals according to their needs and as far as possible their wishes, and the development of their potential according to their capacities.

The elderly will not all suffer from what has too often been considered an inescapable mental deterioration in old age. But they are subject to serious stresses and face a variety of difficulties that require a variety of management approaches (Simon, 1970). Special mental health problems (in addition to the mental and emotional illnesses that may affect persons of all ages, and the organic brain syndromes that are more characteristic of old age) are related to the aging process and to the overall conditions and circumstances in which the aged live in our society. These problems include alcoholism, drug dependence, suicide (Sainsbury, 1962), nutritional problems that contribute to psychiatric disturbances, depression, isolation and alienation (Lowenthal, 1964), morale problems, arrests (which in this age group are mostly related to drunkenness and so reflect mental health problems [Epstein *et al.*, 1970]), and problems associated with translocation shock resulting from moves such as those from home to hospital or nursing home, or from institution to institution, or moves within the community that may be brought about, for example, by urban renewal projects (Lieberman, 1969; Jasnau, 1967). Our primary mental health goal for these persons is to provide adequate and appropriate preventive, therapeutic, supportive, and rehabilitative programs to help them to live at home or, if necessary, in suitable health care or residential facilities that then become their new homes and communities, with ready availability of a wide range of services required for all levels of physical and mental disability.

While it has been widely held that the elderly are better off in their homes, maintaining themselves or being assisted by family members, the patient and his family should participate in the final decision about home care versus institutional care. Families vary in their willingness and ability to care for their aged members, who frequently are both physically and mentally ill. Too often, however, the decision for institutional placement is forced by lack of supportive services in the community (Grad and Sainsbury, 1968). It has been noted, also, that psychiatrists, other physicians, and welfare agencies may at times underestimate the burden that elderly patients place on their families, and so may tend to exert inappropriate pressure on families to keep an old person at home (Goldfarb, 1967). To be effective, community care must keep the right people out of institutions and do so without causing more misery than it prevents. Institutions are an important point in the continuum of care, to be used when appropriate. At the same time, it is certainly true that many families prefer to care for elderly relatives at home, despite the problems, and would be willing to do so if they know that quick assistance was available from professionals when needed—up to and including hospitalization at times of crisis for the patient or the family (Sainsbury and Grad, 1971).

Only if services of all kinds are available in the community will families be free to make the choice of alternatives that best suits their own situation.

COMPREHENSIVE CARE

Definition

The comprehensive and continuing health care needed by the aged includes not only "the diagnosis and treatment of illness but also its prevention and the supportive and rehabilitative care that helps a person to maintain, or to return to, as high a level of physical and mental well being as he can attain" (A.M.A., 1966, p. 36). The achievement of this goal requires the provision of the necessary number of high quality programs and facilities; the training of adequate numbers of professional, allied health, and administrative personnel; the support of research to provide the basic knowledge and techniques needed for a fuller understanding of the aging process and for the development of specific preventive and treatment programs and efficient and economical methods for the delivery of health services for the aged; and the development and expansion of educational programs for professionals, including continuing education for caretaking personnel in various types of residential care facilities, and for the general public, the aged themselves, and their families. Suitable administrative organization must provide for both centralized and decentralized functions, for establishing standards, licensing, data collection, and monitoring and evaluation of programs.

Comprehensive care further requires the active participation and motivation of the patient, both in the planning and delivery of health services and in developing a sense of responsibility for his own health rather than adopting a passive role and wishing the burden of responsibility to be assumed by a physician or institution. This requirement poses a special problem for the aged mentally ill and for the many elderly persons who are isolated, who rarely initiate efforts to seek medical care until a crisis arises, and who are faced with serious financial and transportation difficulties in relation to seeking health care.

Everything that is known about the treatment of mental illness in general is applicable to the aged. Therapeutic nihilism is not justified; the aged can benefit from all types of psychiatric therapy, although the goals may have to be limited for some. Mental health can be maintained and improved by appropriate medical treatment of the many illnesses to which they are vulnerable. Treatment must be given for the physical illnesses and organic and functional mental disorders that have in the past often been left untreated in the elderly because they were regarded as "just the result of old age."

Anticipated increases in the number of elderly persons in the population will bring an increase in the number of patients with chronic diseases, with accompanying emotional problems and evidence of mental impairment. Adequate programs directed at treatment of chronic and acute physical conditions might well prevent the development of some types of mental illness in these old persons, and slow the deteriorative process by the prevention of acute illness and a consequent forestalling of the acute confusional states so often seen in the elderly. Other preventive programs include efforts to involve older persons in meaningful activities as volunteers or as paid workers, for example as foster grandparents or as workers in identification and information-giving programs; training and educational programs to enable older persons to review skills and learn new ones that may permit employment or the enjoyment of intellectual pursuits; and the general education of the public, including students in schools, colleges, and professional schools, about human development from infancy and childhood through the young adult and middle years, the aging process, and reactions to death and dying.

Effective screening is essential to identify and make suitable referrals of old persons in need of help. Screening must include complete medical evaluation, including psychiatric evaluation; evaluation of socioeconomic resources; and legal evaluation, including determination of the need for conservatorship. Such screening can take place in the community, as casefinding prior to treatment in a hospital or elsewhere; it can take place at the time of hospitalization; and it can take place subsequent to—even years after—hospitalization or placement in some other institutional setting. The primary aim of screening is placement of the patient where he will receive the best available treatment and services in circumstances most appropriate to his condition—physical, mental, social, and economic (Rypins and Clark, 1968).

In its broadest sense, prevention of geriatric mental illness requires the provision of environmental advantages throughout life, minimal exposure to injurious circumstances and agents, including disease, and maximal use of available preventive and remedial medical and social services. Comprehensive care for the aged, then, really should begin early in life and extend into old age and include all those efforts of society that contribute to optimal growth and development, education, and personal integration. The elderly person should be able to feel challenged rather than defeated by adversity and should be able to make use of those resources in the community that can help him to act and to do, within the limits of his capacity, despite a loss of vigor and functional capacity (Goldfarb, 1967).

Resources and Manpower for Comprehensive Mental Health Care

The resources required for a program of comprehensive mental health care for the aged are available in greatly varying quantity and quality in most communities throughout the nation. These may be categorized in a number of ways, although the categories overlap and may be defined differently in different areas and by different groups of health personnel. Table III-I lists the overall hospital and nonhospital residential facilities and extramural services that would constitute a comprehensive mental health care program. Unfortunately, there does not exist in any community an adequate coordination of services and agencies involved with programs for the older population. There is too often overlapping of responsibility and authority, duplication of services, and shifting of patients from one agency to another, with fragmentation of available treatment resources, problems in communication at the professional level, and a too sharp separation of outpatient, inpatient, supportive, and aftercare services.

Inadequacies in present programs of all kinds arise from difficulties relating to too few facilities, manpower shortages, lack of adequate financing, lack of training programs for caretaking per-

TABLE III-1

SERVICES AND FACILITIES
FOR COMPREHENSIVE MENTAL HEALTH CARE

Services

General medical care
Psychiatric treatment and consultation
Therapeutic and rehabilitative programs
Social work services
Social and recreational activity programs
Protective and supportive services

Hospital and Nonhospital Residential Facilities

Mental hospitals: private, county, state
General hospitals: medical and psychiatric units
Nonhospital residential facilities:
    Nursing homes (including intermediate care facilities)
    Boarding homes
    Old age homes
    Residential hotels
    Retirement homes and communities
    Halfway houses

Extramural Services

Treatment services: Outpatient psychiatric services and community mental health
    center psychiatric services
    Neighborhood health centers
    Alcohol treatment centers
    Physicians' and psychiatrists' private services
    Screening program services
    Visiting nurse services
    Day care centers
    Home health care services
    Sheltered workshops
    Outreach programs

Preventive services: Suicide prevention centers
    Health programs in rural areas
    Senior centers and social clubs
    Multipurpose informational and educational services
    Mental health consultation to agencies serving the aged

Protective and supportive services:
    Social work services
    Welfare services
    Conservator services
    Legal aid
    Volunteer services
    Attendant care
    Homemaker services
    "Meals on Wheels"
    Advocates
    Respite services
    Indigenous workers
    Transportation, public and private
    Hobby and activity centers
    Foster Grandparent program
    Telephone contacts

TABLE III-2

MANPOWER FOR COMPREHENSIVE MENTAL HEALTH CARE

General and specialist physicians, including psychiatrists
Psychologists
Social workers
Nurses and nursing aides
Rehabilitation therapists
Legal counselors
Recreation therapists
Volunteers
Advocates (both ombudsmen and those directly serving aged patients)
Indigenous workers
Homemakers and home aides
Bus and car drivers
Well aged as workers

sonnel and of educational programs for the public, and program deficiencies resulting from both lack of knowledge about the best programs to support and lack of personnel to present programs.

Health and allied personnel serving the mentally ill aged are listed in Table III-2. Figures are not available as to the numbers of these workers who are at present providing services to the aged, but government figures show that nurse's aides are the largest single group employed in the field of care for the aged. There is a particularly pressing need for recruiting, training, and retraining a stabilized and well qualified corps of aides who can receive adequate financial compensation and job satisfaction, including career development opportunities, in this type of employment, both in residential care facilities and providing home care.

Relationship of Physical Health and Mental Health Care

Since mental and physical health are essentially inseparable, and this is especially obvious in the aged, it can be argued that mental health and physical health services should not be separated. An alliance of mental and physical health services would provide more opportunity for training of all health personnel in the psychosocial problems of elderly patients, with whom all in the health professions must deal. If well organized and integrated, such a combined program would reduce fragmentation and duplication of services. Proper epidemiologic studies could identify medical and psychiatric problems and social and economic needs, and result in better understanding of the relationships among these problems and needs. Regional medical programs are being developed throughout the country, especially in such categoric areas as heart disease, stroke, and cancer. The concept of such programs is being applied increasingly on statewide and regional bases to encourage the development of regional comprehensive health centers. In itself, this concept more than implies that problems associated with mental health and mental illness should be an integral part of a comprehensive regional health plan (Simon, 1971).

At the same time, many mental health professionals are fearful that if mental health services are part of statewide or even local overall health services, the tremendous mental health needs of the aged, neglected for so many years, will not receive the attention they so desperately need. If mental health services are submerged in overall health programs, they certainly will not have the visibility of separate agencies, and the aged mentally ill, a deprived group even within the field of mental health, might be even worse off than they have been in the past.

However the problems of organization are resolved, the needs of the aged must be emphasized, possibly by the setting up of specific divisions of aging or of identified separate units labeled as mental health units for the aged and specializing in consultation on problems of the aged, program evaluation, manpower training, and research realted to the field. Experts on mental health aspects of aging must be represented in such units in order to achieve necessary coordination and integration.

It has become a truism to emphasize the holistic approach to patient care, and such an attitude is inherent in the concept of comprehensive medical care. Comprehensive care programs for the aged need leadership with an investment in geriatrics and the mental health problems of the aged. Specialists in aging are few in any clinical field, including psychiatry. It is particularly important that the basic concepts of human development, including geriatric medicine and gerontology, be included in the training and experience of all health professionals, so that planning and implementation of programs for the aged, wherever this takes place, will be on a sound basis.

The President's Task Force on the Mentally Handicapped (1970) has recommended as a long-term goal:

> The establishment of community-based geriatric programs, each serving a defined geographical area and providing diagnosis, short-term treatment, and placement. Though separately funded and staffed, these should, wherever possible and appropriate, be affiliated with a comprehensive health center and include psychiatric consultation services. In other facilities and programs now caring for the aged, adequate health care and psychiatric consultation services must be available (p. 2).

Particular attention is needed to certain "high risk" groups in the elderly population—those with low socioeconomic status and low levels of education; certain of those who are retired; the recently bereaved; the single, separated, and divorced and the socially isolated; the alcoholics; the physically ill; and those who have made suicide attempts (Simon *et al.*, 1970).

MULTIPURPOSE GERIATRIC FACILITIES

In some areas, especially in metropolitan centers, consideration may be given to the development of large multipurpose facilities that can provide needed comprehensive services—physical health, mental health, and supportive services of all kinds—to the aged, whether they are in mental hospitals or nursing or boarding homes or are living in the community. Whether such multipurpose facilities are housed under one roof or various aspects of the program are distributed among various facilities depends on the present availability of such facilities and the ability of the community to organize them into a well functioning, coordinated whole. In any case, smaller satellite units may be necessary in certain areas where minority groups live, so that elderly patients can communicate with individuals who are familiar with the health folklore of the group. These satellite units could be part of public health clinics, senior service centers, information centers, and the like.

Where large multipurpose geriatric facilities are developed, they must take into consideration both individual and group differences pertinent to the care of the aged. With respect to mental health needs, for example, there are fundamental differences between the "young old" patients and the "old old" patients, that is, between patients who are depressed, paranoid, alcoholic, or have other functional disorders, who are mostly in the age group sixty-five to seventy-four, and patients suffering from organic brain syndromes, who are mostly aged seventy-five and older. The younger and older types of aged patients require different types of therapeutic approach. The younger patients are more likely to be physically ill and to be in general hospitals, while the older ones often have acute illnesses that are superimposed on chronic illnesses and are more often in nursing homes.

While large facilities in general tend to have less interpersonal contact between staff and patients, they may offer a variety of programs and services that a smaller unit cannot so easily make available. An advantage of the large multipurpose geriatric center is that as a patient's condition changes, moves from one level of care to another are more easily made, both geographically and administratively. When services are scattered in the community, moves from one institutional setting to another are more difficult and may be more upsetting to the patient.

Some way must be provided to make certain that patients in fact receive comprehensive care that is available, that they seek help, understand what is recommended and what is available, are directed to the appropriate help and actually receive the needed services, and are followed to be sure that the help given was effective (Gaitz, 1970). A person who can act as advocate or coordinator for the patient can help to overcome many of the obstacles that may face a sick or confused or just timid or apathetic old person who needs care. Such a coordinator can be of great assistance to family members and to caregivers, also, because his overall view of the patient's needs and resources and of the resources available in the community make it possible for him to give appropriate information and advice and to encourage realistic expectations of what can be accomplished for the patient.

In sparsely populated areas and states it is much more difficult to develop special geriatric programs and it may be necessary for neighboring communities or counties to deal cooperatively. In such areas, transportation is necessary to bring patients to the central facility for examination and treatment, or traveling teams of mental health specialists may make regular visits to such areas.

COMMUNITY MENTAL HEALTH CENTERS

The trend in recent years has been to provide services for the mentally ill, especially the elderly mentally ill, outside mental hospitals, both by screening in the community and making alternative placements and by screening in the mental hospitals and discharging long-term residents to placements in the community (Simon and Epstein, 1970). The result has been a tremendous increase in the number of persons living alone or with families or in resident care facilities who are urgently in need of mental health services.

Responsibility for providing such services is being focused primarily in the community mental health centers, which unfortunately have not given a high priority to the needs of the aged mentally ill. The aged have been underrepresented among users of the centers and there are very few programs that give special attention to the needs of the aged. Community mental health centers have failed to involve themselves with various community groups, agencies, and senior citizens groups dealing with the aged. There are few formalized programs such as preretirement counseling, consultation to housing developments where the elderly reside, or outreach programs and specialized programs for the aged of minority and various ethnic groups. The rural mentally ill aged are an especially neglected group.

To be truly functional in serving the mentally ill aged, the community mental health centers must provide high quality services, they must be easily available, geographically accessible, and comprehensive in approach. Mental health personnel must be available at all hours and for emergencies and must work closely with the police, courts, and social and welfare agencies, as well as with medical facilities of all kinds and with nursing and broading homes. The community mental health center can itself be the comprehensive care unit for the aged, having available to it other aspects of the health care system, and it can at the same time be a part of the system.

Each community mental health center should be required to have a specific, highly visible, specialized, and competent group or team responsible for geriatric comprehensive mental health services (Beigel, 1970). The aims of this group would be:

1. The identification of community needs, especially in the area of development of outreach programs to locate the isolated, "socially invisible" elderly.

2. Identification of resources available in the community, including private and public agencies and individual health service personnel, specialized units such as centers for suicide prevention, alcoholism, drug abuse, and so forth.

3. Development of a coordinated program with other health care agencies utilized by the aged in general and the aged mentally ill in particular.

4. Development of information and counseling centers, including subunits in neighborhoods, ethnically oriented where appropriate, and with the substantial utilization of the services of the well aged to carry out appropriate roles.

5. Service program development, including:
    (a) Screening centers and programs, including outpatient and inpatient facilities for assessment when necessary;
    (b) Use of advocates, including the well aged to assure utilization and continuity of services for the aged;
    (c) Improvements in standards of care in nonhospital residential care facilities, with specific identification of required programs;
    (d) Inservice training programs in all health facilities in which the aged are cared for, and basic educational programs for the general public and for health personnel;
    (e) Supportive-protective services;
    (f) Mental health consultation to public and private agencies; and
    (g) Preventive programs.

6. Basic and operational research programs.

EVALUATION

Evaluation is becoming increasingly important in the development and management of health policies and programs. Despite the obvious need to analyze programs and to measure their success and failure in meeting their goals, the methodologies and systems that can produce such assessments are still in their beginning stages. Nevertheless, provision for evaluation should be a required part of all such programs.

Evaluation of policies and programs dealing with the mental health and mental illness of the aged should extend from the broadest state level down to the specific operation of projects at the local level, including their impact on individuals. Clearly, this cannot be accomplished without adequate funds and personnel with the necessary technical background and experience.

Evaluation is concerned with program effectiveness in reaching its goals more than with its efficiency of operation. Evaluation includes: definition of program objectives, development of measures of progress toward these objectives, assessment of what programs actually accomplish, and projection of what can be expected if programs are continued, expanded, or limited.

Applied to services for the aged, this means first of all that criteria must be determined for the population to be served, which includes not only the aged in various kinds of institutional settings but also other impaired elderly persons living in the community and well elderly persons for whom specially developed programs are needed in order to prevent their entering the group of impaired persons. We must learn what the needs are of this overall population, what services are already available, the extent to which they are utilized by the group they are intended to serve, and what their effects are on the users of the services and their families. We must be able to estimate the extent to which present services fall short of meeting both present and future needs of their target populations.

The present concentration on providing mental health services at the local level, primarily through community mental health centers, makes these centers the basic source of needed information, both through already required reporting and through additional requirements that might be made part of evaluation programs. The community mental health centers, as providers of services, will themselves be the subject of evaluation, both as to the effectiveness of their programs for the aged and as to the comparative effectiveness of different centers in serving the aged within their respective catchment areas. Evaluation strategies must be developed that are readily applicable to and by the community mental health centers.

It is essential, however, that the primary responsibility for seeing that evaluation is required and carried out, and that the results are used appropriately, remain at the state level. A division of aging in each state's department of mental hygiene (or equivalent) should include an evaluation system with adequate staff and money to measure the effectiveness of major programs, and those who plan and implement these programs (whether public or private) should be required to include evaluation plans in their budget proposals.

Responsibility for evaluation at the state level is especially important for programs for the mentally ill aged, inasmuch as they have been and are now being moved in large numbers from facilities (state mental hospitals) in which the state traditionally has cared for them, and placed in a wide variety of other facilities, mostly nursing and boarding homes. It is incumbent upon the state to assure itself that these old people are in fact receiving care of a kind and quality commensurate with their needs. This assurance can be provided only by adequate follow-up studies and by evaluation of facilities and services in relation to the needs of the aged populations of the various local communities.

Among the tasks of evaluation that are needed (and the priorities must be determined) are:

Program impact valuation (assessment of the overall effectiveness of a program in reaching its stated objectives, or of the relative effectiveness of two or more programs in meeting common objectives);

Program strategy evaluation (assessment of the relative effectiveness of different techniques or methods used in a program);

Field experiments and demonstration projects;

Local program evaluation;

Monitoring (assessment of managerial and operational efficiency of programs or projects);
Routine data reporting;
Cost analysis; and
Development of evaluation methodology

Emphasis should be on the development of short-term and long-term indicators of effectiveness, systems for assessing the relative effectiveness of comparable local projects, and standard systems of comparing project costs.

In assessing specific services to the aged, questions that must be considered include (Group for the Advancement of Psychiatry, 1970):

What do the aged, their families, community agencies, and physicians think of the services?

Is a full range of services easily available and well known throughout the community?

Are resources distributed among services on the basis of needs and effectiveness of investment?

What are the costs of the various types of services?

Are aged patients seen in proportion to their number in the population and are efforts made to extend services to racial and ethnic groups that may not previously have been served?

Do new patients get prompt and thorough evaluation and treatment?

Are discharged patients followed up as thoroughly as is clinically indicated?

Is consultation given to agencies and institutions working with the aged and are services for the aged coordinated?

Is there a particular person (an advocate) in the facility or agency who gives special attention to the needs of the aged?

Do staff members have a positive attitude toward treating the aged and do they consistently include the needs of the aged in their planning?

Responsibility for evaluation should be placed at a level appropriate to the decisions it is designed to assist. To the extent possible, major evaluation responsibilities should be directed by independent persons with no vested interest in the outcome. This should take full advantage of the experience of the aged themselves. Full-time evaluation personnel should be assigned to this area, at both the local and state levels, and evaluation strategies should be coordinated for all groups that are the targets for mental health programs, including the aged. Contracting for evaluation studies, field experiments, and demonstration projects will be necessary in many cases, because of limitations of staff time and expertise at the local level.

CONCLUSION

The importance of life and living for everyone is part of our ethic and morality, and the health needs of the entire population must be considered and met to the best of our abilities. But even though one cannot place a higher priority on the needs of any specific group, such groups may represent special problems and long term deprivations that we wish to exert a special effort to remedy. Certainly, the mental health problems of the aged population fall into this category.

The resources of physicians (including those trained largely at public expense) and other health personnel and hospitals are today to a large extent public or community resources and "their allocation and conditions of use are thus a public concern. The escalation from individual need to community crisis to public funding to public decision making is the choreography of social action in a democratic society." (U. S. Department of Health, Education, and Welfare, 1970, p. 5).

In this time of crisis in health care, the tendency is to deal with immediate crisis situations and operational problems related to them, and to give extra emphasis to meeting these situations with the limited funds available. This often is done at the expense of research and training programs. To adopt such an approach, specially as it concerns services for the aged, means that any future change in operational programs that requires the use of increased numbers or different kinds of health care personnel or requires new knowledge would suffer.

Research is particularly likely to suffer from curtailment at times of shortage of money, and basic research is likely to be the first affected, rather than operational and evaluative studies. This is sadly shortsighted, as it is from basic research that real advances in knowledge will come. Basic science studies in the biology of aging, from the biochemical and molecular levels through genetics and the study of organ systems and general organismic functioning, are essential to progress in the field. Behavioral science research includes studies in epidemiology, together with studies that attempt to correlate the physical and mental health, economic, psychologic, psychophysiologic, and social factors concerning the aged and their adjustment.

Difficult as the problems raised by lack of funds may be, a serious effort must be made to provide a well balanced program of services, training, and research, for these are all essential and interdependent elements of an adequate program. Efforts should be directed at finding ways to make our present system of delivery of services more efficient and economical and the providers of services more accountable, always remembering that good quality care requires adequate financial support. Emphasis on preventive and supportive care may have long-range effects in decreasing the amount of expensive institutional care that must be provided. Adequate medical care would help the large numbers of aged who become blind, particularly those with glaucoma, cataracts, and diabetic retinal complications. Adequate attention to visual impairment and hearing defects would decrease the isolation imposed by sensory impairment. Involvement of long-isolated persons in social activity programs might help to reduce the frequency of depression, suicide, and alcoholism. Appropriate social and nutritional programs might lead to increased interpersonal contacts and prevent the lowered tolerance to physical illness associated with a state of malnutrition.

Such preventive programs have been and are grossly inadequate and would seem to merit a high priority, in spite of limited financial resources. Screening programs for the identification of those with handicaps are essential, and once the handicapped have been identified, means must be available to make sure they receive needed help. The requirements for therapeutic services are more widely recognized. The trend toward decreased use of hospitals for the treatment of the aged mentally ill makes it even more imperative that close attention be given to the alternative facilities and services provided. These, because they are more recently developed, are the locus of many problems that will require large expenditures of money and manpower to solve.

The needs are great in all areas relating to the mental well being of the aged—prevention, treatment, training, education, and research. Society has begun to look at the aged from a new perspective, and meeting the needs of this group for community resources presents some of the most urgent challenges facing society today.

BIBLIOGRAPHY

American Medical Association: *The Graduate Education of Physicians.* Chicago, The Association, 1966.

Beigel, A.: Planning for the development of a community mental health center. *Comm Ment Health J, 6*:267-275, 1970.

Epstein, L. J., Mills, C., and Simon, A.: Antisocial behavior of the elderly. *Compr Psychiat, 11*:36-42, 1970.

Gaitz, C. M.: The coordinator: An essential member of a multidisciplinary team delivering health services to aged persons. *Gerontologist, 10*(3):217-220, 1970.

Goldfarb, A. I.: Geriatric psychiatry. In A. Freedman and H. I. Kaplan (Eds.): *Comprehensive Textbook of Psychiatry.* Baltimore, Williams and Wilkins, 1967, pp. 1564-1587.

———: Prevalence of psychiatric disorders in metropolitan old age and nursing homes. *J Am Geriat Soc, 10*:77-84, 1962.

Grad, J. and Sainsbury, P.: The effects that patients have on their families in a community care and a control psychiatric service. A two year follow-up. *Br J Psychiat, 114*:265-278, 1968.

Group for the Advancement of Psychiatry. *Toward A Public Policy on Mental Health Care of the Elderly.* Vol. 7, Report No. 79. New York, Group for the Advancement of Psychiatry, 1970.

Isaacs, B., Livingston, M., and Neville, Y.: *Survival of the Unfittest, A Study of Geriatric Patients in Glasgow.* London, Routledge and Kegan Paul, 1972.

Jasnau, K. F.: Individualized versus mass transfer of non-psychotic geriatric patients from mental hospitals to nursing homes, with special reference to the death rate. *J Am Geriat Soc, 15*:280-284, 1967.

Lieberman, M. A.: Institutionalization of the aged: effects on behavior. *J Gerontol, 24*:330-340, 1969.

Lowenthal, M. F.: Social isolation and mental illness in old age. *Am Sociol Rev, 29*:54-70, 1964.

———— Berkman, P., and Associates: *Aging and Mental Disorder in San Francisco.* San Francisco, Jossey-Bass, 1967.

President's Task Force on the Mentally Handicapped: *Action Against Mental Disability.* Washington, D. C., Government Printing Office, 1970, p. 2.

Rypins, R. F. and Clark, M. L.: A screening project for the geriatric mentally ill. *Calif Med, 109*:273-278, 1968.

Sainsbury, P.: Suicide in the middle and later years. In H. Blumenthal (Ed.): *Medical and Clinical Aspects of Aging.* New York, Columbia University Press, 1962, pp. 97-102.

———— and Grad de Alarcan, J.: The effects of community care on the family of the geriatric patient. *J Geriat Psychiat, 4*:23-41, 1971.

Simon, A. and Epstein, L. J.: Alternatives to mental hospital care for the geriatric patient. In *Current Psychiatric Therapies, Vol. 10.* New York, Grune and Stratton, 1970, pp. 225-231.

———— Lowenthal, M. F., and Epstein, L. J.: *Crisis and Intervention, The Fate of the Elderly Mental Patient.* San Francisco Jossey-Bass, 1970.

Simon, A.: Mental health. In *1971 White House Conference on Aging, Physical and Mental Health, Background and Issues.* Washington, D. C., White House Conference on Aging, March, 1971, 43-83.

————: Physical and socio-psychologic stress in the geriatric mentally ill. *Compr Psychiat, 11*:242-247, 1970.

Stotsky, B. S.: Allegedly non-psychiatric patients in nursing homes. *J Am Geriat Soc, 15*:535-544, 1967.

U.S. Department of Health, Education, and Welfare: *Report of the Task Force on Medicaid and Related Programs.* Washington, D. C., Government Printing Office, 1970, p. 5.

Chapter IV

COPING BEHAVIOR AND THE ENVIRONMENT OF OLDER PEOPLE[1]

M. Powell Lawton

Economists, Planners, architects and politicians have known for years of the importance of the environment, and today the behavior scientists are catching up. To put things into their proper perspective, however, let us acknowledge that the "soft" sciences were, perhaps, forced to retreat into the interiorization of their life view by the too-easy optimism of economic and physical planning. At one time it was possible for some to believe that a life-sustaining income and the razing of slum areas would create a new society. Dynamic psychology and sociology could no more accept this oversimplification then than now, and an unfortunate result may have been their generation-long tendency to overlook the natural and man-made surroundings that are an integral component of the human behavioral system.

It took some lonely souls to recall to us that man behaves in a world of space and objects. Fritz Heider 1959), Isidore Chein (1954), A. H. Maslow (1956), Festinger, Schachter & Back (1950), and others took an occasional look at the environment, while Roger Barker over a period of years quietly trained researchers and produced some empirical data about man and his environ-

1 Parts of this article were presented at the Symposium on Aging. Veterans Administration Hospital, Wadsworth, Kansas, in May 1971.

ment. People in the vanguard of the present surge of interest in social ecology produced a few compelling observations:

Students who sit in the front central region of a classroom participate more in classroom discussions than do those who sit in the rear or peripheral areas (Sommer, 1969).

Pairs of naval recruits undergoing experimental isolation in a limited space establish patterns of marking out and occupying territory that vary with their personalities, the spatial conditions of the isolation, and their expectations regarding the isolation experience (Altman & Haythorn, 1967).

The size of a school—one aspect of its social environment— appears to have predictable consequences for the behavior of the students in it: the large school has a wider range of activities, but a small proportion of students are engaged in the activities; the small school engages a greater proportion of its members, including the marginal student who would almost certainly remain disengaged in a larger school (Barker & Gump, 1964).

Different distances established between two people appear to be appropriate to different types of behavior, relationships between the two people, and cultural standards (Little, 1965). One empirical study, for example, validated Hall's (1966) observation that Arabs interact at closer interpersonal distances than do Americans (Watson & Graves, 1966).

The above examples of knowledge in the area of what I should like to call social ecology suggest that there are several ways of looking at man-environment relationships. One way is to think of environment as a cause of behavior—cold weather, for instance, motivates a search for heavy clothing, shelter, or hot coffee. Conversely, man may change the environment—he builds cities, expressways, temples, and so on in response to inner needs. Stated baldly as cause-and-effect sequences, however, these event chains have a naive sound that does not do justice to the complexity of man-environment relationships. A preferable way of looking at the issue is in transactional terms, that is, as an open system in which man and environment are components, and where the output, behavior, is constantly fed back into the system (Schwartz & Proppe, 1970). In the transactional view, both man and environment are dynamic, and what may appear to be cause in one part of the system may be effect a short step removed. The concepts are old hat in the science of ecology, but necessary to reiterate as we try to apply them to a new area.

The transactional view seems essential to a proper understanding of aging. It is very easy to conceive of the older person as a passive recipient of environmental stimulation. He is said to be "at the mercy of a slum environment", "the victim of economic deprivation", "socially isolated by three flights of steps" and so on. Each of these statements may be true of a given individual or of a large aggregate of older people, but each is only a partial statement of the truth, since none tells us anything about the mutual adaptation process between the older person and his environment. For example, an arthritic lady living on the third floor may exist marginally, awaiting sporadic offers to help from neighbors for basic shopping, and letting her medical needs go untreated. Or, she may systematically organize her errands so that the painful climb occurs only once a week. Or she might demand and organize a cadre of supports, exercising dominance over a social agency, relatives, her doctor and neighbors to help her needs. Or she might change her residence so as to obviate the stair-climbing problem. Each of these behaviors represents an attempt at coping, which can be classified on many dimensions: active vs. passive, social-vs. object oriented, amount of social cost, and adaptive vs. nonadaptive, to name only a few possibilities. Other adaptational efforts may offer more possibilities for the active alteration of the environment, such as a congregate housing project tenant's placing his chair in the center of the pathway of traffic leading into the building.

The relevant components of the behavioral system are the environment, the relatively fixed characteristics of the aging individual, the adaptational styles utilized by the individual, and the inner response of the individual as he copes with his environment. Behavior may be called the result of all these components, yet it is simply another component of the whole system, since the person's inner life is conditioned by his perception of his own behavior, his behavior can directly change his physical environment, and so on. For the present purpose, I should like to linger a while on the coping behavior exhibited by older people in response to differing environmental situations. A close examination of their behavior in adapting to different environments should lead to two types of conclusions that can benefit the older person: first, knowledge of healthy coping mechanisms and ways in which they can be augmented. Second, knowledge of failures in adaptation. This knowledge can lead to the design of supportive or, in Lindsley's terms, prosthetic environments. In the ecological framework, individual adaptation and environmental prosthesis are alternative routes to the production of competent behavior and positive inner states.

I should like to examine two familiar situations of older people in terms of the positive and negative aspects of the environment, the individual's characteristics particularly as affected by the aging process, the competence which he exhibits as he strives to cope with the environment, and his internal sense of well-being in response to this complex of transactions. Two common situations of stress for older people are, first, living in an urban slum and, second, becoming institutionalized.

The Philadelphia Geriatric Center has studied intensively the remaining small population of elderly Jews living in a section of Philadelphia that once contained 30,000 Jews (Lawton, Kleban, & Singer, 1971). This area has a beautiful name—Strawberry Mansion—but is no longer beautiful. The negative aspects of the environment are negative from the point of view not only of our older Jewish subject but from the point of view of younger people and of the black, whether young or old. "Change" in the neighborhood—to use the old euphemism—took place precipitously so that, in only 10 years, the proportion of black residents changed from 64 percent in 1950 to 93 percent in 1960. Disorganization, aided by profiteering real estate owners and scared businessmen, insurance policy writers, and politicians, came in the wake of the change. The most obvious negative environmental stimulus is crime—this area has the highest crime rate in the city. Our research project had trouble finding interviews willing to work in the area, and the residents of the area seem preoccupied with stories of the latest mugging, rape, or armed robbery. The fear blends into the social environment. One is suspicious of one's neighbor, and a sense of common responsibility for others is difficult to establish. Poverty is evident in the physical environment. Housing is substandard for the occupant, and in its collective ambience creates a mood of both suspicion and despair. More concretely, there are bare patches where demolition has occurred, abandoned houses and even whole blocks where people and rodents run wild, and sad attempts to run small businesses tailored to the capabilities of the impoverished. The marginal corner grocery, the check-cashing agency, the luncheonette, and the bar are the residue of the resources that used to be abundant.

Positive environmental features do exist, however. By and large, housing is relatively inexpensive, though in this case the younger black probably fares much worse than the elderly Jew, since the latter either owns his dwelling or has been able to maintain a lower rent without the exploitation that comes when large families come and dwelling units are subdivided. Despite the scarcity of satisfactory resources like a supermarket, a bank, a hospital, library, or post office—none of which exist in the 40-square-block area—the most basic resources are within walking distance: transportation, physician, grocery. There is also a park, whose positive aspect is centered on a small area near a busy street and a park guard's station. For the elderly Jewish resident, there are positive social aspects; despite their rapidly dwindling number, there are still old friends around, and most of the Jewish residents know one another. Finally, the environment is familiar. People have built-in cognitive maps of the area that afford security where the changes have not been too sweeping.

So much for the environment. Now what about the characteristics of the aged individual? Our survey revealed ample evidence of deprived status, even compared with other populations of aged people, as if the survivors remaining in the slum were selected for disability. These people were in poorer health, were less apt to be living with a spouse, were less mobile, and had lower morale than several comparison groups of old people. Evidence from the literature amply documents the likelihood in aged people of chronic illness, limitation on movement, reduced speed of information processing, greater anxiety about new learning, and a greater tendency to fail to respond to appropriate environmental signals. Most of these changes that seem intrinsic to aging are directly traceable to biological aging. While it is by no means true that all older people are impaired, the incidence of illness is greater, and impairment in function thus more widespread.

The behavior expected as a result of the environmental deprivation, the biological limitations, and their combination, are well-known. A whole technology of case-finding and protective services has been developed to take care of older people who live in flats without adequate food supply, medical care, or sanitary facilities. These people may be physically housebound, emotionally disturbed, or simply fearful about walking through a neighborhood preceived as dangerous. Isolation and retreat from human contact is not unusual, particularly where the ethnic or racial composition of the neighborhood has changed. Staying in one's flat every day not only removes the gratification of mutual support and shared experience with others, but it also removes important social monitoring procedures that encourage an individual to maintain his appearance, moderate his behavior in relation to others, and exercise his mental abilities. Poor housing may compound the problems of neighborhood mobility and houseboundedness, particularly where large numbers of steps are involved or where dimly-lit halls with spaces for intruders must be traversed. New York City has hundreds of thousands of 5- and 6-story walkup apartments in older areas where high concentrations of older people occur. Accidents may frequently result from such environmental obstacles.

These are only a few of the maladaptive behaviors that can occur as the single or combined result of multiple deprivations. By no means do all older people exhibit these behaviors, however. In fact, when one goes actually counting, one finds a relatively low rate of American elderly who are either bedfast or housebound—8 percent, (Shanas, 1971); of gross social isolation—5 percent, (Lowenthal, 1964); or of certifiability to mental hospitals—5 percent, (Gruenberg, 1961). Even among our deprived Strawberry Mansioners, 39 percent go out shopping twice a week or more, 54 percent leave the house for some purpose every day, and 23 percent visit neighbors every day. How do they manage so well? One might well have a sense of wonder that 95 percent of older people maintain residence outside institutions, in spite of their biologically and socially-induced aging.

The mechanisms by which such adaptive behavior is maintained are many. By no means are all such mechanisms valued by the larger society, however. I would like to call attention to a few adaptive mechanisms that have varying degrees of social approval. Actually, there is no need at all to attach an evaluative label to any one of them—they are ways of adapting to environmental, biological and social constraints that may, except for extreme instances, preserve independence or even life itself.

Fear of crime in Strawberry Mansion keeps people indoors, as does poor health. Both conditions may reduce the level of social interaction, of participation in organizations, and of other elective, enriching uses of time. The restriction of behavioral space that we found in our subjects was, to be sure, regrettable. On the other hand, what would be the consequences of *not* restricting behavior? There are real dangers in the neighborhood, and the aged are vulnerable physically. There is a real self-protective quality in being able to recognize one's own vulnerability and to act on the basis of it. Even younger people in the neighborhood avoid dark streets at night and learn which areas to bypass in the daytime.

But there may be positive aspects to restricting leisure-time activity that go beyond the simple avoidance of negative consequences. Rationing one's energy theoretically should result in more energy being available for the most critical tasks. This was shown most forcefully in our Strawberry Mansion residents, where evidence of deprivation in status and lower levels of social, organizational, and ambulatory activity were clear. The one area where they did *not* function at a less active level was the area of instrumental activities, such as shopping, cooking, housekeeping and so on. In these area they were as active as anyone, as if they had been very adept in reserving their energies for the behaviors that mattered most in maintaining life.

There is an inner aspect to such behavior, also. Perin (1970) has described coping behavior as being motivated by the need to experience a sense of competence. Experimental psychology has taught us that people modify their expectations so that they remain in accord with their actual potential, and that judgments tend to be made taking account of the level of recent performance on the tasks being judged. People would find it impossible to exist psychologically if, in the face of external or internal limitations on their performing ability, they continued to aspire to levels they may have reached in earlier life, and to feel perpetually incompetent because they could not perform this way. Thus, new "adaptation levels" are formed, new aspirations are set to lie within the range of possible performance. It is behavior of this type that is frequently admired by society—the person who walks to the store regularly in spite of arthritic pain may himself be gratified by the modest achievement of performing in spite of his disability. Substitutions may occur. Housework may become the only area where a housebound woman may exercise her competence. New standards of self-evaluation may be established to be consistent with the limitations on housekeeping ability occasioned by lack of limberness, or by the fact that long flights of steps prevent her emptying trash as often as she may have been accustomed to in the past.

The Strawberry Mansion residents frequently referred to their lack of opportunity for social interaction. By comparison with other groups, they were very dissatisfied with their current level of contact with others. Some verged on a clinical level of depression, expressing feelings of abandonment by the world. These were a distinct minority, however. Far more frequent were people who appraised their present status in negative terms, such as in agreeing with one of our Morale Scale items, "Things keep getting worse as I get older." Yet these people could maintain this low ideological morale without being depressed, while they went about their tasks of daily living. If you want to look at this phenomenon positively, you could call it "another triumph of dogged determination." In any case, while almost everyone in our sample was threatened by social isolation, different people reacted to the situation in different ways. Those who were healthy enough adapted to the threatening environment by finding the safe times and occasions for social interaction. A small "colony" of elderly people lived in houses facing on a busy street; the porches of these houses were frequently populated with elderly people visiting the occupant, using the porch as a safe place for sitting. There are relatively few park guards in the park that the Strawberry Mansion area faces, but one of them stays all day within a few feet of a shelter that has a public toilet and is surrounded by a number of park benches. This area is the major social congregating area for the people of Strawberry Mansion. Thus, the highest coping level in the social domain involves a person in relatively good health seeking out and using the environment in a way that will satisfy his social and possibly locomotor needs, while minimizing the risk of crime or harassment.

Many others do not deal successfully with so many needs. A number of our subjects appeared to have withdrawn more from social contact, either because of poor health, psychological mal-adjustment, or very unfavorable location of residence, from the point of view of security.

One could observe some of the signs of "disengagement" (Cumming and Henry, 1961) in these people. Very frequently, these characteristics, most often viewed very negatively by society, seemed to serve as adaptive cushions between the deprived individual and the onset of clinically diagnosable psychopathology. Active use of reminiscence ("dwelling on the past") was seen. "Interiority", defined by Henry as a heightened cathexis of one's own inner state, as opposed to one's reflected social image, has a very positive aspect; yet, this attitude is probably most often called "self-centeredness" (Henry, 1965). Use of these mechanisms may be deplored if one looks on them as evidence that society, by rejecting the elderly, has forced them to employ desocializing inner processes. On the other hand, those who appear to dwell on their social losses seem to be depressed, or paranoid, or self-hating. A cut above these in the adaptive scale is the person who can be self-centered and enjoy it a bit. Thus, even granting that the social and physical environment may be impoverished, most older people continue to cope and find something satisfying in the perception of their competence in coping.

Poverty is as salient an aspect of the Strawberry Mansion environment as crime or distressed housing. Lack of financial capability to move from relatively cheap housing seems to be the most important single factor in keeping our subjects in Strawberry Mansion. Poverty is both an environmental deprivation and an almost intrinsic aspect of the aging process as programmed by society today. Lack of capacity to buy forces adaptation to a lower level of experienced need. The negative features are obvious: the person may well have his life or his psychological health threatened by not being able to afford life-sustaining or life-enriching goods and services. Adaptation to a lower level of need also protects the individual from the frustration of bitterness of constant awareness of deprivation. This adaptative mechanism—"reality-boundedness"—is very plain in the frequency observed unwillingness of many older people to be able to assume an "as-if" attitude, or to express a wish. The typical response, "How can I tell you what I'd like when I know things have to be this way?" is the bane of a research interviewer's existence. However, this reality-bound attitude is one inner aspect of adaptation to environmental deprivation.

To recapitulate, our look at the older person coping with a slum environment highlights the negative, and sometimes positive, environmental stimuli. Reductions in personal competence due to biological and social aging interact with environmental forces to result in coping behavior and inner responses that vary greatly in style and in adequacy. At worst, the individual dies, exhausts his residual energy, or disintegrates psychologically. The positive side of the continuum ranges from minimally adaptive, threshhold-level competence, to a full, enriched life gained through the overcoming of the environmental, biological, and social obstacles to fulfillment.

The other environmental stress situation to be examined from this transactional viewpoint is the process of ceasing to be a senior citizen and becoming an institutional resident—a "social death", as Glaser and Strauss have called it (1968). The negative aspects of the institutional environment have been identified so often that it seems almost unfair to institutions to dwell on them. The institution constitutes an unfamiliar physical environment whose signals may be unclear. The social environment is also strange. Instead of family members, or a zero social environment, if he lived alone, there are staff and residents who may become involved with the new resident in even the most basic activities of daily living, where previously he was a free agent as he ate, slept, and toileted. Loss of spatial privacy is notorious. The organizational milieu revolves around schedules, seeing to it that large numbers of people do things in a uniform way. There is an extensive genre of architecture, decor, and sensory environment that can be identified as "institutional." If this sort of physical environment is depressing to those of us who can enter and depart from the institution every day, how much more so must it be to those whose total life is spent there?

There are, of course, environmental pluses. Supposedly, the major one is proximity to medical and other types of life-supporting care. There is good evidence that most older people who are admitted to nursing homes or mental hospitals are truly in need of medical care—research shows that people wait too long, if anything, to seek such care (Lowenthal, 1964). For some people, admission to an institution may reintroduce them to an environment that can provide proper food, bathing, sanitary facilities, or shelter from the weather—in short, it may provide asylum for them. Ideally, the institution should also provide a social environment that is benign and help-oriented: staff are trained to anticipate patient needs, to be understanding of the aging process, and to perform patient care in the light of mental health principles. The larger social environment is composed of age peers, so that age-appropriate norms for behavior may become established and common generational experiences may form the basis for more viable interpersonal relationships than occurred when the resident lived in the age-integrated community. Finally, there is the possibility that the institutional environment may be actually more enriching than was the community environment. Some institutions have recreational programs, opportunity for religious observances, or visitors from outside the institution. If a resident was housebound or psychologically isoalted from the social world, institutional life cannot help but be somewhat more stimulating. In fact, Weinstock and Bennett (1969) have presented some evidence that institutionalization may be followed by a rise in the level of cognitive responsiveness of some older people.

Age-related personal liabilities have been detailed in the section on the inner city. People who enter institutions are apt to be physically and mentally vulnerable. The incidence of chronic brain syndrome is very high; therefore, there are many additional disease-related problems such as memory loss, disorientation, decline in personal self-maintenance skills and, sometimes, gross emotional instability.

Behavior typical of the institution is characterized above all by "loss" of behavior, or at least by the loss of behaviors thought to be necessary to the maintenance of life roles. Few institutions have facilities for individual cooking, laundry, or care of one's possessions. There frequently appears to be a conspiracy in policy and practice for staff to assume responsibility for such activities as housekeeping, care of clothing, and the scheduling of the resident's day. Thus, opportunities to exercise one's competence are lost and such decrements in function as may result from physical and mental disorders are further amplified by disuse.

This loss of instrumental roles is one of the most destructive aspects of becoming an institutionalized person. How can a resident develop a positively adaptive response to a pure loss? One does have to look hard, but it is possible to find people developing new roles that are appropriate to the new environment. Social competence is in relatively short supply, and it is possible for the person with modest residual capacities to substitute institution-appropriate functions such as greeter for new residents, assistant in minor clerical or nursing tasks, and so on. Other roles are less obviously positive but, in line with my view of behavior in terms of its ability to sustain the individual above the level of mental and physical collapse, they are not totally maladaptive. Take complaining as a way of life—frustrating to staff, and seemingly self-defeating, chronic complaining sometimes gets one what one wants, in spite of the leveling influence of the institutional environment and the difficulty encountered in trying to get directly what one wants through the use of instrumental skills. Beyond the ability of a complaint to gain the desired need, even where the need can never be satisfied, the mere fact of making the complaint may keep alive the complainer's feeling that he can still discriminate, decide what he wants, and assert his independence by making the complaint.

Social withdrawal has been studied extensively as a phenomenon occurring in the course of aging and has generally been linked to role loss, such as widowhood or retirement, rather than to aging per se. In the institution, social withdrawal seems almost to be the norm. Studies have shown that later-life social behavior in the community predicts to some extent whether one will become quickly socialized into life in the institution (Granick and Nahemow, 1961). The withdrawn, inactive resident is widely seen as a problem: the stimulus poverty of the institution and the marginal energic resources of the resident appear to account for at least some of this behavior. On the other hand, given these two sources of deprivation, how can the institutional resident best cope with the situation? Conserving one's resources is one way and, for the person in marginal health, withdrawal may relieve enough stress to sustain life. One step up the ladder of complexity from simple withdrawal is what I have called the "sitting and watching syndrome." Many of us, made anxious by the thought of any cessation of our own mad pace, are apt to consider the residents who place themselves in chairs near the entrance of an institution or a ward to be indulging in totally null behavior. However, a closer look reveals that, for many of these people, this behavior constitutes the most active life of which they are capable. They are participating in life by means of observation, while leaving more physical or verbal behaving to others. On the lowest level, watching the passing scene varies the sensory stimulus field; people- and activity-watching engender less mental atrophy than would blank staring at the wall opposite one's bed. Other sitter-watchers are not totally withdrawn, but simply more discriminating: they wait for a status-giving conversation with a board member or administrator while finding no stimulation in conversing with a fellow resident.

Territorial behavior has received considerable attention through the easy analogy that animal behavior provides exemplified by the seemingly irrational behavior of fighting men or suburban landowners. Rather than utilizing a wide variety of spaces and physical resources in an institution, many patients will occupy the same space in public areas repeatedly, to the point of becoming very upset if someone else places his coat on the preferred chair, or worse yet, occupies it. Therapeutically-oriented staff may view this behavior as introducing further rigidity into an already too-rigid life, depriving the occupant of the opportunity to exercise his competence elsewhere, and depriving other residents of the variety that might come with their use of the "owner's" space. At worst, fighting may occasionally erupt in defense of what has come to be the squatter's-right property of the owner. Again, the origin of the behavior may be found in the loss of privacy and unique posession of spaces and objects occasioned by entry into an institution and in the physical and mental inability of the resident to range freely in all areas of the institution. In particular, memory loss, disorientation, undependable bladder control and other impairments may heighten the importance of an individual's staking out a location that he knows intimately and in whose close environs he can locate himself. The adaptive nature of territorial behavior and other forms of spatial regression has been described extensively by Hall (1966), Sommer (1967), Esser and others. The level at which territoriality functions adaptively is neatly demonstrated in a study, by Esser, Chamberlain, Chapple, and Kline (1965), of hospitalized schizophrenics. They developed an index of dominance based on observed social behavior, especially that initiated by the patient. Occupancy of the same ward space for at least 25 percent of the total observations was considered evidence of territorial behavior. They found that the most competent patients did not exhibit territorial behavior—presumably their social skill was such that they ranged freely in space and among people and did not need the security of an area to call their own. The least competent also did not exhibit territorial behavior; they were frequently ejected by more dominant patients from wherever they were sitting. Only the patients of moderate social competence exhibited regular and successful territorial behavior. In our institution, patients at very low levels of competence are observed to stake our particular chairs to occupy regularly. DeLong (1967) observed that chronic brain sydrome patients with single rooms were less likely to act in this manner than those who shared rooms in the Philadelphia Geriatric Center. Thus, it would seem that territoriality is a response that, in the well-functioning human being, is taken for granted in behavior, as are home ownership and love of country. Where personally-owned space is scarce, and particularly in association with lowered personal competence, territorial behavior in public spaces becomes a way of coping both with other people and with the threatened loss of self. Many rooms in institutions for the aged are shared by two or more people. Furniture is standardized and frequently shared, and it is sometimes difficult to keep one's own possessions separate from those of other residents. Therefore, the annexing of a chair, or a corner, or a view from a window, is an attempt to preserve a sense of self in concrete form.

The centrality of the resident's inner response to some of the environmental and personal losses, and to his perception of his own behavioral adaptations, already has been suggested. That is, he may well perceive his own "social death"—research by Lieberman, Prock, and Tobin contains evidence of a rise in negative affect as an applicant to a home awaits admission (1968). The medical adtmosphere of the institution is pervasive, and the high level of mental impairment and depression among other residents are potent stimuli for negative feelings in the perceiver. Far more than the community-dweller does the institution resident have to bear the loss of privacy, personal possessions and territory—additional blows to the perceived self. On the other hand, the inner adaptive mechanisms mentioned earlier are utilized to protect the ego against total dissolution: reminiscence, interiority, and reality-boundedness, to name a few.

Thus far, the emphasis has been on the varieties of adaptational responses, both inner and outer, to deprivations from endogenous and exogenous sources. The responses have been sometimes characterized as of varying quality, but there has been a sort of cloud-with-silver-lining tone to my thoughts: even the lowest-level adaptation may be doing something for the person. One difficulty with this approach is that it can be thought of as too accepting of the *status quo*: never mind poor Smith who lies on his urine-soaked floor all day, he is doing the best he can, given a shoddy institution and his loss of bladder-to-brain signals. Clearly, we do not wish to stop at mere analysis of the current situation.

A prescription for treatment would be the natural next phase. However, aging and chronic illness generally being unidirectional processes, traditional concepts of social intervention or psychotherapy are not always applicable. Too-rigid adherence to therapeutic expectations appropriate to younger people is one of the factors that has led to the attitude of therapeutic nihilism about working the elderly. If you expect too much you are bound to be disappointed and, therefore, this proves it isn't worthwhile to put our resources into treating the aged and therefore children deserve the lion's share . . . we have all heard this line of reasoning.

For the present purpose, environmental change is the aspect of the system that will be examined. The term "prosthetic environment" suggests that even the most inert physical environment may become a dynamic component of a system to counteract the negative influence of deficits of any type on behavior.

In the case of Strawberry Mansion, what can the analysis of deprivations and adaptations lead us to in designing environmental prostheses? Money is the generalized reinforcer—an adequate income, and a raise, rather than the cut proposed by Nixon in Medicare coverage, would buy some supportive services. Beyond this basic necessity, planning on an individual, community, and governmental level may improve the environment so as to make the critical difference between incompetent behavior and behavior at a marginally competent level, and therefore make the difference between a negative and a positive perception of oneself.

In a sense, the burgeoning business of housing for the elderly is a major prosthetic operation. Under some ideal conditions a public housing project for the elderly can do the following:

ameliorate poverty by giving shelter at a rate of 25 percent of one's cash income.

reduce vulnerability to crime by giving a secure physical structure, some monitoring of behavior in proximity to the dwelling and, possibly, local escort services.

provide esthetically and functionally pleasant surroundings.

provide a social environment of people who speak one's language.

provide other basic resources, such as food, medical care, or shopping.

This list looks so good as to seem like a panacea. However, in reality, things are not so good. The need for such housing will not be met for many years; much of it is too expensive for the very poor; the slum locations of some projects keep fear of crime alive; some are located far from resources and provide none of their own; some provide a threatening social environment when they include overactive children or teenagers; and isolation is very possible in such environments, with reference to the larger society or one's significant others outside the housing environment.

Congregate living must be carefully planned with the total community and its future needs in mind. Much of the need in areas like Strawberry Mansion is even more acute for the black aged than for residual white groups. It is almost unthinkable not to plan to serve both groups, which in itself occasions many immediate problems, as does the question of building in areas that are already totally ghettoized—is building for aged blacks in a black area justified because of the great need, or should one fight the harder battle involved in building integrated housing in middle class and suburban areas? Looking further ahead, the areas that now are our suburbs will be very badly planned for the aged of the future, with their spatial dispersion, their total dependence on automobile transportation, and their ranks closed to imaginative uses of land. The only answer may be a federal-level compulsion for municipalities and developers to include plans for low-income and elderly people as they deal with the future.

Going back to the level of the individual in the inner city, another obvious point for prosthetic intervention is in his dwelling unit. Total community planning should be able to do a better job of assisting with both remodeling and change of residence within the neighborhood. In our own research, the necessity for managing steps has turned out to be a formidable determinant of people's seeking a change of residence involving their leaving their familiar neighborhood, or even becoming institutionalized. Federal programs for home rehabilitation would be well advised to try to develop a program to assist an older person both to dispose of his owned or rented dwelling unit where it necessitates stair-climbing, and to relocate himself on a ground-floor level. There should also be assistance provided in the technology of small-scale remodeling so as to substitute ramps for small sets of steps.

At the level of housekeeping skills, a sense of competence seems relatively easy to maintain as long as the housewife remains even minimally mobile. One would want, however, to include in the training of what will probably be a growing number of homemakers a respect for the wish of the elderly housewife to maintain her competence in as many areas as possible. Thus, even with a moderate level of impairment of functioning, basic skills like cleaning, bedmaking, and cooking may be prolonged through the solution of design problems involving the length of handles for brooms, use of bedclothes and bed placement to minimize the amount of stooping required, and imaginativeness in easy-to-cook frozen foods. One would also hope that such devices as low-cost small dishwashers and automatic dialing phones could be developed for use by the marginally competent.

Outside of the dwelling unit, the increasingly critical problem seems to be transportation. In our Strawberry Mansion group, a followup program of service given by Jewish Family Service of Philadelphia included station wagon transportation from the person's door to a shopping center—one of the most successful of the intervention programs. Many variations on such service now are being tried. Some of the issues involve questions of whether the public transportation system should be modified to make travel for the elderly more convenient, or whether special service for the elderly is necessary; whether door-to-door or bus-route style; whether volunteer drivers or paid; whether the vehicle itself should be prosthetically designed or productionline; if public transportation, how much of a subsidy should be provided.

In any case, it is easy to see how transportation ease can directly elevate behavior. A door-to-door pickup in the worst crime area can enable the person to be able to move about without fear. The shopping behavior of our Strawberry Mansion residents was reduced to a bare level partly because of the impoverished stocks of the nearest stores. Thus, the range of options in actual shopping would be increased. Beyond having more things from which to choose, opportunities for window shopping or simply widening the range of one's environmental experience would be increased. Social interaction would receive a boost from the point of view both of being better able to visit friends and relatives in other areas as well as the social occasion of the ride and shopping itself. Finally, medical needs might be much better taken care of with better transportation planning.

Most of our neighborhoods appear to have lost their ability to function as true communities in the sense of assuming mutual voluntary responsibility for services for, and protection of, their own vulnerable members. Solutions to this problem lie far beyond the physical environment or measures tailored to the elderly. However, measures that tend to bind together different segments of the neighborhood cannot help but benefit the elderly. Any kind of service should be beamed to both black and white aged, but this is not really where the problem lies. It lies in generational, rather than racial, differences. Thus, any community service that could enlist the youth of the area in a protective role such as that of escort, friendly visitor, or driver would help build mutual concern.

The physical environment itself can be utilized in the service of social interaction. Large city park areas have become jungles, but small areas near concentrations of the elderly, with some sort of behavior control such as a park guard, can become the center of neighborhood activity. The park guard's house in the Strawberry Mansion area is one such place. Benches placed in the grassy divider of the upper reaches of Broadway in Manhattan are well utilized because there is a lot of action to watch and it is so public as to be very safe. MacArthur Park in Los Angeles is almost ideal in having not only safe space and activity, but a beautiful scene to watch, public rest rooms, and some basic equipment for games.

To summarize, beyond the obvious necessity of adequate income, major prosthetic measures for aged urban dwellers include congregate housing, home rehabilitation and remodeling, land use planning for the future, transportation designed for the elderly, household object design, training of personal service workers in skill maintenance procedures, mobilization of community segments to facilitate community living by the aged person, and design of parks for social purposes. It is important to note that these prosthetic measures vary in the degree of prominence which the purely physical environment plays. Yet, none of them is physically deterministic in its operation; the active effort of a user and frequently of a facilitator is required for the environment to function prosthetically.

In the case of the institution, the level of behavior to be supported is generally lower and, because of the public nature of most institutional behavior, more subject to modification than the community resident's. There are many possibilities for ameliorating the shock effect of the unfamiliar physical and social environment confronting the person entering an institution. Most institutions give an applicant a tour of the premises before admission and provide some orientation to the institution immediately upon admission. However, these procedures seem quite inadequate, considering the completeness of the change and the low level of residual adaptive capacities of many of the residents. It would seem to be a most worthwhile exercise to carry out a research project testing the effect of a time-extended, before-and-after admission orientation procedure. Repeated exposure to the institution prior to admission might help desensitize the applicant to the waiting-list anxiety found by Lieberman, Prock, & Tobin (1968) in their study, as well as begin the process of forming a new network of social relationships. Following admission, a planned program of initiation to and repeated practice in dealing with the mysteries of elevators, the meal bell, a new type of bathroom, and endless corridors should lower anxiety. Similarly, many new residents will require a number of exposures to significant people before they know who can do what for them. They may also be helped by planned social introductions to fellow residents. The effect of such an orientation procedure could be tested in terms of how long it took individuals receiving the orientation to learn the norms of the institution, the names of people, become integrated into activities, as well as in terms of more "distant" criteria such as morale, health, and self-maintenance task performance.

Physical aids to orientation may be helpful throughout the stay of a resident with chronic brain syndrome. Some possible prosthetic devices are: large clocks and calendars; seasonal paintings or posters; large room numbers and names of occupants; color-coded paths, or floor areas; names of staff or doors and uniforms.

Much loss of privacy is inevitable, but too frequently we assume that no privacy is possible and this attitude extends further to the conviction that the resident does not really miss his privacy; it is then only a short jump to the resident's becoming so institutionalized that he adapts to the lack of privacy. There is much evidence that a private room, for example is very highly prized by anyone lucky enough to have one and that, when there is a realistic opportunity to get one, people are almost unanimous in wanting one (Lawton & Bader, 1970). The more accustomed one has been to privacy in earlier life, as the middle-class life style allows, the more important will be privacy in an institution. Yet, cost considerations continue to dictate the building of shared institutional space. Given the structural limitations of occupancy by two or more people, what can be done to maximize the sense of privacy? Furniture dividers can be designed to perform this function to some extent though, frequently, space is too limited even for this minimum provision. Somewhat more possible may be the strict arrangement of personal belongings and furniture into distinct 'his" and "mine" sections, rather than having two dressers side by side for the convenience of space use, or having two people using a single closet. The more differentiation the better. Ideally, each room occupant should bring as many of his own possessions as possible. That way, two roommates' bedspreads will be different, the pictures hanging on their walls will contrast, possibly even their favorite armchairs can be brought in to aid in the distinction of who is who.

Staff is a most important component of the behavior-prosthetic system, most usually for the worst as far as maintaining privacy goes. Staff may feel free to open a resident's closed door without knocking or, more frequently, to insist that doors stay open. Even bathroom doors are frequently propped open, presumably so that proper health or safety surveillance can be maintained. Obviously, active counteracting of the principle of least effort is required to train staff to take the trouble to observe the sanctity of private offstage behavior—knocking, calling to a person to check on his status of the moment, and so on. As continence and personal grooming become impaired, staff is more likely to provide residents with institutional clothing, without regard to how well it fits. Yet, wearing one's own clothing is an aspect of privacy and of maintaining an identity. The extra work of overseeing the upkeep of the impaired resident's clothes and seeing that the right clothes return to the owner from the laundry is a practice that must be mandated administratively.

Much of the physical structure and the pattern of life in the institution seems to force residents into the presence of others. In addition to the shared bedroom, there is group dining, organized activity programs, lines waiting to see the doctor or social worker, and the lounges, lobbies, and outdoor benches for un-programmed sitting. Yet, there is a relative absence of social inter-change in these institutions, enough so as to give much discom-fort to the administrators and professionals responsible for pro-grams.

The maintenance of privacy is in some ways opposite to the encouragement of social interaction. That is, the attainment of one goal seems to preclude satisfaction of the other. However, research by Proshansky, Ittelson & Rivlin (1970) in a mental hospital indicates an interesting paradox in this connection. Actually, there was more observed social behavior going on in single rooms of the wards they studied than in double or multiple rooms, presumably because the single-room occupants felt freer to have both relatives and other patients visit them in their private rooms than was the case with patients in multiple rooms. This finding may also suggest, though there are as yet no empirical data to support it, that an economy operates so as to balance offstage with onstage time. When offstage time is impossible physically, people may retreat psychologically, while still being physically in direct contact with others. Alan Lipman, a British architect and sociologist, described in some detail the behavior in homes for aged where there was a total lack of physical privacy (1968). Residents sat around the periphery of a sitting room, side by side. There was occasional conversation, usually done while looking straight ahead. The end of conversations could be signaled simply by a logical ending sentence, a glance away from a second party, or a closing of the eyes. All appeared to understand and respect these signals. Thus, offstage time was indeed carved out of enforced interpersonal proximity. It may well be that, if adequate provision is made for physical privacy and for the choice between times for privacy and times for social contact to be made by the resident himself, a greater amount of true interaction would occur.

In any case, the institution is a natural place for experimentation with physical space as a facilitator of interpersonal contact, so long as we recognize that not all residents have the same capacity for interaction, and that all residents need their times and places to be alone, as well. The sitting-rooms studied by Lipman are found in every institution. The behavior of residents in them is certainly adaptive, but one would want to alter this structure to allow considerable more choice, as Sommer & Ross (1958) did when they arranged such chairs around four-person tables; this arrangement greatly increased interaction. Every public sitting area, whether indoor or outdoor, should have its sociopetal (interaction-facilitating) and its sociofugal (interaction-inhibiting) space and furniture placement. Research with younger adults indicates that, for some purposes, the necessity of sitting face-to-face or at right angles produces discomfort and there is every reason to think the same may be true of older adults.

Similar considerations apply to the design of facilities for recreation and leisure-time activity in the institution. There has probably been a tendency for people engaged in treatment to assume that any activity is better done in social rather than solitary style, if possible. Some of the behavior therapists have ingeniously designed environments that will reward behavior only when performed in a mutually complementing fashion by two or more people. In this way, both instrumental and social functions are reinforced. In less formal fashion, a recreation therapist at the Philadelphia Geriatric Center subdivided the jobs in a teaparty situation for impaired older people so that the consummatory activity was possible only after different people had contributed by pouring, providing sugar and providing cream.

On the other hand, each such task should be carefully analyzed to determine whether performance of the activity can be enhanced by physically increasing or decreasing the potential for social involvement. A projected re-design of the Philadelphia Geriatric Center's occupational therapy area at one point placed four sewing machines around four sides of an imaginary rectangle, with opposite-side operators looking at each other, on the theory that conversation would occur more easily that way. However, the O.T. workers quickly observed that sewing on the machines was a compulsively solitary activity requiring intense concentration. It would be done much better by operators seated side by side, facing a blank wall. If the aim is to increase competence of performance, incidental social interaction may be merely a nuisance, as in the case of a library. Sheltered workshops seem to work better when the work space of a single individual is not only clearly demarcated but also shielded from the direct gaze on one's neighbor. On the other hand, if social therapy is the major goal, deliberate blurring of boundaries between people and subdivision of the task into mutually interdependent parts may be preferable.

The limited mobility of many residents may make necessary the design of spaces near their beds for the performance of recreational activities. Distance itself may be a deterrent to participation. A long, involved process of gathering up materials at the end of a work session, storing them in a locked cabinet, and getting them out again for the next occasion may also discourage both patient and staff. Evenings and weekends are, in general, times of near-total sensory deprivation for the institutionalized person. Thus, combined work and storage space, where some of the materials could be brought out by the resident for use at times when a worker is not on duty, might increase the level of participation.

For the person who is not bothered by other people watching him work, working on crafts within highly-used common spaces may provide something for the less-competent person to watch. In a building designed for the mentally impaired aged (described a greater length elsewhere; Lawton, 1972) a large central area of a ward will be utilized for group and individual activities so that they can be watched by people sitting on the periphery or walking through the high-traffic density central area.

Thus, utilizing space, objects, and the proper training of staff in the use of physical environment, it is possible to bolster failing skills of the elderly. Such programs may include orientation to the new surroundings before and after admission; objects to enhance the sense of time; the enhancement of privacy, whether through providing space for seclusion or the respecting of private occasions; provision of an environment that facilitates social interaction; and making meaningful activity more accessible.

In conclusion, there appears to be in every aged person a motivation to perform at the highest level of which he is capable. At times the performance seems self-defeating or far below the standards deemed "adaptive" by societal standards. Wherever possible, active programmatic intervention should be applied. Environmental intervention is a less obvious and sometimes underutilized route to the elevation of performance. At the very worst, if behavior cannot be changed, understanding of how low-level behavior *is* adaptive for the individual may improve our service programs and planning for older people.

REFERENCES

Altman, I. and Haythorn, W.: The ecology of isolated groups. *Behav Sci, 12*:169-182, 1967.

Barker, R. and Gump, P.: *Big School, Small School.* Stanford, California, Stanford University Press, 1964.

Chein, I.: The environment as a determinant of behavior. *J Soc Psychol, 39*:115-127, 1954.

Cumming, E. and Henry, W. E.: *Growing Old.* New York, Basic Books, 1961.

De Long, A.: *A Preliminary Analysis of the Structure Points of Interpersonal and Environmental Transactions Among the Mentally Impaired Elderly.* Philadelphia, Philadelphia Geriatric Center, 1967. (Mimeo report).

Esser, A. H., Chamberlain, A. S., Chapple, E. D., and Kline, N. S.: Territoriality of patients on a research ward. In Proshansky, H. M., Ittelson, W. H., and Rivlin, L. G.: *Environmental Psychology.* New York, Holt, Rinehart & Winston, 1970.

Festinger, L., Schachter, S., and Back, K.: *Social Pressures in Informal Groups: A Study of Human Factors in Housing.* New York, Harper, 1950.

Glaser, B. G. and Strauss, A. L.: *A Time for Dying.* Chicago, Aldine, 1968.

Granick, R. and Nahemow, L.: Preadmission isolation as a factor in adjustment to an old age home. In Hoch, P. H. and Zubin, J. (Eds.): *Psychopathology of Aging.* New York, Gruner & Stratton, 1961.

Gruenberg, E. M.: A mental health survey of older persons. In Hoch, P. H. and Zubin, J.: *Comparative Epidemiology of the Mental Disorders.* New York, Grune & Stratton, 1961, pp. 13-23.

Hall, E. T.: *The Hidden Dimension.* New York, Doubleday, 1966.

Heider, F.: On perception and event structure, and the psychological environment. *Psychological Issues.* New York, International Universities Press, 1959 (Part 3).

Henry, W. E.: Engagement and disengagement: Toward a theory of adult development. In Kastenbaum, R. (Ed.): *Controbutions to the Psychobiology of Aging.* New York, Springer, 1965.

Lawton, M. P.: Some beginnings of an ecological psychology of old age. In Wohlwill, J. F. and Carson, D. H. (Eds.): *Behavioral Science and the Problems of Our Environment.* American Psychological Association, 1972.

————— and Bader, J. E.: Wish for privacy by young and old. *J Gerontol,* *25*:48-54, 1970.

—————, Kleban, M. and Singer, M.: The aged Jewish person and the slum environment. *J Gerontol, 26*:231-239, 1971.

Lieberman, M. A., Prock, V. N., and Tobin, S. S.: Psychological effects of institutionalization. *J Gerontol, 23*:343-353, 1968.

Lipman, A.: A socio-architectural view of life in three old people's homes. *Gerontol Clin, 10*:88-101, 1968.

Little, K. B.: Personal space. *J Exp Soc Psychol, 1*:237-247, 1965.

Lowenthal, M. F.: Social isolation and mental illness in old age. *Am Soc Rev, 29*:54-70, 1964.

—————: *Lives in Distress.* New York, Basic Books, 1964.

Maslow, A. and Mintz, N.: Effects of esthetic surroundings. *J Psychol, 41*:247-54, 1956.

Perin, C.: *With Man in Mind.* Cambridge, Massachusetts Institute of Technology Press, 1971.

Proshansky, H. M., Ittelson, W. H., and Rivlin, L. G.: The environmental psychology of the psychiatric ward. In Proshansky, H. M., Ittelson, W. H., and Rivlin, L. G. (Eds.): *Environmental Psychology.* New York, Holt, Rinehart, & Winston, 1970.

Schwartz, A. N. and Proppe, H. G.: Toward person/environment transaction research in aging. *Gerontologist, 10*:228-232, 1970.

Shanas, E.: Measuring the home health needs of the aged in five countries. *J Gerontol, 26*:37-40, 1971.

Sommer, R.: *Personal Space.* Englewood Cliffs, N. J., Prentice-Hall, 1969.

—————: Small group ecology. *Psychol Bull, 67*:145-162, 1967.

————— and Ross, H.: Social interaction in a geriatrics ward. *Int J Soc Psychiat, 4*:128-133, 1958.

Watson, O. M. and Graves, T. D.: Quantitative research in proxemic behavior. *Am Anthropol, 68*:971-985, 1966.

Weinstock, C. and Bennett, R.: A followup study of social isolation, socialization and related cognitive performance in residents of a home for aged. Paper presented at the Eighth International Congress of Gerontology, Washington, D. C., August 1969.

Chapter V

DEATH AND DYING: AN APPROACH TO TRAINING PROFESSIONALS

Frances G. Scott and Saul Toobert

Why Do We Need "Death Education?"

IT IS TEMPTING To one familiar with the development of training in gerontology in this country to see a causal relationship between the burgeoning of gerontological training in the United States since World War II and a similar burgeoning of interest in the phenomena of death and dying, including in the past few years scattered attempts at systematic training of professionals to cope with these phenomena. Developments in the two fields of study have been parallel, if not causally related. A paper by James E. Birren traces the historical development of the field of gerontology, with an emphasis upon research in the psychology of aging,[1] and a paper prepared by the same author for the 1971 White House Conference on Aging builds on this discussion and provides documentation of the growth of gerontological training programs in this nation.[2] Several efforts have been made recently by the news media to identify and discuss new developments in training of professionals for coping with the phenomena of death and dying among their patients or clients, but to our knowledge

---

[1] Birren, James E.: A brief history of the psychology of aging. *Gerontologist, 1* (2): 69-77, 1961. Birren, J. E.: Insight and progress in the psychology of aging *Gerontologist, 8* (2):126-128, 1968.

[2] Birren, James: *Training Background.* 1971 White House Conference on Aging. Washington, D. C., Govt. Printing Office 1972.

these attempts have been unsystematic and have omitted important training components.[3] At the present writing no compendium of training programs, nor a discussion of their philosophies and historical development could be found for the field of training in death and dying such as the material Birren has presented for the field of gerontology. The nearest thing is found in a recent monograph by Green and Irish.[4]

The general conclusion one might draw from efforts along these lines is that interest in and research into the phenomena of death and dying have followed by about fifteen years or so a curve similar to interest and research in the field of aging. If this generalization is true, we can confidently expect the development of training programs in thanatology and related topics, probably supported by federal funding. Certainly, interest at the federal level in the phenomena of death and dying is already apparent.[5]

Since the medical profession is generally thought to have more contact with dying persons than any other professional group in modern society, it is not surprising that much of the early research attempted to assess the methods used by the medical profession to cope with dying patients and with their surviving relatives and friends. Among the earliest were the studies of Herman Feifel, which were conducted in the early 1950s.[6] One facet of Feifel's studies is his commentary that the medical profession seemed unable to grasp the fact that the dying patient not only knows he is dying, but wishes to talk about this fact with a sympathetic listener, probably someone outside his family, and that because of denial and repression on the part of the physician, the physician almost never will talk with the patient directly about the impend-

[3] Dempsay, David: Learning how to die. *N Y Times Mag*, November 14, 1971. p. 58. Shea, Terence, New seminar helps take the sting out of death. *National Observer*, January 5, 1970, p. 22.

A Course on Death. *Newsweek*, May 8, 1972, p. 7.

How America Lives with Death. *Newsweek*, April 6, 1970, p. 81.

Dying the Taboo Subject. *Harpers*, June, 1971.

[4] Green, Betty R., and Irish, Donald P., (Eds.): *Death Education: Preparation for Living*. Cambridge, Mass., Schenkman, 1971.

[5] U.S. Congress. Senate. Special Committee on Aging: *Death with Dignity: An Inquiry into Related Public Issues*. Hearings. 91st Congress, 2nd Session. Washington, D. C., Govt. Printing Office, 1972.

[6] Feifel, Herman, (Ed.): *The Meaning of Death*. New York, McGraw-Hill, 1959.

ing death of the patient. Indeed, Feifel commented on the fact that patients talked with him (a researcher) so freely and seemed to feel so much better emotionally after these discussions. His reports to the physicians in the hospital where he was making his investigations were almost universally unacceptable to them, because they simply did not believe patients so readily talked with a stranger about their own impending deaths.

Without tracing further Feifel's early research and its possible effect on the medical profession, we should note that at least some physicians began examining their own feelings about dying and death, and how these feelings impinged upon dying patients to the frequent detriment of the patient and his family. It is interesting to note that prominent among these physicians were psychiatrists, most of whom do not in the normal course of their practice encounter a large proportion of dying persons among their patients. However, it is perhaps because he does not encounter death as frequently as the surgeon, the internist, or the general practitioner, that the psychiatrist is in a unique position to investigate the clinical management of the dying patient in a manner productive of a more enlightened, humanistic, and existential approach to the dying. At any rate, the culmination of this point of view among physicians is contained in the work of Elisabeth Kübler-Ross, who encountered more intensive opposition and criticism from her peers than did Feifel (who, after all, was a psychologist, not a physician) and who had a great deal of difficulty in gaining a sympathetic understanding of her views by her fellow physicians.[7]

Perhaps the work which has had the most significant recent impact upon medical schools, nursing schools, and the training of medical personnel is that of Glaser and Strauss.[8] In a major sociological study of several large hospitals, Glaser and Strauss investigated the social system composed of the physician, the nurse, the dying patient, the patient's family, and persons occupying other revelant social roles. They discovered that for very sound social-psychological reasons, the patient was quite likely to die in a situation described by Glaser and Strauss as "closed awareness," in

7 Kübler-Ross, Elisabeth: *On Death and Dying.* London, Macmillan, 1969.
8 Glaser, Barney, and Strauss, A. L.: *Awareness of Dying.* Chicago, Aldine, 1968.

which everybody, including the patient, knows he is about to die, but no one would talk about it to anyone else. It is this kind of situation which marks the traditional hospital social system within which most persons in the United States are placed to die.

WHO NEEDS EDUCATION IN THE PHENOMENA OF DEATH AND DYING? The work of Glaser and Strauss also pointed out that the physician, who is regarded by most persons as the responsible professional and considered the one who should cope with feelings as well as facts about the impending death, is likely more often than not to abrogate this role expectation. He is likely to transfer these responsibilities, either clearly or ambiguously, to the nurse. She, then, must talk with the patient and/or the family about the patient's impending death. The nurse, no better equipped by her professional training than is the physician, is likely to handle this serious matter in an unsystematic, probably highly emotionally-charged manner, which may or may not benefit the patient and the family.

In fact, nearly all professionals who might be expected to have a relationship with dying patients and/or their families seem to be just as lacking in systematic professional training to cope with the phenomena of death and dying as are physicians and nurses. These training lacunae are discussed with various degrees of self-consciousness by professionals in such fields as psychology, social work, and even religion.[9] The phenomena of death and dying are usually considered relevant to the training of gerontologists, however, since gerontologists supposedly study old people, and old people are more likely to die than younger ones. However, the systematic inclusion of course work on death and dying is just as lacking in the curricula of training programs in gerontology as it is in that of medical schools, nursing schools, and psychology departments.[10]

[9] *The Doctor and the Dying Patient.* Proceedings of a Seminar, University of Southern California Gerontology Center, Los Angeles, The Center, 1971.

Bentz, Thomas O.: Living with dying. Condensed from the writings of Robert E. Neale: *Presbyterian Life.* May, 1972, p. 32.

[10] The University of Oregon is a notable exception. The gerontology training program there was activated in 1968, and that same year the first "Confrontations of Death" seminar was conducted. See Scott, Frances G. and Brewer, Ruth M., (Eds.): *Confrontations of Death.* Corvallis, Oregon, Continuing Education Publications, 1971.

We suggest that to examine the phenomena of death and dying, including the professional's reaction to the death of a patient, and the ways in which he might help the dying patient and the family, is very nearly mandatory subject matter for training in the "helping professions."

Death is a universal experience. It not only happens to all of us ultimately (which statement might be regarded as a *non sequitur* if it were not necessary to restate it in order to overcome attitudes and feelings of grandiosity and denial on the part of large segments of modern populations) but all of us as adult members of society are called upon from once to several times to cope with a death in the family. Hence, even if we are not professionals who expect to work with dying patients or with their families, we need to know more about the phenomena of death and dying. We need to examine our own feelings about death. As part of our general education and personal growth as adults we need to be aware of the fact that not only will we ourselves die, but before that event takes place we will likely to be called upon to help other persons die, or to manage the consequences of their dying for someone who is near and dear to us personally.

To the extent that we are able to carry out these adult responsibilities in a humanistic, emotionally healthy and mutually therapeutic manner, to that same extent will we be promoting good mental health not only for ourselves, but for those around us, regardless of whether or not we are "professionals."

Therefore, we regard the inclusion of studies of death and dying in university and college curricula in much the same way as we regard studies of philosophy, history, scientific method, literature; while these studies are not absolutely necessary to the education of *all* students, they are certainly relevant to the experiences of *most* students who are seeking a well-rounded education and a knowledge of the cultural background from which their intellectual and emotional heritage has come. We need to study death and dying because these have been "taboo topics" for too long.[11] They have been taboo because our society is afraid of death and dying; it denies that death and dying will happen; it

11 See Farberow, Norman L., (Ed.): *Taboo Topics.* New York, Atherton, 1963.

provides a philosophical basis for regarding death as an obscenity and as a tragedy, and as an unjust imposition upon human life. The entire thrust of medical science and technology has been to overcome death, to increase the longevity of mankind, to prevent the death at an early age of even grossly abnormal members of the human race. At the same time, the folkways and mores surrounding the care of the dying, the disposal of the dead, and other adjustments of the society to the loss of an individual have become in the modern world increasingly inhumane, unrealistic, and indicative of massive guilt, anxiety, and denial.[12] What seems to be needed, then, in the general education of university and college students, in the professional training of those in the "helping professions," is not desensitization as practiced in medical schools to accustom the young physician to the dead body through constant exposure to corpses, but *sensitization* as implied in the term "sensitivity group," or the ability to be in immediate contact with one's own feelings on the subject and to express these effectively to another person. We should, on the one hand, be made intellectually aware of the differences between our perpetrated social mythologies and stereotypes and what are really the facts of the matter as people approach death and as those surviving them mourn; on the other hand, one needs to come to terms with his own feelings about his own death (mortality), not only because one's joy in life is thereby enhanced, but because otherwise one cannot comfortably or sensitively deal with the deaths of others.

THE "CONFRONTATIONS OF DEATH" SEMINAR AS TAUGHT AT THE UNIVERSITY OF OREGON

The historical background of the University of Oregon seminar called "Confrontations of Death" is described in the book by Scott and Brewer.[13] Our concern in this chapter is to describe what we try to accomplish in the seminar, particularly the rationale for the mixture of cognitive inputs and existential inputs, or what our students of today call "the head trip" as contrasted with "the

---

12 Among other books on these subjects, Jessica Mitford's seems most relevant and precisely (if floridly) stated. See *The American Way of Death*. New York, Simon and Schuster, 1962.

13 Scott and Brewer, *op. cit.*

feeling trip." It is not accidental, but deliberate and purposive, that the seminar as conceived by the faculty introducing it at the University of Oregon contains both of these elements. The intent of the seminar is definitely to change the *feelings* that the student has about his own death. The reader may recognize this approach as basic to the old psychoanalytical principle: if one is to be a good therapist, he must beforehand undergo therapy himself. Although this approach has been discredited to some extent, and although the student does not, of course, actually die (which would be a strict analogy to the psychoanalytic example), we nevertheless insist upon the validity of our point of view. It should be emphasized that what we are attempting to do is *sensitize* rather than *desensitize* our students to the phenomena of death, dying, mourning, and bereavement, through the medium of a deliberate and structured experience which enables the student to consider very seriously, and to consider his feelings about, his own death and dying.

COGNITIVE INPUTS. The very first thing that happens in a new class of "Confrontations of Death" is that each student writes a position paper on his own philosophy of life and death. A suggested outline for this position paper is given to the student, and most of them stay within the confines of this outline in their discussions, although this is not required. The outline suggests that one might want to examine what it is he wants out of life, why he has these beliefs and desires, how he thinks he will react to his own death, and why he thinks so. In addition, he is asked if he has had any prior experience with the death of others close to him, e.g., parents, grandparents, etc. Students write this position paper before anything else in the course has occurred. The papers are then taken up. Students are told that if they wish, they may re-examine their own papers at the end of the course, and at the end of the course they will be asked to do a similar position paper, simply for the purpose of judging for themselves if they think they have changed as a result of the course.[14]

After all students have finished the position paper, a human relations warmup is conducted. This separates the students into

14 These data, although not collected for research purposes, were utilized in an evaluation study reported later in this paper. See the section on "Student Reaction."

working small groups which continue throughout the course.[15] The warmup ends the first session of the seminar. Students normally leave talking animatedly with their peers. Thus far, we have had no cognitive inputs; the position paper is considered, by most students, to be very similar to exercises conducted in other courses.

We begin cognitive inputs in the second week of the class. These continue through five weeks of instruction. The intent is to start consideration of death and dying "out there" in the realm of the "the patient," "the other," "the not-me." This seems to be less threatening than consideration of one's own death. In fact, students seem almost totally unable to consider their own deaths in the first session or so, as will be evident from the discussion on "Method of Instruction," when we give details of some of the difficulties encountered in the initial roleplaying situations during the human relations warmup.

Although we start "out there," we attempt to come closer "in here," by which we mean within the feelings of the student himself/herself. The culmination of this process is in the laboratory weekend group experience, more fully described in the next section of this paper. Between the first meeting of the seminar and the laboratory weekend, the series of cognitive inputs, psychologically drawing ever closer to confrontation of one's own feelings about one's own death, continues.

There is an excellent film, called *Ikiru,* which depicts the meaning of life in the context of impending death. We normally show this film about the second class meeting. The film, of course, is an "out there" experience. The protagonist, an humble civil service department head, finds he is dying of cancer, without having ever accomplished anything meaningful. He almost single-handedly railroads through the hierarchy of local government the necessary approvals, regulations, and requisitions to construct a small park for the neighborhood children. The film ends with the funeral of this man, who was posthumously considered a great hero by the parents of the children living in the neighborhood. This film, better than any other we have found, makes the point that death

---

[15] This is discussed in detail in the section on "Method of Instruction."

is intolerable unless one's life can be justified as worthwhile and meaningful.

On two successive evenings, intellectual inputs based upon the theme of death in poetry and in classical and contemporary music are presented to the class. These inputs vary from time to time. We try to have a person come and read poetry to the class; the reader and the poetry vary from one year to the next. The music is generally presented via an audio tape, and we try to make new tapes every year or so, to include contemporary music. It is interesting to note that contemporary (late 1960's—early 1970's) popular music has produced some interesting titles on the theme of death. An examination of the popular music of the 1940's and 1950's produced no useable titles, although one might think World War II would have inspired many such songs. War songs were examined, but nothing emerged which has an analogous philosophical insight and existential meaning to, for example, the Beatles' version of "Eleanor Rigby," or the version by Blood, Sweat, and Tears of "When I Die." Blues songs of far earlier eras, for example, the "St. James' Infirmary Blues," frequently have more existential meaning for life and death.

We have been fortunate in the "Confrontations of Death" seminar to have a physician, Robert I. Daugherty, of Lebanon, Oregon, interested from the beginning in working with us. Dr. Daugherty is able almost every quarter to provide a seminar input on the effects of death upon a physician, and how one physician tries to deal with dying patients and their families.[16] We have for several years wanted to present the students a video tape or movie of Dr. Daugherty interviewing one of his patients who is dying. This has not been possible until recently; a videotape will be used in our Winter, 1973, seminar, although Dr. Daugherty will also be present. An interview, or a film or video tape interview, showing a physician and a dying patient discussing the patient's impending death will be a very valuable input to the seminar.[17]

---

16 Dr. Daugherty's role in the development of the seminar is detailed in the book *Confrontations of Death, op. cit.*

17 Dr. Robert E. Taubman, Department of Psychiatry and Division of Family Practice, University of Oregon Medical School, also has recently made some video-

The final intellectual input, just preceding the laboratory weekend group experience, where the feeling component is stressed, is a PBL documentary film on death. This is part of the larger PBL documentary entitled "Birth and Death."[18] This video tape is a very powerful presentation of the death of a cancer patient. The protagonist is shown from the time he enters a hospital for terminally ill cancer patients until he is wrapped in his shroud. The physical deterioration and increments in weakness and nearness to death are very graphically displayed. While this film still is "out there," it is nevertheless a visual and intellectual input with which most students can readily identify; the result is generally an increase in one's awareness that one does indeed have feelings about death, and most of these are focused on fear of one's own death. Admiration of the protagonist for still being able to talk about his impending death is frequently expressed by students in the small group discussions following the documentary.

We should mention at this point that following each intellectual input there is a discussion in the small working groups of the class about what the input seemed to mean to the individuals involved, and what feelings were stimulated by the input. The small group process is described in detail in the following section. A word is in order here about the "non-allowable" or "cop-out" topics which are likely to be brought up in the small group throughout the five or six weeks of intellectual inputs we have just described.

"Cop-out" topics. Among the "non-allowable" topics brought up most frequently is that of religion. The unsophisticated student is likely to base his opinions about death upon the concepts of afterlife that rather straightforwardly follow from "living a good life" in Christian terms. The more sophisticated advocate of the "religious cop-out" is likely to bring up the comparative religion point of view, with the suggestion that one is likely to face death differently depending upon his religious beliefs, no matter whether these are Christian, Confucian, Taoist, or whatever. We feel both

---

tapes of such interviews; we anticipate their usefulness in the "Confrontations of Death" seminar, once they have been edited to a length reasonable for classroom use.

[18] "Birth and Death" produced by Arthur Barron for Public Broadcasting Laboratory on December 1, 1968.

of these approaches are denials or "cop-outs," for this reason: We are interested in helping the student confront his own feelings about his own death; even more explicitly, we are interested in confronting him *with* his own death, as nearly as is possible in a laboratory T-group situation. His feelings about his own death are logically (and emotionally, we insist) separable from his beliefs about religious practices or about "life after death." We feel that discussions of religious beliefs and practices are therefore irrelevant and constitute denial of an earnest attempt to examine feelings about one's own death.

Research on the subject of religious beliefs and the manner in which people confront death is quite ambiguous; if anything, it demonstrates that the religious person is even more afraid of death than the atheist or the non-believer.[19] Our own feelings is that judgment should be suspended and the statement should go something like this: There is no relationship between one's religious beliefs and his feelings about his own death; therefore, religious beliefs and practices are irrelevant to this course, since the course is concerned with identifying one's *feelings* about one's own death. Parenthetically, the first author has had discussions with several religious leaders, among them both priests and ministers, who tend to agree with this point of view. One priest, particularly, who is engaged in working with dying patients in a local hospital, feels that how one meets death, and his feelings about it, are almost totally unrelated to his professed religion, or to his religious practices when he was in good health.

A second "cop-out" subject, almost always brought up, is that of comparative funeral practices. As the reader might suppose, one could teach an entire course on comparative funeral practices. In the extreme version, this form of "cop-out" or denial goes so far as to motivate the student to arrange for a visit to a local mortician, for example, inviting class members or small group members along, so that they can observe current funeral practices in the local community. While we feel this is extremely important, and probably every adult should have this experience, we do not

---

19 Feifel, Herman: Attitudes Toward Death. In Feifel, Herman, (Ed.): *The Meaning of Death.* New York, McGraw-Hill, 1959.

feel it is relevant to confronting one's feelings about one's own death. Therefore, when a student actually arranges with a local mortician for himself or other students to make such a visit, the instructor simply takes note of this fact and advises students they may go or not as they wish. Instructors never participate in these activities.

Needless to say, we would like very much for some relevant department in the university, for example, anthropology, to conduct a course on comparative funeral practices. Interested students then could simply be referred to this course, which is a quite legitimate area of intellectual inquiry.

Murder and suicide usually arise in conjunction with one another as denial or "cop-out" topics. Entire courses are, of course, devoted to considerations of homicide and suicide in American society, to comparative studies of homicide and suicide, and the interrelationships between these two methods of ending human life. However, we know that although most people are not going to die thus violently, whether or not one actually dies in this manner is as irrelevant to his *feelings* about his own death as is whether or not he believes in the Christian God.

Feelings about war and other types of violence, while they are extremely relevant to the problems of modern society, are not particularly relevant to one's feelings about one's own death. We feel it is an extreme "cop-out" if the student simply gives up and insists upon an attitude which can be paraphrased like this: "I am convinced I shall die by an atomic bomb blast, therefore I do not wish to think about it any more." All this leads to is clinical depression, not to the realistic confrontation of one's feelings about one's own death which we are seeking in this seminar. We should note parenthetically that such "cop-outs" on the subject of war are more typical of the younger student. Graduate students, and those who are not university students at all, do not generally bring up this particular subject.

A word is in order about what the instructors do when confronted with these kinds of intellectualized "cop-outs." The instructor tells the student in a gentle but straightforward manner that we do not deal with this topic or subject in this course. If the students wants to know why, which is generally the case, he is told much the same thing we have said here: These topics are not relevant to one's simulated confrontation of his own death or to his feelings about his own death. The instructor generally does not argue the point, but moves ahead to some other "allowable" subject matter. At worst, the student is urged to "wait until the weekend," at which point the human relations trainer is left with the job of coping with the over-intellectualizing student.

EXISTENTIAL INPUTS. The "feeling trip" which we try to provide for our students begins during the six weeks of intellectual inputs we just outlined. In fact, as the reader may have noticed, the intellectual inputs are somewhat existential in their orientation. To put this another way, we could have selected other materials which would have been more research-oriented, more cognitive, and less feeling-oriented than the ones we did select. The book by Scott and Brewer, *Confrontations of Death*, which is used as a text, with assigned readings each week, is of the same nature. The readings for the most part are deliberately selected for their existential components.

Perhaps the most relevant source of "feeling trip" inputs is from the small group discussions which follow the didactic or intellectual material presented each meeting. In the small group discussions, the instructors (to the extent to which they themselves are comfortable) discuss feelings stimulated by all cognitive inputs made that evening or at other sessions of the seminar. Students are encouraged by role modeling on the part of the instructor to describe feelings about, for example, the documentary on death, depicting the patient dying of cancer. Aspects of the film are examined, and students are encouraged to shudder, to express dismay, to express depression or feeling ill, if these are authentic reactions. Some instructors, of course, are more comfortable with this type of material than are others, and we never expect an instructor to lead his group into areas with which he feels uncomfortable himself.

The emphasis is always upon allowing the group to go as far as it can (and as the instructor can) in relating the cognitive material to feelings about oneself, about the death of oneself, about one's own non-existence. If the student cannot quite do this, he is encouraged to relate the materials to his feelings about these aspects of another's existence—a meaningful other, such as a close friend, a cherished relative, or a spouse or child.

We have briefly reviewed in this section the usual type of cognitive and existential inputs made in the seminar "Confrontations of Death," up to the time when the small groups experience the laboratory group weekend. It has been somewhat stilted, and artificial to talk about these inputs without at the same time mentioning the method of instruction utilized, and we have at times referred to this. In the next section, we will explicitly deal with the method of instruction, and relate it back in varying degrees to the cognitive and existential inputs.

Method of Instruction

SCREENING AND SELECTION OF STUDENTS. In our introductory statements, we expressed the opinion that all university students should be allowed to examine their own feelings about death, and particularly about their own deaths, as part of their general education or as a personal growth experience. We now wish to modify this statement. If the "death education" course is taught as a "task-oriented T-group" as at the University of Oregon, a certain amount of screening is indicated to insure the best utilization of staff time and effort. Therefore, we screen students who wish to register for this course. A word is in order about our screening criteria.

First of all, we screen to eliminate the obviously psychotic or pre-psychotic student. This student is screened out, no matter how well-integrated or how much in remission he seems to be at the time. The screening is done by a staff member with a graduate degree in counseling psychology. We feel that the screening has been successful; the only time such a student was admitted was the very first semester we offered the course, before we had initiated the screening procedure. The student did not complete the course, refusing at the end to attend the laboratory group. The import of this is, of course, that the space occupied by such a student is "wasted," since we always have a long waiting list of students who are able to complete the course, and presumably profit from it. In subsequent terms, screening of students has eliminated several who were considered pre-psychotic or pre-schizophrenic, and we have never since had a student fail to complete the weekend experience. This has been the case, despite various physical injuries, e.g., we have had at least four students appear for the weekend in casts and/or on crutches with broken bones, usually acquired in skiing accidents. The level of their discomfort was exceeded only by their desire not to be left out of their group during the weekend experience. In fact, laboratory group members have carried the handicapped person up and down stairs all weekend, in retreat situations in which there is no elevator, so that the injured one could attend sessions.

A second screening criterion is whether or not the student is in bereavement. There are very good psychological reasons for the age-old requirement of a full year's mourning.[20] For example, the person in mourning or bereavement may be emotionally unstable, even though he may be quite stable at other times. His emotional lability may lead him to do or say things which are atypical and not necessarily very rational. Such a person may be more in need of group therapy than anything else. But the "Confrontations of Death" seminar is not a therapy group, it is a learning experience. For this reason, persons in mourning are asked to wait until about a year has passed, and then to register for the course. They are given preference in registration at that time, if they remain on the waiting list.

A third criterion, and probably the one most often abrogated, is that a student should be either a graduate student or a graduating senior. We have allowed students who were juniors into the seminar, depending upon their assessed degree of emotional maturity. It is essentially emotional maturity, however one measures this elusive variable, for which we screen. This is not entirely a function of chronological age, although chronological age is probably the best single indicator, and one's status as a graduate or undergraduate student is probably the best single

20 Jackson, Edgar, N.: Grief and Religions. In Feifel, Herman, (Ed.): *The Meaning of Death*. New York, McGraw-Hill, 1959, p. 218.

indicator of chronological age in a university setting. However, it is interesting to note that usually younger men, and older women, are more interested in the course. While we do have a sprinkling of younger women, most of the women who apply for registration in this course are past 35.[21]

The question has frequently arisen in discussing this seminar with our colleagues as to whether we would attempt the same kind of approach if we were offering the course to the general public, or if we were requiring the course of students of any given type or academic discipline. With respect to this latter point, we strongly recommend that no students anywhere be *required* to take any course which involves T-group, sensitivity or laboratory methods. We feel very strongly that students should not be put into these kinds of situations against their wills, not to mention the fact that the pre-psychotic student simply will not be entrapped in such group situations in any event. He likely will discover some method of escape even if he is forced to escape into irreality. Other students may be quite uncomfortable, even though they are relatively normal emotionally, if for some reason they are especially shy or simply do not enjoy expressing themselves before groups. Therefore, we would never *require* this course, or any other taught with a similar method.

The question of presenting the cognitive inputs to the general public is something else again. We certainly do not feel, in principle, that the general public should be "T-grouped" any more than should students. Therefore, we do not present this seminar in the same way when we present it to the general public. One of our graduate students, who has also been a trainer in the "Confrontations of Death" course, recently developed a course syllabus and outline for a lecture series approach to the cognitive and existential inputs which does not utilize the T-group method.[22] We feel this lecture course can readily be offered to students in classes of any size, even several hundred, and it can be given for

---

21 This phenomenon is discussed in the section on "Student Reaction."

22 This lecture series, "Issues in Death and Dying," has been offered by James H. Lynch in Roseburg and in Portland, Oregon, through the Division of Continuing Education. The series attracted large audiences in both locales.

the general public. In fact, in such situations, we advocate the lecture approach.

RATIONALE FOR THE "TASK-ORIENTED T-GROUP" APPROACH. In view of the ultimate aim of the seminar, that of offering the student a simulated confrontation with his own death, plus an examination of his own feelings about his own death and a sharing of these with others, the method selected from the inception of the seminar has included a laboratory experience away from the campus. During this experience, an attempt is made to offer each student a simulated death experience in the small group, although these experiences are not always the same.[23] The data generated from each experience is then debriefed in the group, facilitated by a skilled human relations trainer. This technique offers the advantage, suggested above, of completing the progression of exploration from death "outside," or happening to others, to a consideration of death "in here," or "my own death." The method has the additional advantage of providing the student with the possibility of a very close human interaction experience with the members of his group as well as feedback and self-understanding from others in the group about their perceptions of him. Furthermore, as will be seen in the following description of specific exercises, the experiences devised to deal with death offer the participant the antithesis, viz., a hard look at his life. While the goal of the method is a confrontation of one's own death, the side-effects of the method are often a first, warm, supportive, confrontative, close and loving experience with members of a peer group who, at the beginning of the course are almost always total strangers.[24] This of course implies the possibility of transferring

23 For example, only three or four students in a 10-person group experience the "zap" exercise, another four or five have their eulogies read, and the rest may have leading roles in the family role-play exercise (see below for specific descriptions). For each student, the specific event simulating his "death" is somewhat different, but each one *gets a chance* for an experience. Occasionally, a student or two does not have such a chance; this is inevitable because the emotional problems of some group members require more time and may usurp the attention which the staff planned to direct to each student in turn.

24 Bradford, Leland P., Gibb, Jack R., and Benne, Kenneth D., (Eds.): *T-Group Theory and Laboratory Methods: Innovation in Re-Education.* New York, John Wiley, 1964.

these warm and close feelings to other human beings. Not surprisingly, students often report, "This course has been the highlight of my college career."

DESCRIPTION OF METHOD. The reader will recall that the "Confrontations of Death" seminar meets for six weeks with a schedule resembling that of most seminars: meetings last for three hours, one evening each week, a cognitive input of some kind is made, followed by a discussion. The principle difference between this and an ordinary seminar is that an effort is made in the discussion to elicit *feelings* about the cognitive input. The small discussion groups frequently go beyond the three-hour meeting time and continue discussions at a tavern near the campus or in some other informal setting. At the laboratory group experience, two full days, from 8-10 hours each day, are scheduled. Again, in this situation, students are likely to continue their discussions far into the evening. In short, considerably more than the 33 clock hours of instruction considered as the standard for an 11-week, 3-credit-unit course at the University of Oregon is experienced.

Beginning with the human relations warm-up, which occurs the first evening the seminar meets, we will now describe more fully some of the laboratory exercises. The reader should keep in mind that these exercises are changed from time to time—in fact, we seldom use the same exercise in precisely the same form more than once. However, the goals of each exercise remain essentially unchanged, even though the specific components of the exercises may change.

The *human relations warm-up* has been described in detail elsewhere.[25] The goal of the warm-up is essentially threefold: (1) to get the class acquainted with each other in a brief period of time, (2) to socially "unfreeze" the students during the first class meeting and to teach communication skills in the process, and (3) to arrange the class into three permanent small groups wherein age, sex, race, experience, and other personal and interpersonal resources are distributed equally. The exercises in the warm-up and the debriefing are actually an attempt to offer the student

[25] Toobert, Saul: The Simulation of Personal Death: A T-Group Experience. In Scott, Frances G., and Brewer, Ruth M. op. cit.

experience in attending to his own feelings and reporting them to others so that they are understood. Experience in receiving feedback as well as offering it to others is included. Role playing is introduced as a skill which will be utilized later at the laboratory weekend.

Typically, a warm-up will begin with several "rounds" of "pairing." Students are told to go to someone else in the room with whom they are not acquainted, and to talk with this person about whatever they wish. Such pairings are allowed to continue for about 2 minutes and then another pairing is requested. In this manner, students get to meet many of the persons in the class for the first time, and to become aware of their names and some of their characteristics. When several rounds have been completed, students are asked to pair up again, but this time, one of the pair is to pretend blindness by keeping his eyes closed. They go ahead and talk. Midway in the exercise, the trainer requests that the pair switch roles, with the previously sighted person now pretending blindness. Following this, the pair is asked to join another pair for "de-briefing" or discussing their feelings about the experience just undergone. In short, they are to discuss in a foursome how it felt to be blind and how it felt to talk with a blind person. They are also encouraged to share in the foursome any feelings or thoughts they might have had about the other person in the pair during the role-play situation. This variation in the "pairing" exercise introduces rudimentary role-play, and practice in attending to one's own feelings and sharing these with other members of the group.

An attempt is also made during the warm-up to introduce the subject of death into the sessions, usually through the role-play device of having one student in a pair role-play a physician who is telling the other member of the pair that he has a terminal illness. This experience is also debriefed in a foursome, or sometimes in a small group of six. Variations on this exercise can include more sophisticated role-playing; for example, one member of a pair may role-play a husband or wife who has just been told of the death of a spouse and the other member may role-play the messenger. Other situations involving the death of oneself or a relevant other may be devised.

The ultimate goal of the warm-up is to leave the students and their instructors in three small groups (we have never used more than three instructors, and we limit enrollment to 30-36 students). Beginning with a foursome, which has just been formed for purposes of de-briefing a prior exercise, e.g., the exercise involving the theme of death, foursomes are asked to join each other, and to discuss further their feelings about death, or about what has transpired in the seminar so far, or some other revelant subject selected by the trainer. After a short (5-6 minutes) discussion in a group of eight, the instructors are asked to stand out (leave the groups). The groups are then asked to divide themselves into only three small groups, whereas there are currently some four or five, depending upon the number of students enrolled. The three small groups should be relatively equivalent in terms of resources. "Resources" are defined for the students as age, sex, experience, etc. The trainer attempts to see that the ensuing milling process results in a relatively equal division of students into three groups. With very little assistance from the trainer, the groups are usually able to accomplish it. The instructors then select the small groups with which they will work for the term. Instructors are asked to select groups containing a minimum number of students already known to them.

The trainer then gives the reconstituted groups the task of discussing their own position papers, addressing themselves primarily to the twin issues of *"what did you think about it"* (cognitive attitudes) and *"how did it make you feel"* (awareness of and sharing of feeling). During the ensuing five weeks, following every stimulus input (music, films, poetry, etc.,) the small groups again meet and follow the pattern set for debriefing the stimulus data in the small groups. Instructors try to keep both cognitive and feeling awareness before their groups.

At the *laboratory weekend,* three human relations trainers are introduced, one for each group. Usually, one of these trainers has conducted the warm-up, and is therefore not a stranger to the students. The other two are generally strangers. The trainers design and execute a set of exercises which offer the student a simulated confrontation with his own death or the death of someone close to him. Notice that the trainers do not involve the participants (students) in the design of their own laboratory, as is sometimes done in laboratory training. The weekend is considered too short for such an enterprise; furthermore, the students are not fully trained in operating as self-directing, task-oriented T-groups or sensitivity groups, and hence should not be given such an overwhelming task.

The trainers themselves (who need not be experts on death and dying) must be experts on group process. It is particularly important that they are skilled in handling the de-briefing of a group. It is advisable that skilled trainers be selected, who do not themselves have "hang-ups" or serious denial problems with the phenomena of death and dying. Regrettably, we are unable to specify how one can ascertain this about a trainer without watching him work; this is about the only way, in our experience. We have, at the present writing, utilized some 12-14 different trainers; at least three of them have manifested such difficulties. Such trainers do not actually harm their groups, but if the trainer has reservations about the subject matter of death and dying, he is likely to prevent the group's movement toward a meaningful simulation of the confrontation of death.

We have presented details of a typical laboratory weekend elsewhere,[26] but we shall review briefly some of the exercises that have been used in the past. The goal of these exercises, as we have stated above, is to confront the student with a simulation of his own death, which tends to produce a new evaluation of himself (by himself) as a person and of his life to date. Among the exercises we have used are the following:

> 1. The *eulogy exercise* is very effective. The student is instructed to write down what he thinks people will say about him when he dies, or what he would like people to say about him; variations we have used include specifying that he first write what a *friendly* person would say about him, and then what a *critical* person might say. In completing the eulogy, the student is really reviewing his own life. When each person in the small group

26 *Ibid.*

has completed the written eulogy, one person, usually a volunteer or a person selected randomly by the trainer, is asked to pick out a member of the group to read his eulogy. The "dying" person then lies on his back in the center of the group, is covered over with a sheet simulating a shroud, and hears his own eulogy read. The group then de-briefs his eulogy and talks about him and his life as it was shared with them. He is then interviewed from the "grave" after which he is brought "back to life," having been offered the rare opportunity of hearing people discuss him in his own presence. This, too, has the effect of allowing others to share with him in the validation of his own life. Since he is "brought back to life" after the eulogy experience, and is then free to de-brief his own feelings with the group, he usually experiences the full support of the group as they attempt to deal with his feelings and with the summary of his life as it was shared with them.

2. The *lifeline* exercise is frequently used. This exercise is generally a preliminary one, but it can be extremely meaningful for some participants. Students are given a piece of paper and asked to draw a line, which need not be straight or of any given shape, representing their life from birth to death. They are then asked to place an "X" on the line indicating where they think they now are in respect to that lifeline. The group then de-briefs commonalities and eccentricities as they appear on the drawings and discusses feelings about why they made the "X" marks where they did.

3. The *"zap"* exercise is sometimes used. In this exercise the trainer puts an "X" or other marker under a chair or under a plate at the dining table, or in some other random fashion marks a location where someone will sit or stand. (The locus of the "zap" site is never disclosed to others.) The person so marked then is "dead" for a specified period of time, such as an hour or two, or for the remainder of a meal if this is done at mealtime. The person at the end of the specified time rejoins his group and de-briefs how it felt to be thus "dead." During the time he is "dead," the student is not to have eye contact or to talk to or in any sense communicate with any other living person, either in his small group or outside of it. The exercise is reported as providing very intense experiences by those who have gone through it. Sharing of feelings about the experience with the small group tends to produce insights into a state of non-being rarely experienced by the average person.

4. The *"death machine"* exercise has been used upon occasion, and variations of it are readily brought to mind. The small

group is given the simple instruction of constructing a "living machine" with some kind of function, decided upon by the group, by distributing themselves in an arrangement which makes this machine "work." They are given time to get the machine into operation, and to make sure that it is "debugged" and seems to be working as they intend it, i.e., performing the kind of function or movement that the group intended it to do. The instruction then is that persons will be selected by the trainer to "die," thus being removed from the "living machine." The machine, however, is to keep on functioning as best it can without the members who "die." The trainer continues to select out group members until the machine breaks down entirely. Members who are "dead" are required to sit with their backs to the group, so that they are not fully aware of what is happening to the machine. De-briefing this exercise gives rise to many productive feelings about how remaining group members feel as each deserts the group through "death," and how the group member feels when he must thus give up responsibility which he perhaps found enjoyable and meaningful.

5. The *family role-play* exercise has been one of the most productive of the exercises we use. It offers a full experience for all participants, through a simulation of what a family goes through when death strikes a significant member. The members of a small group, aside from the trainer and the instructor, who are usually needed as "stage managers," are asked to organize themselves into an extended family group. It may have a mother, father, brothers, sisters, aunts, uncles, grandparents—in short, whatever composition it desires, including family friends and household pets. The group is then to interact upon some controversial subject, established by the trainer, and not at all concerned with death or dying. Subjects that have been used are such things as reactions of the family to the revelation that the daughter is living with a man to whom she is not married, and yet expecting financial support from the family; what the family should do about a son who wishes to avoid the draft, in a family where the father is a strong member of the American Legion; and other such topics of family concern. When the family role-play is in full process, and it is possible for the trainer to determine which member of the group is the communication center, he then instructs this significant member to "die." The group is expected to cope with what happens after that.

Participants have role-played for several hours, starting with the sudden death of a member, calling of an ambulance, removal to the hospital, being pronounced dead by the physician, arranging for the funeral and burial, dealing with friends, helpful neighbors, lodge members, insurance agents, morticians, newspaper reporters, and ending with the funeral and the situation in the family which occurs after the funeral. This exercise always generates rich amounts of data for de-briefing and feedback.

SPECIAL PROBLEMS ENCOUNTERED BY TRAINERS. The laboratory weekend experience presents an unusual situation for the skilled human relations laboratory trainer to master. A trainer's skill lies primarily in his knowledge of group process and in his ability to lead a group through a meaningful sequence of experiences in the examination of and sharing of feelings about the data generated, regardless of *how* that data was generated. Often, the trainer is called upon to assist in the generation of data by presenting the group with a stimulus task designed to produce behaviors which can then be examined. This can be referred to as the "task-oriented T-group" approach as contrasted with the "encounter group" approach in which the trainer presents no definable stimulus but rather allows and facilitates the group's production of its own interaction data. Furthermore, in most laboratory groups the trainer starts afresh with a group of people who have never worked together as an organized group, although the expectation is that they will share feelings with one another. The trainer is thus able, as an initial participating member of the group, to begin as a member in full standing to assume the task of creating an atmosphere of trust and freedom where a sharing of feelings can take place. Whether the group's interaction concerns data generated by a specific task or concerns the unspecific task of allowing data to unfold from the interaction itself, the trainer is part of the group from the start.

An important problem faced by the trainer at the "Confrontations of Death" laboratory lies in the fact that the trainer enters an already established group by whom he is perceived as a stranger, an outsider. Perceptions of him seem to range from a Messiah who will solve all of the group's problems to an unwelcome foreigner or authority whose mettle must be tested. Added to this is the fact that the groups are composed primarily of young people, some of whom are still struggling with problems of identity and of self. Moreover, there may be resistance in the group to dealing with the task of confronting one's own death. Taken together, these factors easily can lead the trainer to spend the weekend establishing himself in the group rather than in facilitating the group's goals. For example, one way of finding out "Who I am" as a group member is to challenge the authority of the trainer, who has just entered the group. This challenge also serves the dual purpose of avoiding the task of confronting feelings about death, if the unsuspecting trainer accepts the challenge at its face value. The second author of this paper has, with very few exceptions, been the Dean of the laboratory weekend and has always instructed the other trainers to be particularly wary of this possibility lest one group member be allowed to "blow" his group's whole weekend with unending challenges of the trainer's authority and methods. Thus it is advocated that any such challenges from group members be dealt with firmly and quickly in accordance with the trainer's style.

Another special problem (which may not be specific to a "Confrontations of Death" laboratory) is the question of the "death" of the group at the end of the weekend. Since the participants are all members of the University campus, there was originally a strong tendency for the groups to plan campus meetings and reunions long after the weekend. This phenomenon is not unusual, in that group members do tend to become extremely close friends after sharing the adventure of the laboratory weekend. Yet, the groups can never be the same unless each and every group member can appear at subsequent meetings. Trainers are usually imported from other cities and from neighboring states and cannot reappear; furthermore, instructors usually have other commitments and cannot meet regularly after the class is over. In short, it rarely happens that a group can meet again completely intact.

To deal with this problem, it was decided to introduce a ritual "death" of the group at the end of the weekend and to indicate early to the participants that this will happen so that all business proper to the group has to be finished before the weekend is over. The rationale here is that if the possibility of future meetings is held forth, the group may—at a level of awareness or non-awareness—decide not to deal with its problems at the laboratory, but to hold them in abeyance for the future. Farewell rituals have been devised, prefaced by the trainer's remarks concerning "re-entry" back home, viz., "It is important to consider that we have gotten very close to each other here and have shared our feelings openly and honestly. The world out there does not always behave in this way and maybe it is good that it doesn't. One of the most important things about a honeymoon is that it comes to an end, else the pace might kill off the newly married couple. This group can never again meet as a group since it will not be the same without one person and I will not be there. Let's plan some way of saying goodbye."

Groups have been very imaginative about designing the end of the laboratory. One group, for example, locked arms and then had individuals leave singly in the order in which they had indicated they would die in an earlier exercise. Another group formed a tight circle, arms about each other; the circle was then expanded as each member stretched his arms out until only finger tips were touching. Individuals then allowed their arms to drop, turned, and left the group, until all had departed.

STUDENT REACTION. What does all this mean to the student? Is the "death education" seminar a significant learning experience? We have made no systematic attempt to evaluate the seminar, but some data do exist, gleaned from reports in the Position Papers written by students as the very first seminar experience and as the very last one. While Position Papers I and II (reproduced here in the Appendix) were not intended for research purposes, we did an analysis of some of these papers, and report the simple statistical findings, along with some direct quotations which are of a more existential nature. These data give the reader an idea of student reaction to this course. Needless to say, we have for the most part selected examples favorable to the seminar and its goals; it would have been difficult to do otherwise, since almost without exception student reaction to the seminar is highly favorable.

AN EVALUATION OF SOME DIMENSIONS OF CHANGE AS REPORTED

IN THE POSITION PAPERS. Position papers, pre- and post-seminar, of students enrolled in four different quarters in 1969-71, resulting in a total of N of 126, were examined.[27] The following variables were elicited from these data: (1) Did the respondent change his philosophy of life and/or death after the seminar? (Changers vs. Non-Changers); (2) If the philosophy of life and/or death did in fact change, what was the content of change? (3) Does the respondent state a belief in a formal religious idea concerning death, or a "hereafter?" (4) What are the respondent's feelings and thoughts about the death of people close to him before the seminar?

Demographic data descriptive of characteristics of the students were utilized in examining attitudes, feelings, and thoughts concerning death before and after the seminar. These included age, sex, marital status, religious preference, and college major as independent variables.

Age was found related to change in philosophy of life and/or death and to content of philosophy of life and/or death. Younger people, primarily those aged 20 to 24, feel living each moment to the fullest extent is most important in life, as well as having close interpersonal relationships or honest, open exchanges of feelings with others. Age was not related to belief in an afterlife.

Sex was not related to change in philosophy, content of change, attitudes concerning one's own death, nor attitudes concerning the death of close others. However, when age was controlled, sex was found related to feelings toward one's own death after the seminar. "Men under 30 tend to accept death as a natural culmination of life, while women under 30, in addition to this acceptance, also express less fear of death after the seminar than before."[28]

Change in philosophy as a consequence of the seminar was related to the student's feelings and thoughts (before the seminar) about the death of people close to him. Changers were able to accept the death of close others while non-changers seemed to pre-

---

[27] For additional details, see Saul Toobert and Frances G. Scott, Confrontations of death, a report of an innovative seminar, unpublished paper presented to the *XVIII Congrès International de Psychologie Appliquée, Liège*, Belgium, 1971. Portions of this paper are reproduced here.

[28] *Ibid.*

fer to think there is an afterlife or a transmigration rather than accept the stark fact of death.

Belief in a formal religious idea concerning death or an afterlife was found related to feelings and thoughts (after the seminar) about one's own death. Non-believers tended to be fearful about their own deaths, but not as fearful as *before* the seminar, while believers seemed less fearful but nevertheless still looked forward to a hereafter or a "non-death" of the self. The same afterlife belief was also related to feelings and thoughts about the death of close others. Non-believers in afterlife were more accepting of death as a natural (even desirable) culmination of life; believers did not accept death but felt the close others would go to an "afterlife" of some type.

Eighty-one percent of the total sample changed their philosophies of life and/or death as a result of the seminar. Of those who changed, 35% thought it most important to live life more fully; 33% thought the most important experiences in life are close interpersonal relationships (or honest, open feelings toward others); 11% thought their most important change was toward valuing self-realization or self-awareness.

Of those subjects who changed, 59% denied belief in an afterlife or other religious idea concerning death and 41% believed in an afterlife. Of those who did *not* change, 52% denied belief while 48% were believers. Hence belief in an afterlife is not a factor in changing one's philosophy of life and/or death. Age seems to be the most important factor here, with younger students (under 30) becoming "changers."

Table V-I summarizes the findings of this analysis.

SOME DIRECT QUOTATIONS. Let us now examine the replies of a few students who indicate in Position Paper II that they consider themselves "changers," or among those who either *have* changed in their point of view about death, or feel they *are going to change* but have not had time to do so yet, as a result of the seminar. Here are quotations from "changers":

> (From a young women): My orientation towards life has changed as a result of this seminar. I've become more realistic about my goals in terms of "helping others." Earlier, I was obsessed

TABLE V-1

SUMMARY OF SIGNIFICANT RELATIONSHIPS

Significant Relationships *Discovered Between Age and:*	*Chi Square* *Significance* *Level*	
1. Change in philosophy of life/death	.05	
2. Content of change in philosophy	.01*	
3. Sex	.05	
4. Marital status	.01	
Between Sex and:		
1. Belief in afterlife	.10	(trend)
2. Belief in afterlife (age controlled)	.02	
3. Feelings about own death (age controlled)	.05	
Between College Major and:		
1. Change in philosophy of life/death	.01	
2. Marital status	.01	
3. Feelings about own death	.10	(trend)
Significant Relationships Between Other Variables:		
1. Change philosophy and feelings about death of close others	.01	
2. Belief in afterlife and feelings about own death	.01	
3. Belief in afterlife and feelings about death of close others	.01	
4. Feelings about own death and feelings about death of close others	.001	
*Based on Kendall's Tau rather than Chi Square.		

with the *number* of people who need help without realizing
the intense personal effort which each contact demands. I've
now accepted the fact that the best I can do for mankind as a
whole is to, first, know and accept myself, and then to share
myself with others in a meaningful, intense way. Change cannot be accomplished in brief, superficial contact, but requires
the exchange of feeling. My perception of death has changed
also as I realized the duality of it. It implies grief over the loss
of a loved one for those who live on, and yet it is completely a
personal thing, perhaps the only personal moment in one's life.
(A young man reports): My feelings of death have changed a
lot. I have never had someone close to me die (since) I was old
enough to remember, so I was not at all aware of what goes into
an American death. I thought the body stayed where it was
(someone takes it away when you aren't looking) and the people
close to the deceased deal with their grief in their own ways,
some waiting for friends to be comforted by, some wanting to
be alone to work things out with themselves. Instead, I learned
that the whole world wants into the act: friends, relatives, colleagues, chums, funeral people, newspapermen, neighbors, insurance men, and many more. The family is burdened with
much more than the death itself.

And a few from "non-changers:"

(An older woman): I don't think my philosophy of life has changed. Perhaps I see more clearly the need to tear down the reserve and control I wrap myself in . . . I realize my relatedness (or need for it, perhaps) a bit more. I'm now aware I do *not* wish to die alone. If someone could help me over death as Laura helped Aldous Huxley . . . that would be beautiful. I don't fear death except dying in pain or alone. . . .

(A younger male): I do not *want* to die, but I will; and I *could now*. Knowing that I have touched people in deep and subtle ways. That *is* important. . . . If I should perceive that I have not touched, then it will be a hard death.

(Another young man): I . . . feel that the past experiences in this course, and especially the weekend, will play a significant role in my life and in my death . . . I guess what I am rather awkwardly trying to say is that my death and the death of people I am close to seemed to be an extremely frightening obstacle to life, one that I had no idea how to deal with. Right now, I do not feel that . . . fear. One of my personal objectives for this course was to obtain a better grasp of the death of my parents. I think I have accomplished this goal, in that I now feel able and comfortable to discuss with them the reality of their death.

And a final excerpt, from the protocol of a young man who says he has not yet changed, but wants to:

I don't want to die alone. And I do want to know when I'm going to die so I can finish what I must. But now I just want a chance so I can start. I'm going to change. I'm going to say to the living what is on my mind. I'm going to explore others and not run or hide or stand like some stump. I can, and I will!

To the instructors, perhaps the most gratifying of all such remarks is the student who makes a point of saying "thank you" for the course, either verbally or in the context of the Position Paper II. One tends not to expect such reactions from students, but it is good when it happens, and a high proportion of our students thus thank us.

Recommendations for Training Professionals in the Area of Death and Dying

Aside from the obvious gratification of the teacher who has accomplished the instructional goals which he has held forth for himself, we do feel that the "Confrontations of Death" seminar is worthwhile in training young professionals who intend to work with aging clientele, as well as clientele of all ages who must confront death. As we said in the beginning of the chapter, while the aged are not the only ones who die, by any means, one's statistical chances of dying in the near future increase as one becomes older. The "Confrontations of Death" seminar does not focus on the aged; rather, it focusses upon the feelings of the individual himself about his own death. Nevertheless, some of the reading material, and some of the group discussions, involve the question of the death of an elderly person. Students, whether they are gerontology students or not, become aware of the special problems of the dying elderly person. Such patients are more likely than are young patients to be left alone, to be bereft of the human companionship that they need at the end of their lives, and to be generally ignored in the hospital setting. Students who have taken the "Confrontations of Death" seminar are sensitized to these points.

DEVELOPING A COURSE. The instructor wishing to initiate a course in thanatology or "death education" is confronted with several problems. One of these is where to get satisfactory materials. If the reader is interested in developing a course similar to the University of Oregon's seminar, materials are available which can be of assistance. The book, *Confrontations of Death,* has been adopted by several instructors, not all of whom use the laboratory method.[29] In addition, a documentary movie of the same title was released early in 1972 and is available for rental or sale.[30] Our recommendation with regard to the documentary movie is that the instructor contemplating using this method first view the movie for himself. The intent of the movie is to enable the viewer to "feel" along with the group the same kinds of experiences that the small group had in the seminar. In our perception, the movie has caught this feeling very well. We do not use this movie in our own classes, except *after* the laboratory weekend experience. The final follow-up or "wrap-up" session, which is held at the regular class time following the laboratory weekend, is

---

[29] *Confrontations of Death, op. cit.*

[30] The 16mm color film, *Confrontations of Death,* is available for rental or sale from Audio-Visual Instruction Center, 133 Gill Coliseum, Corvallis, Oregon 97331.

a good place to use the movie. A short discussion of the movie, how it tends to capture and universalize the experience, and one's reaction to the movie itself make a good ending point for the seminar.

OTHER RELEVANT AVAILABLE MATERIALS. New materials which are useful in various approaches to the topic of death education are available. For example, Elisabeth Kübler-Ross has made video-tapes showing her methods of instructing students in the phenomena of death and dying.[31] These videotapes are very useful in certain types of training endeavors. In addition, Robert I Daugherty, M.D., who has assisted us in the "Confrontations of Death" seminar, has recently produced a videotape giving an interview with one of his patients. This tape is available in limited circulation.[32] Robert E. Taubman, M.D., and a group of his fellow physicians, have developed a series of videotapes on the subject of death and dying; these doctors are available for consultation or can conduct short-term conferences and workshops on the subject.[33] Recently, a new film strip series, "Perspectives in Dying," has been developed for the training of nurses and other medical personnel to cope with the phenomena of death and dying.[34] The reader may very well know of local physicians who are engaged in similar endeavors, and from whom videotapes or films can be rented or borrowed.

The literature on thanatology is rapidly increasing. The prospective teacher will want to develop materials of his own, to fit his own frame of reference and his own method of teaching. We have suggested above that popular music is a rich source of relevant material. Newspapers and magazines frequently carry good feature articles. New books are appearing frequently. In short, the news media, the television and film productions, scholarly books and articles, biographies, film strips, and other teaching

[31] Kübler-Ross, Elisabeth: Death and the Dying Patient. One-hour audio tape available from the Minnesota Nursing Home Association, 2950 Metro Drive, Suite 101, Minneapolis, Minnesota 55420.

[32] Write to Robert I. Daugherty, M.D., 191 N. Main Street, Lebanon, Oregon 97355.

[33] Write to Robert E. Taubman, Division of Family Practice, University of Oregon Medical School, 3181 S.W. Sam Jackson Park Road, Portland, Oregon 97201.

[34] Write to Concept Media, 1500 Adams Avenue, Costa Mesa, California 92626.

materials are becoming much more available than they were a few years ago. The teacher can find a number of good resources. We are appending to this article a short bibliography of the current basic literature we have found most helpful. This bibliography is not intended to be exhaustive, but merely suggestive.

LEGAL POSITION OF SPONSORING AGENCY. The reader, especially if he is relatively unfamiliar with the laboratory method, may wonder what would happen if, despite screening efforts, a person participating in the seminar has an extremely unpleasant or even dangerous reaction to the seminar, e.g., if a person who is emotionally unstable resorts to a psychotic response. Is it not dangerous to utilize this method in dealing with a topic as potentially emotionally-laden as death and dying? We have reported our fortunate experiences. We feel there are essentially two reasons for this success: one is the fact that we screen students carefully, the other is the fact that we have a staff/student ratio of about one to five on the weekend experience. In other words, the seminar is richly loaded with faculty.

In addition, to protect the legal position of the University of Oregon, we have always had at least one psychologist certified by the State of Oregon among the trainers who were present for the laboratory weekend. In fact, the first time we taught the course, we had two trainers, one of them a certified psychologist, in *each* of the three groups, plus the instructors, or a total of three staff members for each small group of ten students. Now, we consider it sufficient to have one instructor plus the trainer, or two staff members for each small group of ten students. Only one trainer must be a certified psychologist. We have never found it necessary to utilize the services of our trainers in the capacity of therapists to help students having unpleasant reactions. As a precaution, however, we suggest that persons utilizing this method follow a similar procedure. The presence of a certified psychologist is not difficult to obtain and is a comforting "insurance factor."

We reiterate that students should never be forced or required to take a course which uses laboratory group methods. In addition, we feel that such courses should always be taught ungraded if they are in a university setting. If this method is utilized in some other setting, e.g., if you are conducting a short-term workshop or conference for in-service training, potential participants should be made aware of the methods before they are asked to attend the first session, and they should be given the privilege of not attending.

In other words, we do not feel it is ethical to insist that a person participate in a laboratory experience. He should be given the opportunity, but he should not be *required* to do so as a part of his job or by virtue of his student status, whichever is applicable. If you are engaged in a training effort which requires the attendance of all potential participants, for example, in-service staff training at a hospital or nursing home, we suggest that you utilize a lecture method, perhaps with more conventional group discussions following the various inputs. Audiovisual materials are very good in these situations, and may be readily used. In short, we caution that the laboratory method, even though we have found it to be extremely effective, is not necessarily for everyone or for use with every group of persons desiring training in coping with the phenomena of death and dying. We cannot overstress too that if the laboratory method is used there is no substitute for capable trainers.

SUMMATION OF AN EXISTENTIAL PHILOSOPHY. Rather than summarize the ideas presented in this chapter, we will close with a poem, which to us describes the growing awareness of the naive student that he is himself involved in the processes of death and dying, that he is inevitably interwoven with all of the human race in this final endeavor, and that he must somehow share his feelings of compassion with those around him. In short, the poem is a summary of the philosophy expressed in the "Confrontations of Death" seminar. Presented below are the lines of Dylan Thomas' *Fern Hill*:[35]

Fern Hill

Now as I was young and easy under the apple boughs
About the lilting house and happy as the grass was green,
The night above the dingle starry,

[35] Thomas, Dylan: *The Collected Poems of Dylan Thomas.* New York, James Laughlin, 1953, pp. 178-180.

Time let me hail and climb
Golden in the heydays of his eyes,
And honored among wagons I was prince of the apple towns
And once below a time I lordly had the trees and leaves
Trail with daisies and barley
Down the rivers of the windfall light.

And as I was green and carefree, famous among the barns
About the happy yard and singing as the farm was home,
In the sun that is young once only,
Time let me play and be
Golden in the mercy of his means,
And green and golden I was huntsman and herdsman, the calves,
Sang to my horn, the foxes on the hills barked clear and cold,
And the sabbath rang slowly
In the pebbles of the holy streams.

All the sun long it was running, it was lovely, the hay-
Fields high as the house, the tunes from the chimneys, it was air
And playing, lovely and watery
And fire green as grass.
And nightly under the simple stars
As I rode to sleep the owls were bearing the farm away,
All the moon long I heard, blessed among stables, the nightjars
Flying with the ricks, and horses
Flashing into the dark.

And then to awake, and the farm, like a wanderer white
With the dew, come back, the cock on his shoulder: it was all
Shining, it was Adam and maiden,
The sky gathered again
And the sun grew round that very day.
So it must have been after the birth of the simple light
In the first, spinning place, the spellbound horses walking warm
Out of the whinnying stable
On to the fields of praise.

And honored among foxes and pheasants by the gay house
Under the new-made clouds and happy as the heart was long
In the sun born over and over

I ran my heedless ways,
My wishes raced through the house-high hay
And nothing I cared, at my sky blue trades, that time allows
In all his tuneful turning so few and such morning songs
Before the children green and golden
Follow him out of grace.

Nothing I cared, in the lamb white days, that time would take me
Up to the swallow-thronged loft by the shadow of my hand,
In the moon that is always rising,
Nor that riding to sleep
I should hear him fly with the high fields
And wake to the farm forever fled from the childless land.
Oh as I was young and easy in the mercy of his means,
Time held me green and dying
Though I sang in my chains like the sea.

—Dylan Thomas

APPENDIX

Outline For Position Paper I

I. Your philosophy of life, or orientation toward life.
    A. What do you want of life?
    B. How do you go about the process of living?

II. Your philosophy of death, or orientation toward death.
    A. What do you think happens after death?
       What is your rationale for thinking this?
    B. How is your philosophy of life related to your
        philosophy of death,

III. Your experience with death.
    A. Your feelings and reactions when a parent, close relative
        or friend died.
    B. Your feelings and reactions when your own life was in
        danger.

IV. Your feelings and thoughts about your own death.

Outline For Position Paper II

During this seminar, you have been exposed to various literary, empirical, philosophical and theological notions about life and death, as well as to certain types of interpersonal and group experiences conducive to discussing with others your feelings about life and death. Admittedly, the seminar was short and you have not had much time to think or ponder, or to put into action any new ideas you may have adopted. At this point, however, you probably feel either that you *have* changed in your point of view about death, that you are going to change but have not had time to do so yet, or that you *have not* changed and probably won't.

If you are of the frame of mind signified in the first two alternatives, consider yourself a "Changer." If you are of the last-mentioned frame of mind, consider yourself a "Non-Changer." The Outlines below attempt to cover the same points but pose the points somewhat differently for "Changers" and "Non-Changers."

For "Changers"

I. What now is your philosophy of life, or orientation toward life, and how does it differ from before the seminar?
  A. What do you now want of life that is different from before?
  B. How do you go about the process of living (or think you will in the future) that is different from before?
II. What now is your philosophy of death, or orientation toward death, and how does it differ from before the seminar?
  A. What do you now think happens after death, and how is this different from what you thought before?
  B. How has the relation of your philosophy of life to your philosophy of death changed?
  C. How have your feelings and thoughts about the death of people important to you changed?
  D. How have your feelings and thoughts about your own death changed?

For "Non-Changers"

I. What is your philosophy of life, or orientation toward life?
  A. What do you want of life?
  B. How do you go about the process of living?

II. What is your philosophy of death, or orientation toward death?
  A. What do you think happens after death?
  B. What is the relation of your philosophy of life to your philosophy of death?
  C. What are your feelings and thoughts about the death of people important to you?
  D. What are your feelings and thoughts about your own death?

Please put your name on your paper somewhere so we will know you completed the work.

BIBLIOGRAPHY

Books

Brim, Orville and others, (Eds.): *The Dying Patient.* New York, Russell Sage Foundation, 1970.

Choron, Jacques: *Death and Western Thought.* New York, Collier-Macmillan, 1963.

————: *Modern Man and Mortality.* New York, Macmillan, 1964.

Dumont, Richard C. and Foss, Dennis C.: *The American View of Death.* Morristown, N. J., General Learning, 1972.

Feifel, Herman, (Ed.): *The Meaning of Death,* New York, McGraw-Hill, 1959.

Fulton, Robert Lester, (Ed.): *Death and Identity.* New York, John Wiley, 1965.

Glaser, Barney: *Time for Dying.* Chicago, Aldine, 1968.

———— and Strauss, A. L.: *Awareness of Dying.* Chicago, Aldine, 1965.

Green, Betty R. and Irish, Donald P., (Eds.): *Death Education: Preparation for Living.* Cambridge, Mass., Schenkman, 1971.

Group for the Advancement of Psychiatry: *Death and Dying: Attitudes of Patient and Doctor.* New York, Mental Health Materials Center, 1966.

Herzog, Edgar: *Psyche and Death.* New York, G. P. Putnam's Sons, 1967.

Hinton, John: *Dying.* Baltimore, Pengiun Books, 1967.

Huxley, Laura Archera: *This Timeless Moment: A Personal View of Aldous Huxley.* New York, Farrar, Strauss and Giroux, 1968.

Kastenbaum, Robert and Aisenberg, Ruth: *The Psychology of Death.* New York, Springer, 1972.

Kübler-Ross, Elisabeth: *On Death and Dying.* London, Macmillan, 1969.

Kutscher, Austin, (Ed.): *Death and Bereavement.* Springfield, Ill., Thomas, 1969.

Lepp, Ignace: *Death and Its Mysteries.* New York, Macmillan, 1968.

Mills, Liston, (Ed.): *Perspectives on Death.* Nashville, Abingdon, 1969.

Mitford, Jessica: *The American Way of Death.* New York, Simon and Schuster, 1963.

Parkes, Colin Murray: *Bereavement: Studies of Grief in Adult Life.* New York, International Universities, 1972.

Pearson, Leonard, (Ed.): *Death and Dying.* Cleveland, Case Western, 1969.

Quint, Jeanne C.: *The Nurse and the Dying Patient.* New York, Macmillan, 1967.

Schoenberg, Bernard and others, (Eds.): *Psychosocial Aspects of Terminal Care.* New York, Columbia University, 1972.

Scott, Frances G. and Brewer, Ruth: *Confrontations of Death: A Book of Readings and a Suggested Method of Instruction.* Corvallis, Oregon, Continuing Education Publications, 1971.

Shneidman, Edwin S., (Ed.): *Death and the College Student.* New York, Behavioral Publications, 1972.

Sudnow, David: *Passing On.* Englewood Cliffs, N. J., Prentice-Hall, 1967.

Toynbee, Arnold, and others: *Man's Concern With Death.* St. Louis, McGraw-Hill, 1968.

U.S. Congress. Senate. Special Committee on Aging: *Death with Dignity: An Inquiry into Related Public Issues.* 3 parts. Hearings, 91st Congress, 2nd Session, Washington, D. C., Govt. Print. Office, 1972.

Vernick, Joel J.: *Selected Bibliography on Death and Dying.* Washington, D. C., Govt. Print. Office, 1970.

Weisman, Avery D.: *On Dying and Denying: A Psychiatric Study of Terminality.* New York, Behavioral Publications, 1972.

Wertenbaker, Lael: *Death of a Man.* New York, Random House, 1957.

Periodicals

Aring, C. D.: Intimations of mortality. An appreciation of death and dying, *Ann Int Med, 69*:137-152, July, 1968.

Averill, James: Grief: its nature and significance. *Psychol Bull, 70*:(6) 721-748, 1968.

Banks, Sam A.: Dialogue on death: Freudian and Christian views. *Pastoral Psychol, 14*:41-49, 1963.

Collett, Lora J. and Lester, David: The fear of death and the fear of dying. *J Psychol, 72*:(2)179-181, 1969.

Drummond, Eleanor and Blumberg, Jeanne: Death and the curriculum. *J Nurs Educ, 1*:21-28, May-June, 1962.

Eaton, Joseph W.: The art of aging and dying. *Gerontologist, 4*:94-100, 1964.

Faunce, William A. and Fulton, Robert: The sociology of death: a neglected area of research. *Social Forces, 36*:205-209.

Feifel, Herman: Attitudes toward death: a psychological perspective. *J Consult Clin Psychol, 33*:292-295, 1969.

Folta, Jeannette R.: The perception of death. *Nurs Res, 14*:232-235, Summer 1965.

Hinton, J. M.: Facing death. *J Psychosom Res, 10*:22-28, July 1966.

Hobart, C. W.: The meaning of death. *J Existent Psychiat, 4*:219-224, 1964.

Kastenbaum, Robert: Cognitive and personal futurity in later life. *J Indiv Psychol, 19*:216-222, Nov., 1963.

————: The foreshortened life perspective. *Geriatrics, 24*:126-133, 1969.

Martin, David and Wrightsman, Lawrence: Religion and fears about death: a critical review of research. *Relig Educ, 59*:174-176, 1964.

———— and others: The relationship between religious behavior and concern about death. *J Social Psychol, 65*:317-323, April, 1965.

Peniston, D. H.: The importance of death education in family life. *Family Life Coordinator, 11*:15-18, 1962.

Shneidman, Edwin S.: You and death. *Psychol Today, 5*:(1)43 ff, June 1971.

Sociological Symposium, Vol. 1 (Fall, 1968), Entire issue on the sociology of death. Bowling Green, Kentucky: Western Kentucky University. 98 pp.

Vanden Bergh, R. L.: Let's talk about death to overcome inhibiting emotions. *Am J Nurs, 66*:71-73, January 1966.

Walker, J. V.: Attitudes to death. *Gerontol Clin, 10*:304-308, 1968.

Wohlford, Paul: Extension of personal time, affective states, and expectation of personal death. *J Pers Soc Psychol, 3*:559-566, 1966.

The process of dying. Entire Issue of *Voices: Art and Science of Psychotherapy,* Spring-Summer 1969.

Chapter VI

RETIREMENT INCOME ADEQUACY[*]

Yung-Ping Chen

Title 1 Of The *Older Americans Act,* Public Law 89-73, effective since July 1965, lists ten objectives in which Congress recognized the general responsibility of all levels of government toward the well-being of the elderly. The first objective enunciated is "[A]n adequate income in retirement in accordance with the American standard of living." Discussions of retirement income before and since then are replete with such expressions as "abolishing poverty," "sufficient income to live on a standard of health, decency, and comfort," "enough income to provide a living with a certain amount of dignity," and the like. Neither the adequate level of income nor the American standard of living are specified in public pronouncements on the goal of retirement income.

Income need is a relative and not an absolute concept and, therefore, one person's adequacy may be another person's inadequacy. Likewise, the American standard of living is a condition of life that is changing with time; the standard of living in the 1970's is certainly going to be different from that in earlier decades. Although there may never be any consensus, some operationally useful definitions are required, if the goal on retirement income

*Excerpted from the author's *Income: Background and Issues,* 1971 White House Conference on Aging (Washington: General Services Administration; March 1971), 104 pp. (Reprinted by the Institute of Industrial Relations, University of California, Los Angeles, June 1971 and by the U.S. Government Printing Office, October 1971.)

as stated in the *Older Americans Act* is to be translated into reality.

The purpose of this paper, then, is two-fold: to provide a basis for defining the contents of the goal of income adequacy; and to identify certain issues and possibilities with regard to the sources of income. In Section I, the concept of income adequacy as a policy goal is defined. In Section II, the implications of alternative means of obtaining income adequacy are discussed. This is followed by Section III in which the present income situation of the aged is summarized. Finally, the issues and possibilities in the five sources of income support in old age—Social Security, public assistance, private pensions, private savings, and employment—are identified and briefly analyzed.

DEFINITION OF INCOME ADEQUACY

Adequacy of income might be construed as those levels of income that would avoid poverty (thus eliminating "absolute deprivation") according to the income benchmarks defined by the Social Security Administration. Or it might be interpreted as those levels of income that would meet other standards of living, such as the various standard budgets estimated by the Bureau of Labor Statistics. Since income adequacy is a relative notion with social, psychological, as well as economic dimensions, adequate retirement income might be expected to bear a "reasonable relationship" to income before retirement in order to avoid feelings of "relative deprivation." A level of income that is adequate at the start of retirement, however, may become inadequate if its purchasing power declines with inflation. An adequate income when retirement begins may also become inadequate if economic growth raises the standard of living of the working population in general but offers no improvements for the retired. In both instances, feelings of relative deprivation would result.

As pointed out above, "American standard of living," too, is a relative and a dynamic rather than an absolute and a static notion. Perceptions of what the American standard of living is likewise vary among individuals. This is particularly true when this standard of living is discussed in the context of assuring sufficient income for the retired, because at least part of that assurance comes from transferring income from the working to the retired.

One of the first important questions is what level of income may be considered as providing "minimum adequacy." There seems to exist a wide agreement that a poverty-level income is inconsistent with the so-called American standard of living. As a working definition, the poverty thresholds as suggested by the Social Security Administration may be taken to approximate those levels of income required for minimum physical subsistence.

Although it is comparatively easier to suggest a minimum adequacy of income that might eliminate "absolute deprivation," it is far more difficult to suggest what level of income provides psychological sustenance beyond the minimum physical subsistence—a level of income necessary to avoid "relative deprivation."

"The "relative adequacy" level of income is a highly variable and debatable notion; it depends upon the preferences of individuals with respect to their lifetime allocation of income and consumption. Some prefer to consume more when they are young and less when they become old, while others would want to moderate their consumption in early stages of life in preparation for more income in retirement. In a society in which there is a strong belief in personal preferences and a heavy reliance on individual initiatives, it may be argued that choices about distribution of income and expenditures over a life cycle should be left to the individual. However, the ideal of maintaining as much freedom of choice as possible in the management of one's financial and other matters may never become a reality for some people, either because they may suffer from miscalculations or because they may fall victim to forces beyond their control. A compromise between these two points of view may be acceptable to society at large.

Such an approach would call for a compulsory public retirement program to provide income *up to a level*. Beyond that, individuals would be expected to provide for their own. This is in fact the system of divided responsibility for providing retirement income that exists today in this country. However, this crucial question remains: What level of income is a compulsory public retirement program designed to provide? Is it the 'minimum adequacy," designed for the avoidance of poverty? Surely a level of income below the poverty line is contradictory to the American standard of living; but does the American standard *merely* call for the abolition of poverty or absolute deprivation?

It seems equally clear that the American standard of living cannot be based on what the most fortunate members of society may attain ("maximum adequacy"). Thus, the objective of assuring provision of "an adequate and secure retirement income in accordance with the American standard of living" may imply a system of retirement income provision, under which the retired will be able to achieve (1) a "minimum adequacy" of income which is guaranteed by society, (2) a "relative adequacy" level of income to be generated from group plans (both government and non-government) and, (3) a "maximum adequacy" level of income to be determined by and planned for the individual himself.

ALTERNATIVE MEANS OF OBTAINING INCOME ADEQUACY

Even when some measure of agreement is reached on what constitutes adequacy of income, there remains the all-important question of how to provide it. At the present time, retirement income is derived from a variety of sources—those sponsored by Government programs, those under auspices of labor and business group plans, and those built up through the personal efforts by the individuals and their families. Given this *system of shared responsibility,* the question naturally arises as to what are respective roles of collective actions (both government and nongovernment) and individual personal efforts. There may never be any consensus on the proper mix of this responsibility. However, assuming personal preferences and individual initiatives are to be encouraged, it would seem appropriate to suggest that the multiple system that now exisits be maintained and expanded to widen the range of choices and extend as much flexibility as possible. On the other hand, recognizing that (1) income adequacy in accordance with the American standard of living is a desirable goal, (2) the ideal of maximum freedom of choice may not become a reality for some people, and (3) below-poverty level of income is inconsistent with the American standard of living, it appears clear that the provision of a "minimum adequacy" level of income in order to eradicate poverty or absolute deprivation is a program the society as a whole would underwrite.

Provision of relative adequacy level of income would be a much simpler problem to handle if there were only one mechanism, for example, Social Security, instead of many mechanisms of which Social Security is a part. Under a system of multiple programs, coordination among them is a significant question: What is the optimal mix of these programs? The difficulty is also compounded when retirement income is derived from voluntary actions as well as from compulsory programs. The reason is that the previous question of the optimal mix is made complex by the degree or scope of available choice. To be more specific, the complexity in terms of how to provide or generate relative adequacy level of income lies squarely in the relationship between these competing as well as complementary methods of income provision. For example, more contributions into Social Security would result in higher benefit payments for retirement, and the same holds true for private pension plans. However, some choice has to be made between contributing more into one or the other in cases where both methods are available to a worker. Moreover, more contributions into either or both of these programs will of necessity reduce one's ability to save privately by accumulating assets after meeting the many expenses for daily living.

THE PRESENT INCOME SITUATION

During the last decade or so, the aged as a group have improved their economic status as measured by the decline in the incidence of poverty, by the rise in money income (despite declining labor force participation or increased leisure, whether voluntary or involuntary), or by the increase in asset holdings (real asset in the form of homeownership, for example, and financial assets). This has been a consequence of larger Social Security payments, the spread of private pension plans, the absorption of most of their medical and hospitalization costs by Medicare and Medicaid and other programs, the various special favorable income and property tax provisions and other subsidies, though limited), more ample private savings and investment incomes (in spite of greater compulsory saving under Social Securtiy which might be expected to reduce private savings), and public welfare.

This has been a noteworthy if not remarkable achievement,

for all of this has been accomplished in the absence of a well-coordinated national policy with respect to the Nation's aged population. Although the economic position of the aged as a group improved greatly in absolute terms (having shared in the rising income brought about by a growing economy) in the last 10-12 years, other age groups enhanced their economic status to a greater extent; therefore, it has worsened relative to that of the rest of the population. The price inflation since 1965 has helped to account for this deterioration. Had the Nation had a basic national policy toward the aging during all this time, the aged would have been better situated economically vis-a-vis the nonaged. The improving economic circumstances of the elderly in the last decade relate only to them *as a whole;* certain sub-groups among the aged have fared very poorly either in terms of poverty rates, or money receipts, or asset holdings. Had a basic national policy toward the aging been in existence, these sub-groups of the aged would have been more favorably circumstanced economically vis-a-vis other subgroups in the same age cohort.

Therefore, the keynote on the present income position of the elderly may be characterized by *urgency and hope*—the situation is *urgent* because, unless a comprehensive national policy of income maintenance is formulated soon, retirement income position of the aged will lack the kind and degree of adequacy and security which would help to make retirement period truly "golden years" in life; the situation is *hopeful* because this nation possesses not only the ingenuity but by now also the awareness of the real dimensions of the problem with which to design and implement the long overdue national policy.

The first element of a basic national income policy would seem to be the elimination of poverty among the aged (and others), as officially defined. This is the minimum adequacy level of income discussed above.

Another important ingredient in such a comprehensive retirement income policy would appear to be the creation and maintenance of financial mechanisms which would help provide a reasonable relationship between post-retirement income to pre-retirement income and which would also help provide a reasonable relationship between income of the retired to the income of the working population in general. This is the relative adequacy level of income also discussed above. Still another component in a national income policy for the elderly would call for provisions of the opportunity for considerable individual decision-making (to complement collective, compulsory decision-making) to accommodate personal preferences and initiatives. This is the "maximum adequacy" level of income likewise mentioned earlier. The high and uneven incidence of poverty among the aged today has been amply documented, despite very significant decline in the poverty population, aged and others, since 1959.

SOURCES OF INCOME: ISSUES AND POSSIBILITIES

Social Security

Social Security clearly is a basic program, but the present system contains certain features which have been regarded as undesirable by some, though not by all, students of Social Security. If there is no reform plan which aims at preserving the desirable and reducing the undesirable characteristics of the existing system, Social Security faces the dangers of (1) constantly being criticized from the conservative as well as the liberal for the weaknesses in its tax-benefit framework; (2) gradually causing ever-increasing tax burdens on the workers, especially those who are young and those with low earnings; and (3) possibly developing into another public welfare measure which runs counter to the original objective and, more significantly, to the commonly-held belief of a self-supporting group protection program.

Many features of the present tax-benefit structure require change. One candidate for reform is the regressive payroll taxation. Although the well-entrenched beliefs of earned rights and self-support have made past increases in social security taxes acceptable to a large number of persons in the system, further raises in the rates may represent too great a burden for the low-earning individuals and families. As a possible substitute, general revenue financing, which is progressive on the whole, possesses the advantages of relieving regressivity, injecting more effective income redistribution, and contributing to fiscal stabilization. However, there are offsetting disadvantages, such as (1) removing the foundation of self-financing and thus the feeling of earned rights; (2) losing the basis of "cost control" or the fiscal discipline on benefit increases; (3) having to compete with other users of general revenue, and (4) compelling the high income individuals and corporations to contribute a good deal more (due to progressivity alone) to a system which was predicated upon self-help. These considerations have prompted some writers to suggest that future benefit increases, which are particularly weak as related to contributions, be financed by general revenues, leaving the existing (regressive) tax system unaltered. Other analysts are far more impressed with the virtues of general revenue financing than its problems. Some of these persons would advocate strongly the use of general revenues, but others in this group would concede to suggestions of (1) refunding the payroll tax to workers with incomes below poverty; (2) allowing individuals to credit all or part of their payroll taxes against their personal income taxes with refunds for those whose payroll tax credit exceeds their income tax liabilities; (3) using a vanishing exemption for payroll tax purposes; and (4) possibly integrating the social security system with an improved system of transfer payments to the poor.

However, using general revenues as a supplement, in the manner described above, would reduce regressivity of the present tax structure rather insignificantly. Moreover, these refund and credit devices would make the social security benefits paid to low-income persons a *de-facto* welfare payment. By contrast, nothing would change the complexion of Social Security more than a complete replacement of payroll taxes with general revenues. This would result in an overt system of public welfare. There is a serious question as to whether or not the American public is ready to accept either a *de-facto* or an overt system of Social Security with such a strong scent of welfare.

The following are some of the frequently mentioned or discussed possibilities for strengthening the present program. (1) One effective way of reducing the regressivity of the social security tax would be to significantly raise the taxable wage ceilings. (2) A provision for relating benefit payments to the length of time of employment or the period of contributions. This feature would provide incentive for persons to remain in the labor force longer than they might otherwise. (3) A policy to relax (perhaps gradually on a timetable) the earnings test for benefit receipt. This would gradually remove the disincentive effect on work-leisure choices. It would also eliminate the rather common and underhanded practice of older workers remaining at work for wages below the level which the present earnings tests allow, in order to avoid losing some or all of the Socal Security benefits. (4) Women workers would receive benefits in their own right as contributors to Social Security, depending upon the history of their attachment to the labor force. An advantage of this provision would be to improve the allocation of resources as it relates to women. So long as a woman is entitled to benefits on account of her husband's earning record, her scale of choice between work and leisure may tip in the direction of leisure. Of course, work-leisure choice of a woman (as well as that of a man) is not very significantly affected by social security taxes and benefits in and of themselves. But this observation points to a capricious, "discriminatory" element against the present working wife, in cases (more frequent than not) when her own earnings are lower than those of her husband. In such a case, she would be entitled to a smaller amount of benefits than those she would receive as a wife. At present, she only receives whichever benefit is higher. Under the existing system, this type of treatment "discriminates" against those women who work for a few years before marriage and who resume work after the child-rearing period is over—a pattern quite prevalent in America. As an alternative, it has been proposed that credits toward Social Security be based on a husband-wife combined basis.

Public Assistance

When it was first created in 1935, Old Age Assistance programs (OAA) were designed to be a joint federal-state-local program to provide relief for the aged, along with other welfare programs to cope with the poverty problems among all the poor. Because existing OAA programs are operated by various State and local governmental units, they vary greatly in terms of financing bases, administrative procedures, standards of eligibility, and coverage of beneficiaries, as well as level of payment.

Despite its contributions to the income position of the elderly, OAA, along with other welfare programs, has met a large number of criticisms from many individuals and study groups such as the President's Commission on Income Maintenance Programs, Committee for Economic Development, and others, on grounds of financing, administration and related problems. Consensus seems to exist so far as reforming the existing welfare system is concerned; disagreements exist as to how.

If the elimination of poverty by providing a "minimum adequacy" level of income is to be assured under a public program, there could be a number of policy options, such as improving the existing Old Age Assistance programs (OAA), extending the existing Social Security to cover OAA cases, instituting some form of negative income tax, or establishing a nationally administered, nationally financed Federal assistance program along the line of the Family Assistance Plan as proposed by the present Administration.

The existing OAA programs are operated by various State and local governmental units. While it is possible to improve the existing programs, a successful revamping of the system would appear very difficult to achieve because of the widely diffused governmental jurisdictions with a general problem of revenue sources and with different degrees of inclination toward reform.

Another alternative would be to use the existing Social Security program to perform the function of fighting poverty. Social Security is without a question a most effective income-transfer mechanism which can deliver incomes very quickly. This approach to solving the problem of poverty raises some fundamental questions about the nature of Social Security, however.

As pointed out earlier, Social Security is generally regarded as a contributory system for providing partial income replacement in the event of old-age, death, or disability for those covered wage earners and their families. These wage earners have had a fairly normal and substantial employment history and have contributed to the program's financing. Social Security can prevent or reduce poverty as it moderates the decline in living standards by partial income replacement. However, the role of Social Security in fighting poverty is merely incidental to its role in partially restoring income losses. Attempting to use Social Security as a means of fighting the poverty (or providing minimum adequacy of income) among those persons who receive meager Social Security benefits because of very limited labor force participation or non-participation in the world of work would raise basic questions concerning benefit levels and financing methods.

Unless one is prepared to impose additional taxes upon the workers and their employers as well as upon the self-employed, Social Security could not be expected to make payments to the poverty-stricken. Social Security taxes already are quite burdensome on young and low-wage earners; imposing additional taxes to make Social Security a poverty-fighter would further raise the burden to an extent that may prove difficult to bear by some if not many younger participants in Social Security. Some fear that such an extension of the role of Social Security may so undermine the contributory nature of the system as to make the program unpalatable or even unacceptable to the worker-participants.

In order to remove the problem of heavier tax burden, it has been proposed that general revenues be used as a funding basis. This is a possibility. However, when general revenue funds are transfused into Social Security, the wage-relatedness and the contributory feature would be blurred. Since it appears that the earnings-related rights to Social Security benefits, more than any other characteristic of the system, lie at the core of public acceptance, some observers feel that the support of the system will be substantially reduced as a result of general revenue financing.

Still another alternative would be to institute some form of negative income tax (NIT), under which persons or families whose incomes are below a certain level would receive payments from the Federal Treasury either on a flat rate or a graduated basis (the latter depending upon the degree of the income gap between their income and the level of income NIT supports). NIT approach to solving the problem of poverty in the general population (with its incidental result of providing "minimum adequacy" level of income for the aged) has gathered considerable support in recent years. This approach utilizes the general revenues of the Federal Treasury, and it has several commendable attractions such as simplicity and widespread coverage. As a national program to fight poverty, however, NIT (as a generic term to describe its many variants) is not free of certain problems. One difficulty of as yet undetermined magnitude relates to the potential adverse effect on the incentive to work. A more important difficulty has to do with setting the level of minimum support under NIT. If the payments to all the poor persons and families are set at the current poverty threshold incomes, the program cost would be so large as to result in a very significant income redistribution. The redistributive process thus involved is most likely to impose on the middle-income groups a rather large burden if NIT is erected on the Federal income tax base now in existence. If the size of income redistribution is reduced so as to make it economically and politically acceptable to the majority of the taxpayers, then NIT would fall short of its purpose of eradicating poverty because reduction of income redistribution requires setting NIT payments below that which would be necessary. Of course, the incentive issue is of little or no relevance with regard to the retired or the aged as a group. But payments under NIT are of great concern in assessing its effectiveness to remove poverty. This leads to the final alternative discussed in this section.

It may be argued that a nationally financed, nationally administered Federal assistance program along the line of the Family Assistance Plan (FAP) is a viable alternative. As compared with the three alternatives discussed above, an approach like that of FAP would remove the fragmentation in administration, unevenness in coverage, and the differentials in payments which are the major problems with OAA; it would not impose a role of income guarantor on Social Security for persons with little or no wage-related contribution into the system's funding; it would reduce the possible or potential disincentive effects on work efforts which NIT might bring about, because the FAP approach stipulates the requirements of work on certain individuals, and it would utilize general revenues. Since the concern here is with the aged, it is the Adult Categories of FAP which hold the central interest. However, FAP as an overall instrument to remove poverty has the advantage of not singling out a particular population group for special treatment.

Private Retirement Plans

Private retirement plans today are a very important economic and social mechanism for providing income in old age. They have shown significant growth since 1950, when pension plans first became accepted as a proper issue for collective bargaining as a result of a decision by the U. S. Supreme Court in the Inland Steel case in 1949.

The most recent Survey of the Aged (1968) shows the extent to which private pensions contributed to the income of the aged in 1967. In that year, 19 percent of married couples, 13 percent of nonmarried men, and 5 percent of nonmarried women received private pension payments. More than 95 percent of private pension beneficiaries also received Social Security benefits. Actually private pensioners are a group of the economically-advantaged among the aged since their 1967 median total income, as shown below, was more than $1,000 over that of those without private pension income.

	Median Income of		
Aged Population	Married Couples	Nonmarried Persons	
		Men	Women
(1967)			
With private pension income	$4,255	$2,580	$2,330
Without private pension income	3,080	1,520	1,200

The median pension payment in 1967 was about $900 a year. Private pensions were an important source of income for those in the higher income brackets—25-30 percent of married couples in the income levels of $3,000 or more received such payments; 16-23 percent of nonmarried persons in the income levels between $2,000 and $5,000 had pension payments.

Private retirement plans have indeed made a very significant contribution toward income maintenance in retirement. While further growth of these plans may be expected, the rate of growth in the 1960's was slower than it was in the 1950's. Growth of coverage under private pension plans during the 1960's was primarily attributable to the growth of employment in companies where such plans had already existed.

The fact that private pensions were an important source of income for those in the higher income brackets, together with the earier reference to the relatively small number of the aged who received private pensions as the economically-advantaged, raises several important questions. For example, why is the number of beneficiaries so small in relation to covered employees? And why has the growth of pension plans slowed down during the 1960's ?

The gap between the large number of employees covered and the relatively small number of pensioners can be explained in large part by vesting and eligibility requirements. A related and more fundamental question relates to portability of pension rights.

Vesting refers to the right of a participant of a pension plan to receive his accrued pension benefits if he leaves the plan before he is eligible for retirement benefits. Until the mid-1950's vesting provisions were limited largely to contributory plans not under collective bargaining. The prevalence of vesting has been on the rise. It was estimated that 25 percent of the plans had vesting provisions in 1952; 60 percent in 1954, 67 percent in 1962-63, 74 percent in mid-1967, and 77 percent in 1969. It bears emphasis that even now about one-quarter of the plans do not have vesting provisions.

Not only has there been an increase in vesting provisions but they have also been liberalized. Of those plans with vesting in 1969, only 1 percent required less than 5 years of service; 45 percent required 5-10 years, 39 percent 11-15 years, 12 percent 16-20 years, and 3 percent more than 20 years. In addition to the minimum service requirement, slightly less than half (49%) of the plans also had an age requirement for vesting. Of those plans with age requirements, about one-half required 40 years of age or less while the other half required more than age 40.

The slowing down of pension plan growth has been due to the

fact that the most accessible groups of workers already have been covered. The reason that workers in small- and medium-sized enterprises are not covered by similar plans can be explained by the cost of initial establishment and subsequent administration of such plans.

It seems entirely likely that, if financial mechanisms such as the following were available to facilitate such establishment, the adoption of pension plans would be accelerated. The Industrial Union Department (IUD) of the American Federation of Labor-Congress of Industrial Organization has designed a National Industrial Group Pension Plan (NIGPP) for small plants, which is made available to unions to provide retirement income for their members. Currently 24 International unions are using this program in varying degrees. There are at present more than 180 units covered, each unit having slightly less than 40 employees on the average. Contributions from all units total approximately $200,000 per month. Funds under these plans are received and invested by the funding underwriters; at present, only five funding underwriters are involved. Originally (May 10, 1966), the Trustees of the National Industrial Group Pension Trust Fund appointed the Prudential Insurance Company as Administrative Agency for the Plan. In addition, the following insurance companies are also designated as Funding Agencies: Aetna; Bankers of Iowa; Connecticut General; Equitable; John Hancock; Mutual Benefit; Mutual of New York; State Life; Travelers; and Union Central.

The basic goals for developing NIGPP were the achievement of low expenses, simplified administration, simplified bargaining mechanism for employers and unions, flexibility of benefit levels and contributions rates, flexibility in admitting new groups or changing the participation basis of groups, and maximum pooling of experience and protection of benefit expectations. In short, the goals are simplification, flexibility, and protection. This approach is desirable and should be studied, even though the experiences under this plan have not been overly encouraging in view of the relatively small number of participating units.

Portability of pension rights was earlier mentioned. Pension portability refers to the transfer of pension rights from one plan to another when a worker changes employment. The question of pension portability is intimately related to the nature of pension payments. If pensions to a worker were considered as gratuities from an employer as rewards for loyal service over a long tenure, the question of an employee's rights to his pensions theoretically does not even exist either under voluntary or involuntary termination of employment. However, if pensions are viewed as part of a worker's compensation, consisting of current payment of wages, deferred payment of wages in the form of retirement pensions, and other health and welfare fringe benefits including paid vacation and the like, then the question of pension portability takes on a new dimension. Either voluntary or involuntary departure from employment may disqualify a worker for any rights to a pension if the worker has not met the age and/or service eligibility for vesting. A worker who voluntarily quits the job may not be too concerned with forfeiting part or all of pension rights because presumably the new employment has offered better terms. However, for a worker who is involuntarily discharged from the job, forfeiture of pension rights will certainly add to the aggravation of job loss. In either case, so long as pensions are part of a compensation package, giving up of that portion of wages that is deferred raises the question of equitable treatment of workers with shorter tenure and younger ages vis-a-vis those with longer tenure and older ages. Trends toward more liberalized vesting requirements, as cited earlier, do not offer protection to a large percentage of workers who average less than ten years in a job. It is recognized that a payment of employee benefits (including pensions) is just as much a production cost as is a direct payment for wages. In that light, there is a strong case for portability of pension rights as well as for much more liberalized conditions for vesting. However, it should also be recognized that age and service eligibility requirements for vesting have been argued in terms of flexibility and choice in pension planning.

In the public sector, Social Security is the best example of complete portability because credits toward benefits under the system accumulate for the worker no mater how many times he changes jobs. In the private sector, Teachers Insurance and Annuity Association (TIAA) offers the same system for university teachers and researchers to carry their pension credits from one college to another. Even if portability is considered as a desirable goal, there is the problem of implementing it. The private pension system consists of a number of more or less basic patterns with large numbers of variations under each pattern.

Despite the difficulties with implementing it and arguments about its merits and demerits, portability has been a key issue in the pension literature. Congressional bills in both the House and the Senate have been introduced in the last several Congresses. Portability promises to be an active issue in the coming years, along with continued efforts in behalf of early vesting and sound funding.

Private Savings

As an additional source of financial means in retirement, private savings are represented by "income from assets". According to the 1968 Survey of the Aged, this source of income represented approximately 25 percent of the aggregate income received by the aged in 1967.

Although it may be agreed that individuals should be encouraged to save for retirement because private planning allows for preferences and flexibility, there remains the all-important question of whether they are financially able to do so assuming they are willing. For a large number of people it can be rather difficult—under prevailing institutional circumstances—to save for their old age because of a variety of financial obligations, such as buying and replacing household durables, paying off mortgages or making rental payments, paying for various insurance premiums, medical and educational costs, in addition to contributing to the treasuries of all levels of government. This does not include daily living expenses such as food, transportation, and the like.

The advantage of private savings for retirement use should be considered along with the disadvantages of this method. There are several drawbacks that affect the stability and accessibility of savings. Savings may be used up before retirement, for medical (costs not covered by insurance) and other emergencies if not for pleasure. Another drawback concerns people with modest means who typically save in those forms of financial assets (savings accounts, savings bonds, for example) that do not appreciate in value beyond interest payments and that, in fact, might depreciate in terms of purchasing power during inflation. Still another drawback exists. For a large number of people any substantial amount of savings is in the form of home equity which is locked in the house so long as homeownership is maintained.

Another drawback to reliance on private savings may be a lack of will to save on the part of some individuals and families. But that willingness may be enhanced if individuals are better able to save. Although ability to save does not ensure action, inability to save surely guarantees inaction. If conditions become more favorable for private savings, they could generate more support for retirement income. For example: (1) The tax systems currently in use at the State and local levels, which often are regressive and impose a heavy drain on the financial resources of many individuals, could be reformed. (2) The occurrence of uneven, unpredictable, and sometimes catastrophic medical expenses that may drive persons into poverty or, at the very least, make them financially insecure could be prevented by some form of national health insurance; (3) Public policy to prevent inflation or to reverse inflationary tendencies once they appear could be effective so as to preserve the value of personal savings and therefore encourage more savings. As a hedge against inflation, the perennial suggestion of a Constant Purchasing Power Bond deserves more than just another mention. (4) If savings in the form of house equity—a good protection against inflation—could be utilized when more types of shelter would be available or when savings in this form could be utilized without an outright sale of the house. (5) If income tax provisions could be revised to offer inducements to savings for retirement. Exclusion from taxation of payments made into a retirement fund, public or private, and inclusion in taxable income of withdrawals from that fund during retirement would provide such inducements. It should be emphasized that this suggestion applies only to *retirement* funds but not to all savings. To the extent that this practice would reduce income tax receipts to the Treasury, such reductions could well be justified in terms of the social purpose that is served by this approach. Not only would this kind of tax treatment enhance individual *incentive* to prepare for retirement income, but it would also improve the *ability* of many persons to accumulate more funds during their working years for retirement needs.

Either as a substitute or as a supplement to pension plans, individual savings programs restricted to retirement use (with penalty stipulated for withdrawals before retirement, similar to the "Registered Retirement Saving Plan" in Canada) should be further studied. These programs could be handled through existing financial intermediaries. With a view to protection from inflation, individual restricted savings programs (handled by existing financial intermediaries) could also use the variable annuity approach by linking such savings with a mutual fund mechanism.

Employment

Employment as a source of income after age 65 has declined in its importance over the years. Nonetheless, employment still has a very important effect on the income position of older persons. For example, in March 1970, families headed by an aged person had a median income of $4,803 which was a little more than 50 percent of the median income for all families. Unrelated aged individuals had a median income of $1,855, a little more than 60 percent of the median income for all single persons. However, employment greatly enhanced the income position of these categories. For aged families headed by a full-time worker, the median income was $8,935, which was slightly more than 80 percent of the median income of all families headed by a full-time worker. On the other hand, aged single individuals who were full-time workers had a median income of $4,687, which was 75 percent of the median of all full-time working single persons.

While income from employment is of course highly desirable, employment in old age as a means of bolstering financial status is unlikely to be of major significance. Aside from the fact that earnings as a percentage of the total income received by the aged have declined during the last decade, the following review of the labor force status of the aged suggests that only relatively low expectations should be attached to employment as a purely economic matter in old age. Working for reasons other than economic would be an entirely different situation.

In 1970, aged persons numbered just under 19 million. Seventeen percent were in the labor force with 83 percent out of the labor force. One-half of 1 percent were unemployed. The great bulk of the elderly who worked were employed in nonagricultural jobs: of these, approximately 2.4 million, more than 57 percent had a full-time job; almost 40 percent worked part-time by choice; and a little more than 3 percent held part-time jobs but would have liked to work full-time.

Among those more than 15.7 million remaining aged persons not in the labor force, nearly 15.4 million gave such reasons for not working as ill health, keeping house, and retirement. There were 97,000 persons who thought they could not get jobs; for convenience sake, they may be described as "Type I discouraged job-seekers." In addition, there were 282,000 persons who gave an assortment of reasons for not being in the labor force. Since no knowledge is available as to how many of this latter group were too discouraged to seek jobs, about half of them (probably too large an estimate) may be termed "Type II discouraged job-seekers," again for the sake of convenience.

When the numbers of aged persons who are unemployed (104,000) and others on "involuntary" part-time jobs (81,000) plus the two types of discouraged job seekers (Type I, 97,000 and Type II, 141,000) are included, the total number of aged persons who might be assisted by increased employment opportunities in 1970 was in the neighborhood of 423,000. This number represents more than 2 percent of the aged but, while it would increase the ranks of the employed aged by more than 13.5 percent, it would also reduce the number of the unemployed aged to zero as a result.

To view the employment problem of the aged in proper perspective it may be enlightening to compare it with the status of younger persons (16 to 64 years of age). In 1970, the aged represented 13.9 percent of all persons 16 years old or over. The unemployed aged constituted only a little over 2.5 percent of the total unemployed. The number of aged "involuntary nonagricultural" part-time workers made up 3.7 percent of all workers in this category; aged "Type II discouraged job-seekers" were 9 percent of the total. In all three groups, the share of the aged in the employment problem was less than their share of the total population 16 years old or older. However, the aged's experience with respect to "Type I discouraged job-seekers"—more than 15 percent of the total were among the aged—showed a ratio that was larger than their share of the total population 16 years old and over. Moreover, this proportion was much larger than those other three ratios just cited above.

Although employment would not be relied upon to contribute significantly to the income position of the elderly, discouragement and barriers to work should not be part of a public policy. The nation can ill afford the loss of contributions by elderly workers.

CONCLUDING REMARKS

In this paper, the question of adequate retirement income has been dealt with in two broad respects. First, what is meant by retirement income adequacy has been given a definitional as well as a conceptual treatment. Hopefully, the delineation of "minimum adequacy", "relative adequacy", and "maximum adequacy" will be useful as an operational guide in formulating policy measures aimed at assuring adequate income for the nation's elderly. Second, a number of issues and possibilities relating to the five sources of income during old age have been identified and briefly analyzed. It is hoped that a coherent national policy for the assurance of adequate income for the aged may emerge in the not too distant future.

Part III

INTERVENTION PATTERNS

Chapter VII

COMMUNITY STRATEGIES AND THE AGED*

Albert G. Feldman and Frances Lomas Feldman

Loneliness is the worst aspect of old age, women say. Poverty is the worst, say men. Death is, according to young people of both sexes.[1]

T HE LAST SEVERAL decades have witnessed gigantic steps forward in scientific and medical knowledge to cope with physiological and biological impacts of disease and aging. Steady development and expansion are evident in certain income and health supports provided the elderly by our society. Increased availability and accessibility of resources, services, and goods have supplied older persons with companionship, leisure-time activities, improvements in individual levels of living and comforts. There has been rapid accretion in the number and variety of facilities for the care of the elderly who for various reasons require out-of-home care, with considerable attention to regulatory measures for the establishment and maintenance of standards.

And yet, loneliness, poverty, sickness and death continue in their centuries-old places of primacy in the fears, realistically or

*Some of the material for this chapter is drawn from the authors' forthcoming *The Social Worker in the Community*. Aldine-Atherton Press.

[1] The *Los Angeles Times*, March 24, 1973, reporting the results of a survey conducted for it among 650 respondents by a public opinion organization on attitudes about aging.

neurotically acquired, both among those who anticipate becoming old some far-distant future day and those who have achieved this state. For the extended longevity, the mobile and changing work and life styles in an industrial society, the technical developments that facilitate rapid and graphic communication of the physical, mental, social, and economic deficits observable in old age—these and others tend to underscore a stereotype of inevitability. This is a stereotype shaped by awareness that the expanded life span is subject to a waning capacity for self-support and self-care. It is a stereotype that is responsive to the impatience and reduced tolerance with which anxious aged as well as younger persons meet the increasing frailty which may accompany some external evidence of slow-down in mental processes with or without qualitative alteration. And it is a stereotype that is further strengthened because the prolonged life span often evokes guilty uneasiness in the elderly, and others surrounding them, about economic, psychological and physical dependence.

"There is nothing to look forward to," a 25-year old woman said of the elderly and advancing years in a recent survey. "Their life is finished."

"My life is finished, I have nothing to look forward to," was the comment of the 65-year old widower on his mandatory retirement from the job he had held for more than thirty years. "For all those years, my job decided when I'd get up and where I'd go each day; it decided when I would eat; it decided what I would do; it gave me my companions. Now they are there, and I am out. There is no purpose to my day. I've been cast aside, outdated and useless."

Both comments are germinated from seeds of hopelessness nurtured by the prevalent perception that the older years are characterized by myriad personal and social problems. This perception incorporates the idea that such problems include physical and/or economic dependence, or mental or emotional inadequacy, or some combination of these that leads to, or are the consequences of, isolation or sufferance by relatives, neighbors, caretaker, or others. Uncommon indeed are portrayals of aging as a process accompanied by enhanced life satisfactions and contentment, unabated social contributions, continued mastery over one's accustomed life style and personal circumstances, and graduation to new forms of independence and self-reliance after successful termination of an established pace of economic, psychological, and social achievement.

The common stress on deficits of old age holds particular implications (1) for educating the young and reeducating the middle-aged on how to be happy though old; (2) for the economic planfulness and the mental health of those in their middle years advancing into the next stage of the life cycle; (3) for the development and implementation of social policy that permits freedom from fear among those who, on becoming old, are without personal resources for maintenance of their economic and physical health. Clearly these are long-range implications.

How can this stereotype built on hopelessness, be modified more immediately to one that acknowledges the complex of learnings from the physical and behavioral and social sciences, and the positive impact of these learnings on individual and community health? Does the tendency to underscore deficits of old age serve to center community attention and concern on the poignancy of the state to which a sizeable segment of the population is relegated? How accelerate efforts to transform research findings into practice, knowledge and strategies that can be aggregated into a force to maximize qualitative improvements in the life styles and opportunities of older adults? Does it encourage empirical efforts to improve the quality of their lives? Where does initiative rest for stimulating community responsiveness to these deficits through responsible development of new approaches to the old, for attacking the realities that underpin the apprehensions with which aging so often is associated?

It goes without saying that the prerogative and responsibility for ameliorating factors adversely affecting the comfort and the optimum self-esteem of the elderly are not limited to any single discipline or profession or segment of the community. This chapter, however, will confine itself to the role and efforts of the helping professions in effecting change both in the stereotype and in the actuality of the troubled and, sometimes, troubling older person. Moreover, without in any way minimizing the importance of direct services to older individuals or groups of older persons, the chapter focuses only one one method: community organization approaches to meeting or reducing the needs of the elderly which are associated with loneliness, poverty, and other conditions that have significance for the physical, mental, and social health of the aging person.

Accordingly, in the following pages, attention is given, first, to defining community organization in the context of problems, needs, and services relevant to the aged; and then to identifying community organization models and strategies applicable to and in behalf of the aged. From these models will be drawn principles pertinent to any community organization undertaking that aims to alleviate the fears and problems that are centered in the arena of aging.

Community Organization Defined

Social movements as community organization

Any social movement involves some elements of community organization, no matter how primitive or complex its form, or unsophisticated or systematic its skills-level. Characteristically, a social movement proceeds through four identifiable phases (generally more readily discernible retrospectively) in most of which community organization strategies, singly or in combination, become a facilitating force either deliberately or fortuitously. So has it been with the social movement that has focused on the elderly, whether it be designated as a senior citizens movement, senior power, geriatrics, or simply the older persons movement.

The first phase is recognition by a group of people or by a community that *a problem exists,* that it is a problem affecting more than an individual or a few people in its causal or consequential aspects, and that the problem requires control or solution beyond the capacity of an individual or of several persons regardless of the manifest degree of their readiness or of the level of their ability. Thus, the steadily lessening ability of nuclear families in an industrial society and of local communities experiencing related accelerated population mobility to cope with the economic and social needs of aging relatives led to sporadic development in some states of early tax-supported programs of assistance to the aged who met means tests and other specified conditions of eligibility.

The second phase is the *emergence of leadership* among individuals and organizations ready, willing, and able to focus attention on the nature and extent of the problem, and to insist that our society find and/or implement answers to the identified problem. The Depression of the 'Thirties contains many instances of such rise in leadership with respect to the economic needs of the elderly. The circumstances confronting the elderly in the third decade of the century had changed rapidly from even the first two decades, let alone the conditions in the prior century. The older population had been expanding dramatically both in absolute numbers and in percentage of the population. Increasingly, they were involuntarily entering the status of retired workers—a status that required individuals who held it to refrain from working for income and promised them, in return, such rewards as leisure and community respect. This trend had begun in the 1920s, and growing numbers of elderly found they were unable to stretch the meager retirement income to maintain themselves. In the 1930s, their ejection from the labor pool into dependency was accelerated. Their grown children, also victims of the Depression, could not aid them; financial resources husbanded during a lifetime of hard work and saving for the "sunset years" quickly were depleted.

Millions of elderly Americans became convinced that their financial circumstances were unbearable. They rallied around leaders like Dr. Francis Townsend, who created and led the largest group within the ranks of the elderly.[2] Although the goal sought by Dr. Townsend and other leaders in the older persons movement of the time was not attained, there can be no doubt that his successful efforts at organizing the aged in their own interests was a potent force in bringing about the characteristic third phase of a social movement: the *creation of a program or service* purporting to deal with the specific social problem. In this case, of course, the program developed was the Social Security Act's dual approach

---

[2] Dr. Townsend proposed that older retired workers would receive large regular incomes from the federal government, provided only that they not work and that they spend their government grants in their entirety.

to meeting the economic needs of the retired worker: through the contributory social insurance program (Old-age Insurance Benefits), and through public assistance (Old Age Assistance) for those elderly whose economic need would not be met by the insurance program.

The fourth phase is the *development of other programs and services* addressed to reducing or solving social problems. Such development is discernible in the expansion of the social insurance program successively to include survivors of the elderly, to reduce the age of eligibility for the retired and their widow[3], and to provide Medicare to the over-65 through the social insurance mechanism. Such development is apparent also in the addition of increasingly broadened provisions for medical care for the needy aged, first by way of Medical Assistance to the Aged and then through Medicaid. Such development is seen further in the Social Security Act amendments in the 1960s that encouraged states to extend social services to help the needy elderly to attain or regain capacity for self-care.

Each phase of the older persons' movement seeking to relieve economic and medical want among the elderly has involved the mobilization of citizen interest and concern around facts and possible solutions to problems in a vast community organization effort. This is not to say that senior power *per se* as an organized movement was the crucial or even *the* major force in each of the four phases ascribed above to the development of a social movement, for other forces were swirling around as well, including the interest and actions of friends, relatives, and politicians. They knew from their own experiences and associates the impact of an economic depression on even the most provident of citizens. They had a common understanding of the individual's need for money and the effect of its absence or paucity on the individual and the nation. They had personal sensitivity to the prospect of elderly and near-elderly Americans facing a life of lonely pauperism because of reasons beyond their control, dependent on some form of in-

3 The 1972 Amendments to the Social Security Act recognized both the element of equity and the needs of dependent widowers by likewise enabling the dependent widower of a retired woman worker to apply for Old-Age Insurance Survivors, Disability and Health Benefits at age 60.

adequate charity. The conditions that make possible these empathetic responses to recognition of a social problem and to the leaders seeking or offering solutions to the problem, as well as supportive pressure for adopting the proposed solution or program and then for expanding the scope of the established solutions or refining the service available, are essential tools in the community organization process.

What, then, is community organization?

Just as there is no unanimity of conviction that the older persons movement was the single instrumental force in the development of existing income maintenance and health programs for the elderly, so is there no universal agreement as to a definition of community organization. It is variously regarded as (1) community development, which focuses on effecting social and economic change in a neighborhood or larger community through the process of planning and decision-making by its residents, with emphasis on self-determination and participatory democracy; (2) social engineering or planning; (3) a problem-solving process aiming to reduce or control community social problems through the expansion, elimination, or modification of existing services, or through the establishment of new services or new ways for service delivery to meet changing needs and conditions, or through coordination of services or through social action, including the enactment of social legislation; or (4) stimulating interest in participation in community affairs among the various population segments.

Any or all of these views of community organization might be employed appropriately in the arena of aging, depending upon specific and immediate goals, resources, motives, and other circumstances existing at any given point in time. For purposes of this chapter, community organization is defined as a process which seeks to engage the community in a planning and coordinating activity proposing both to prevent the development of social problems and, through social planning, social action, and mobilization of resources for service delivery or social policy implementation, to reduce the impact of social problems. In the context of the older persons' movement, community organization, accordingly, is viewed here not simply as community development or as social planning or as social action, but as incorporating any or all of these activities at different stages.

Some basic ingredients

This definition is predicated on several widely-accepted assumptions apparent in the foregoing delineation of the phases of a social movement in the field of aging and the program outcomes of the community organization efforts in the various stages of the movement. One of the assumptions is that a community is a vital, changeable, and changing social system with interrelated smaller systems or subsystems. A concerned community, or a community that is the target of concern, may be geographical or cultural or social or functional in nature; or it may be a population segment—aged, minority-group membership, poor, or a coupling of any of these or of other population characteristics. The community comprises individuals, groups, neighborhoods, or small or large aggregates of these.

Another assumption is that productive and effective change—and change is both the immediate and ultimate goal of community organization endeavors—rarely occurs at the behest of a single individual or organization. Rather, it comes from the participation of a community's citizens who perceive meaning and value to themselves in the goals sought and are willing and able to mobilize their interest and energies in the pursuit of these goals.

A third assumption is that the techniques to be utilized are contingent upon actual and potential manpower, material resources, timing, the nature of a particular problem to be attacked, the setting in which it is lodged, the level of sensitization of the community to the nature and implications of the given social problem, and the priority resolution the particular problem can claim or be accorded in relation to the range of other social problems compelling public attention and response.

The transformation of the stated definition into practice, especially with reference to needs, problems and services in the field of aging, requires acknowledgment of the importance of three primary ingredients. The first is that any effective achievement depends in large measure on the recruitment or availability of *a coalition of power* sufficient to attain the particular purpose. This power might represent the political or official segment of the community. It might comprise leaders in business or the professions. It might be a concentration of members from an ethnic or economic minority. It might consist of volunteers in civic and philanthropic organizations. It might be a cadre of elderly persons with a common need and/or objective. It might comprise articulate poor or non-poor consumers of health and social service or their advocates. Or it might constitute a cluster of any of these or other key persons and groups.

A second essential ingredient is respect for the democratic tradition of *participation, representation, and self-determination.* All of these imply some trust, some esteem, and some acceptance that people are capable and reasonably desirous of effecting constructive social change and that, as humane and sensible beings, they are reluctant to permit suffering in a particular population segment with whose members they can identify. This ingredient holds special import for a community organization activity centering around a problem or interest of the elderly who have demonstrated self-reliance and achievement in some form. In our culture, self-reliance and achievement are the hallmarks of adequacy that commands respect.

The third important ingredient is that the *tasks and the goals must be rational, hold some expectation of achievement, and be capable of serving as a basis for a concerted action* even though differences may persist about the tasks or goals.

Five Models of Practice

How these three fundamental ingredients can be measured and integrated to facilitate achievement of a goal that reflects improvement of the quality of the older person's life varies, of course, with a number of circumstances: (1) the receptiveness of the public and private sectors of the community at any given point in time or place to coping with the social problem; (2) the resources— material, technical developments and knowledge, and requisite lay and professional manpower; (3) the expertise and commitment of the community organizer for correcting the plight of the aged and often, (4) the receptiveness of legislative bodies to proposals that seek to bring the goal closer.

There is no single approach that can or should be employed for reaching the goal of improving the quality of life for the elderly. The state of the art is such that, even though traditional community organization method has produced some solid successful outcomes in effecting social change in the interest of human betterment, the need for such change with respect to older citizens is so great and so multi-dimensional, that much—outside, perhaps, of some health and income maintenance developments—is purely experimental or on a scale too small to make an impact that is essential.

Five models of community organization pertinent to the needs of the older segment of the population will be presented below, albeit briefly. They are not offered as *new* approaches, although some, in their application to older persons, have innovative aspects or variations. They are not presented as *discrete* categories, for there is considerable necessary overlapping in many ways, and some models develop from or lead to others. Nor are they proffered as substitutes for "traditional" community organization approaches, although the student of community organization in the field of social work will discern its seminal nature in these descriptions. They have been selected for inclusion here for two notable reasons. One is their potential for supplying at least some partial answers to the questions posed earlier in this chapter. The other is that they lend themselves readily as illustrative of some community organization principles and strategies that will comprise the final section of this chapter.

Social planning model

In recent years, the new social movement in behalf of older persons has stimulated a variety of activities designed to meet needs of this population. Private and public agencies have undertaken programs—sporadically, generally on a small scale, and often to meet a pressing and crisis-like need—without much, if any, attention to any ordering of service or other priorities in the expenditure of available dollars and manpower.

Continuing problems of social and economic deprivation have sensitized community service agencies to the limited benefit of traditional methods of service delivery in relation to their cost. Escalating costs of public health and welfare programs have led to sharp questioning of the cost-benefit ratios of human service programs. The growing awareness that money and legislation have not produced maximal positive results has stimulated social planners in the public and voluntary sectors of the social welfare network to develop new and improved ways of planning, organizing, and evaluating the effectiveness of human service programs.

Services to older persons, while not attacked in some legislative quarters with the kind of anger directed toward younger family groups receiving or in need of services, nevertheless have been the target of considerable rethinking.[4] During the 1960's, four important measures addressed the needs of older people: (1) a wide range of social services could be made available to the economically dependent elderly under the Social Security Act's Title I (Old-age Assistance) or Title XVI (combined adult public assistance categories); (2) Social Security benefits were increased by fifty percent; (3) Medicare and Medicaid were introduced in 1965; and (4) the Older Americans Act was passed in that same year. The pace of expansion of services to the elderly increased considerably under the first and last of these measures. Under Title I of the Social Security Act about thirty states significantly expanded their service plans to provide a wider range of services to a larger eligible older population. Title III of the Older Americans Act made grants in aid available to states for projects to provide a wide array of time-limited service activities to or in behalf of the aged. But these programs and services were uneven and sporadic in their coverage and emerged in a piece-meal, uncoordinated and unconnected fashion.

The 1971 White House Conference on Aging—itself the cumulative outgrowth of an extensive community organization effort at local, state, and national levels—formulated its recommenda-

4 At this writing, the Social Security Act has been amended to create a new Title XVI that provides for federal fiscal and administrative responsibility for the Adult Aids, including aid to the elderly; the scope and financing of mandatory and/or optional social services to this target group have not yet been established.

tions after a systematic examination of needs, values and goals revelant to the aged. It advocated an orderly assessment of needs and resources as a basis for rational delineation of goals and the development of programs to implement attainment of the goals.

There has been a further expansion of services to the elderly since the White House Conference. Congress increased the 1972 appropriation for the community service programs of the Older Americans Act from $21 to $45 million, and the Nutrition Act for the Elderly (P.L. 92-258) was signed into law in March of 1972, presumably to be funded to the extent of $100 million.[5] Both in the Administration on Aging, which administers these programs, and in amendments proposed by Congress to the Older Americans Act,[6] there has been continuing emphasis on social planning, particularly with regard to planning and service areas.

Accordingly, a comprehensive array of services may be established and funded in selected target areas which already have a plan for services based on an assessment of social needs and resources. This planning and service approach envisions that responsibility will rest with the individual state's designated unit on aging (Commisson on Aging, or Department or other official entity) to develop a plan for the state as a whole and to provide smaller regions or local communities with guidelines for regional or local implementation of the plan. Each region or community desiring funds in turn must devise a plan derived from an examination of needs, resources and capacity, and the plan must include evaluation of the effort and outcomes of the programs established. Thus, the federal government provides financial incentives and leadership to states in the development of social planning guidelines. Within the framework of these guidelines, the state assumes leadership and responsibility for state-wide implementation of the planning function. But within the guidelines developed by the state for local application, the ultimate responsibility rests with the

[5] This appropriation was included in the Department of Health, Education, and Welfare appropriation for Fiscal Year 1973 but was vetoed by the President when he declared the Department's budget to be too high. At this point no new action has occurred.

[6] The Amendments to the Older Americans Act was passed by Congress in 1972 but vetoed; it subsequently has been reintroduced into Congress.

local community or region for consumer involvement, participation and decision-making in developing and implementing social planning in the field of aging.

States have flexibility in determining how they will approach the social planning responsibility. As an example, California's unit on aging—the State Commission on Aging—divided the State into regions, and Commission staff undertook to stimulate interest in these regions for the development of planning grants. Those approached were organizations with demonstrated interest and/or experience in social planning in behalf of the elderly: community planning councils, official county department of senior citizen affairs, federated financing organizations like United Way, community action agencies, and committees of senior citizens in combination with voluntary or public agencies.

How does the old Title III of the 1965 Older Americans Act differ from the intent and provisions of the new one and of the nutrition program? It intends that the haphazard development of senior citizen programs will give place to a systematic surveying of the needs and problems that require amelioration or solution through social planning and program development for a designated area. A rational approach is called for, one which takes into account available and potential community resources and an ordering of priorities which are publicly established and are accorded citizen consensus. As under the former provision of the Act, the services are not offered by a single agency. However, one agency has monitoring responsibility and authority, thereby offering reasonable assurance of program coordination that avoids unnecessary duplication or gaps in services to the elderly, and of maintenance of standards of quality and quantity of services proffered. Also new is the essential fact that funds are available at the state level for the administration of the programs. It goes without saying that there is a direct relationship between the adequacy of such funding and the quality and quantity of staff that can be expected to provide the state-wide program with competent leadership. It is noteworthy in this connection that, despite the criticisms leveled at the unplanned, and sometimes-aborted, programs for the aged that were started under the earlier legislation, pockets of the Title III programs in some states have clung to life persistently, though often feebly. The sophisticated social planner in the state unit on aging as well as at the local level can productively regard these programs as constituting a nucleus of needed service to be incorporated into the comprehensive plan being developed.

The concept of social planning for service, as intended in the Older Americans Act and the Nutrition Program for the Elderly, is not unique to the field of aging. It has been demonstrated in comprehensive health planning, for example. But it does underscore the application of several important community organization principles to the area of social planning with respect to the aging: (1) the coalition of public agency interests and actions at several levels of government, and of voluntary and public sectors, to plan and establish an effective and comprehensive and coordinated network of services to meet the myriad and diverse needs of the elderly; (2) the recognition of differences in community needs, resources, and capabilities that can be translated into differences in programs and program priorities without jeopardizing or violating criteria established on a broader base for the effective utilization of public and private monies devoted to human services; (3) the provision for staffing that can provide competent leadership and discriminating use of judgment and skill in assessing and coopting the strengths and interests of community leaders and organizations in carrying out the social planning objective; and (4) the effective involvement of consumers and other citizens in priority-setting to assure logical and optimal use of the available yet scarce dollar for services.

Social action model

In general, the term social action implies an actual or potential conflict situation, and the promotion of a cause or objective by a party to the conflict. Although variously defined, the general thrust of social action is to effect change that is both legal and socially desirable by influencing the power or decision-making structure, particularly in the governmental arena. It may be a consequence of social planning; namely, to prevail upon a legislative body to introduce or alter existing legislation for the purpose of putting into operation some program or program phase in keeping with social planning built on the orderly assessment of needs, resources, and capabilities. Social action may lead to social planning as, for example, the successful creation in some communities of official committees or departments to undertake planning to meet the needs of the senior citizens who demanded that local governing bodies institute this measure. Social action is not synonymous with community organization but may be a modality planned and carried out under the community organization rubric.

The target of social action with respect to aging may be the agency director or board of directors of a voluntary agency having authority to institute, alter or delete a policy of interest and concern to this affected group. The target may be a legislative body or a public agency administrator with policy-interpretation or rule-making authority. The target person or body may be at local, state, or national levels. The techniques employed may range from traditional ones of rational persuasion, on the basis of facts, by an individual or a group or a coalition of groups; to confrontation, with or without facts, by an individual, a committee, or a coalition of groups and interests.

Social action may take many forms: letters to Congressmen, delegations of petitioners appearing personally to press for the desired action, standing or *ad hoc* legislative committee, lobbying, hearings before Congressional and other legislative committees and others. And social action may be undertaken by senior citizens themselves, or by others in behalf of the older persons, or by groups or coalitions containing older people as well as others concerned about them.

Unlike almost any other population group seeking social change by social action, senior citizens have a potent power base for the conduct of social action. The sheer weight of numbers of actual and potential voters among them is fortified further by the personal and psychological elements associated with the expectation held by most people that one day they will themselves be senior citizens or the anticipation by many that they will carry some personal or familial responsibility for one or more older persons. Therefore, a letter-writing campaign organized among older persons to call attention of Congress or of a state legislature to the merits or deficits of pending legislation affecting the aged is apt to evoke more than a perfunctory response by the recipients of this correspondence.

This approach is not an uncommon one in the program of the National Association of Retired Teachers/American Association of Retired Persons. Through its regular newsletter, this organization keeps its five million members informed on legislative matters such as changes in retirement programs, reformation of the private pension system, and others. A legislative committee exists in every state, and a lobbyist is located in the national capital. From time to time the newsletter or the legislative committee issues a call for letter-writing on a specific issue. The responsiveness of the members generally is too substantial to be simply disregarded.

In addition to the correspondence campaigns, the legislative committees of this organization at the state level take positions on issues and keep members and the legislators informed about these. However, as appears to be true in most social action involving older adults, confrontation *per se* is not utilized: senior citizens tend to work within the established structure and to use concensus rather than conflict.[7] A notable exception is the Gray Panther organization, which prefers a more militant approach in presenting its range of social action interests, and which has a relatively small membership of older persons.

Reference already has been made illustratively to the impact of the older persons movement on the federal level of government and the enactment of income maintenance and health programs for this group. At local levels, senior citizens have been effective social activists. Independently or with the help of public or private agency staff, they have organized themselves as free-standing units, or they have become part of a network of public and/or private organizations to influence local governmental officials in providing concrete programs for the elderly: reduced or free public transportation, reduced admissions to theaters and other recreational facilities, establishment of recreation areas or senior citizens centers. Most recently, their interests have been directed to the utilization of general revenue-sharing funds for the provision of

---

[7] Campbell, Angus: Politics Through the Life Cycle, *Gerontologist, 11* (2):112-117, Summer, 1971.

services to the elderly in local communities.[8] Whether on their own or with professional assistance, the older persons groups possess important capability for effecting social change especially at the local levels of government.

Many coalitions for purposes of social action have begun to develop between senior citizen groups and other organizations with some commonality of interests. The three-million member National Council of Senior Citizens, for instance, has strong labor support. Some religious groups with committees or programs centering around aging, and already with a stake in social action, have begun to collaborate in social action designed to improve services for the aging. But neither these religious groups nor voluntary agencies at national or state local levels have begun to realize their potential in working together in joint action in behalf of social legislation affecting the welfare of the aged. The new approach to area-wide coordinated social planning described in the preceding section should serve to produce more coalitions between the senior citizens groups and agencies that deliver health and social services.

The social action model as a viable community organization approach, however, poses some questions that merit careful consideration. One question centers on whether a cohesive identity can be established among older persons for social action purposes. Do the more affluent older persons identify themselves as aged, or identify with the problems of the disadvantaged aged? Can the severely disadvantaged aged be mobilized into a concerted force for change? Can aged of various racial minorities bring themselves (or be brought) to a unity of interests than can be channeled into productive social action? Such questions of different self-perceptions and, consequently, variations in common purpose, suggest that the elderly in actuality constitute not a *single* force for social action but, rather, represent a spectrum of interests and identifications that require special recognition by the community organization specialist who desires to bring into being a coalition of older persons themselves.

---

[8] The State and Local Fiscal Assistance Act of 1972 identifies "the poor or aged" as a priority area in which states and local communities can use some of the general revenue-sharing funds allocated to them on a population basis.

Apparent in the social action model is the fact that many kinds of individuals and groups, singly or together, participate in community organization—not only specially trained community organization practitioners, but also other social workers and other professionals, public officials, consumers and citizens who are elderly or not, and public and voluntary organizations of many kinds. Social action may be carried on in certain circumstances by laymen—older or younger—without the help of professionals. In many situations, professional intervention may be required in order that the available facts about community needs and resources and about the community's political and social organization can be taken into account by the social activists, and the strategies for social action be coordinated with the form and objectives of a comprehensive social plan for meeting the needs of the aged. In the latter situation, the professional may provide information and guidance to those engaged in social action, or actively engage in social action in behalf of the committee or group of interested elderly.

Discernible in the social action model are some of the community organization principles enumerated in the discussion about the social planning model: (1) the importance of coalitions; (2) the necessity for considering and selecting differential approaches related to achieving desired results in light of a community's overall picture of needs and resources; and (3) the validity of involvement of the elderly in social action in behalf of their own population segment.

However, other factors also are of special importance with respect to the social action model. One is that the very size and strength of senior power constitute a valuable vehicle for progress toward achievement of a social action objective connected with the needs of older persons, and social action is aided by the volume of its support. Another is that coalitions more often will need to be confined to voluntary groups and organizations because, in many instances, possible conflict in interests will reduce the likelihood that a public organization committee or group will enter sincerely into a coalition addressed to producing some kind of change in the policy or program of its employing agency.

Advocacy model

Advocacy as a concept and as a strategy has evoked considerable attention in recent years. This attention has grown markedly since the advent of the Economic Opportunity Act of 1964 and the concentration of human and material resources on the effort to relieve the plight of the poor and otherwise disadvantaged by reducing or eliminating the powerlessness that was perceived as a major block to their more effective social and economic functioning. The advocacy model of community organization (and of other helping modalities) is the prototype of social reform efforts observable in earlier decades. However, under the impact of new sensitization to the needs of special groups—minority-group members, elderly poor, or others—advocacy has assumed some new forms and moved in some new directions.

Traditionally, the community organizer was expected to be an enabler and facilitator with special skills to help people and social institutions toward change as a consequence of clarifying a social problem, identifying needs, and developing or stimulating the development, in a given group or community, of the capacity to deal effectively with the problem through the formulation and implementation of an appropriate answer for the social problem. In the climate of the last decade there has been a natural transition from enabler-facilitator to advocate, whereby the community organizer, or person in some other helping role, has become the agent seeking resources or redress of grievances in behalf of individuals or a target population or community. This agent, or advocate, might be intent on building a new power base for and with a target group, or he might undertake to attain any of a variety of other objectives.

Characteristically, the advocacy model is built on (1) the identification of the advocate with the needs and aspirations of those being served, and (2) a readiness to take action on their behalf in confrontation with social institutions and persons controlling resources or decision-making. Although some elements of the social planning or social action models also may be present in the advocacy model—and, indeed, social planning or social action may be outcomes of the advocacy-model strategies—the *objective* is different.

Thus the advocate, aware of a social problem and possible ways of effecting a solution, may have to mobilize those who are the victims of the situation, rallying and unifying them around issues he can identify and that he can represent as amenable to improvement. He may thereby be thrust, at least initially, into a leadership role. He also may serve as a general advocate for social protest, social change, and/or social action. He may function directly as organizer, strategist, tactitian. Whereas the advocate, like the enabler-facilitator, encourages participation and self-help, he simultaneously is identified with the target population's objectives and is a partisan to their cause.

Advocacy with regard to aged persons and groups has been practiced by social workers and by public health nurses for many years, particularly in intervening with landlords, health delivery systems, income maintenance systems, and fair hearing devices. A relatively recent entrant into the arena of advocacy with respect to the elderly—and, especially, the elderly poor—is the legal profession. Lawyers have long represented the poor—young and old—and otherwise disadvantaged persons with respect to legal problems. However, the last several years have seen a growing concentration of concern centered on legal problems primarily attributable to advancing age. Age discrimination in employment exemplifies this kind of problem. Many persons in their middle years, especially if they have low-level or marginal skills, find it increasingly difficult to find and retain employment in the face of the understandable preference of many employers for younger workers. Their problem is exacerbated with increasing age. To be sure, age discrimination is unlawful under state and federal statutes, but enforcement is weak.[9]

Elderly poor experience problems brought on by probate laws that do not enable this group to dispose of their small estates quickly and inexpensively. They also have difficulties with regard to protection of their rights in connection with disability or re-

[9] Marlin, David H. and Brown, Robert N.: The elderly poor; an overview of the legal services attorney's responsibility. *Clearinghouse Rev, 6* (4-5):192-193, Aug-Sept. 1972.

tirement benefits under the Social Security Act. Many legal problems are associated with their hospitalization or confinement to nursing homes. Among these are transfer from one facility to another without their consent or without a hearing, and being billed for care when a "fiscal intermediary" under Medicare (Title XVIII of the Social Security Act) determines they are ineligible for the level of care supplied.

Poverty deepens many of the problems of the elderly. Inability to pay rising property taxes not infrequently results in loss of the elderly homeowner's property. He may then have to rely on public assistance not only for maintenance but also for care if he begins to lose the capacity to care for himself without aid. In many states, such an older person may be committed needlessly to facilities for the care of the mentally ill without the benefit of due process. Consumer problems, guardianship and conservatorship problems—these and others are particularly acute among older persons, whether poor or not. The lack of financial resources results in exaggeration of the effects of such problems on the elderly who also are poor.

Developed recently under the auspices of the National Council of Senior Citizens, the National Senior Citizens Law Center was funded by the Office of Economic Opportunity through the Western Center on Law and Poverty[10] to develop the capacity to serve the presently unmet legal needs of the low-income elderly. A major goal is to insure that methods are developed to bring this neglected client group and Legal Services attorneys together as, for example, through outreach programs whereby Legal Services offices send staff to senior citizens centers. Demonstration projects using the advocacy model have been sponsored by this Law Center, one in Venice, California specializing in the elderly's housing problems, and one in San Francisco focusing on their health problems. Out of these experiences, Marlin and Brown report[11] the importance of lawyers investing the time and patience essential to

[10] Established at the University of Southern California as a joint undertaking of the Law Center of USC and the Schools of law at the University of California at Los Angeles and Loyola University of Los Angeles.

[11] Marlin and Brown, *op. cit.*, p. 194.

creating an atmosphere of trust between the attorney and the elderly client. They state:

> To build this kind of trust, to acquaint the elderly community with the availability of legal services, and to overcome the reluctance of the elderly to use these services, lawyers representing the elderly should establish contacts with agencies serving the elderly and with groups of the elderly themselves. Contact of this sort is indispensable, and supplies lawyers with access to senior citizens, sensitizes them to the needs of the elderly, makes the elderly aware of the availability of legal help, and enhances the program's stature.

Thus is set forth a fundamental and early double step in the advocacy model: (1) instilling some *trust* in the elderly person that the lawyer *understands* his need, *wants* to help him, and that the older potential client *can* be helped; and (2) infusing the lawyer with compelling knowledge of the desperation or hopelessness that too often is the concomitant of the isolation that comes with poverty in old age or of the victimization to which the elderly living alone are easy prey, and yet can be amenable to legal redress or protection.

The process of reaching out to elderly persons can be undertaken effectively on many occasions by senior citizens as paraprofessionals provided, of course, that there is careful and appropriate selection, preparation and supervision of persons used in such capacity. Given such conditions, several benefits can obtain. One is that the paraprofessional role can provide the senior citizen with the self-esteem and sense of adequacy that comes from performing a useful task in a work ethic-oriented society, thereby contributing to his own sense of well-being (and the construction of a self-help model). Another is that many elderly persons, as is true in other kinds of instances where personal identification can be a valuable aid in establishing trust, are likely to be more responsive to overtures from other older people they are "certain" have greater understanding of the stress and problems of aging than would be possessed by "a young whippersnapper." A third benefit, of course, accrues from the economical and efficient "stretching" of the available professional manpower.

The use of older persons as lay advocates by legal services

agencies has taken several forms. In one, the paraprofessional acts as an aide to the lawyer in seeking out the elderly clients, notifying them of the availability of legal assistances and helping the attorney to serve the client. This is not necessarily a creative use of paraprofessionals, especially if, as often is the case, they have backgrounds of education and experience that equip them to perform in a status other than "as servants of lawyers."[12]

One illustration of more constructive utilization of paraprofessionals as advocates is that of the Council of Elders in Boston. In this example, older paraprofessionals became aware that the most economically needy elderly, those essentially dependent upon public assistance for their survival needs, lost the benefit of Social Security increases because their public assistance payments were reduced to offset the amount of the Social Security increase. Paraprofessionals organized groups of citizens around this inequitable situation; they in turn sought legal assistance. The lawyer drafted a bill to correct this issue and he arranged for its introduction in the state legislature. The elderly, led by the paraprofessionals, testified at hearings in favor of the bill's passage and in other ways actively supported its enactment until the bill was signed into law.

A similar technique was successfully applied in California when, in 1970, the state attempted to reduce the health care benefits available to the elderly under the state's Medicaid program (Title XIX of the Social Security Act). A lay advocate assisted in the organization of "The Committee Against Medi-Cal Cuts." More than 600 older persons appeared at an administrative hearing of the state health services agency; California Rural Legal Assistance attorneys represented the group at the hearing and also in the subsequent litigation in which the reductions were declared illegal. As a consequence of this organizing effort in the advocacy model, a social action model was developed in the form of the California Legislative Council for Older Americans. This statewide coalition represents the the elderly before the California legislature and frequently relies upon the services of the attorneys of California Rural Legal Assistance Senior Citizens' Project.

[12] *Ibid.*

Contained in the examples cited above are certain elements that suggest the efficacy of the advocacy model as a community organization approach of choice in the effort to tackle certain problems in the field of aging. Elderly persons who are reticent about exposing to others their personal worries, who are sensitive or fearful about how others will regard their adequacy and coping capacity, who in their physical and psychological isolation and separateness from others have come to believe they truly are alone and without hope that their conditions can be improved or corrected—for these and similar others, the advocacy model initially can serve not only to bring relief, but also to move them to the next step of taking action in their own behalf.

The active leadership or, even, directing role assumed by the advocate permits the target older person to move from inertia or lethargy or hopelessness to the support and companionship of persons with like feelings, at a pace he finds manageable and tolerable. He can be transformed from a reluctant follower who must be impelled toward an objective of importance to him, to a self-propelling participant in a joint activity of concern to him personally or to a group of senior citizens.

This model rests on recognition of differences in motivations and capacities among the elderly to participate in planning and action in their own behalf. It also illustrates the importance of selecting a strategy which permits achievement of more than an immediate objective for a group if the organizer hopes the group will have continuity as an organized entity. The leader must strive for a solution which not only relieves the current and immediately urgent problem, but he also must seek to enable the elderly themselves to participate in achieving the objective and to create institutional frameworks lasting beyond the solution of the immediate problem. In representing the elderly, the advocate—whether lawyer, nurse, social worker, or lay paraprofessional drawn from the ranks of the young or old—serves as a resource to groups of the elderly, enabling them to accomplish goals otherwise beyond their grasp. As they move toward meeting their own needs without the advocate's help, the elderly must be prepared to be free to exercise and build on their new-found or renewed capacity for self-determination and self-actualization.[13]

Self-help model

A dearly-prized value in our American culture is independence, with its concomitants of adequacy and self-mastery. It is beyond the scope of this chapter to examine the reasons for this and the circumstances that lead to depreciation of the individual who either is no longer independent economically or psychologically or physically, or is unable to manage his own affairs fully or partially. Suffice it to say that developing or retaining a level of self-help is a condition that mitigates against lapsing into social isolation or despondency. It is a dynamic against the erosion of social participation because of a loss in social role or group membership.

Consequently, with respect to the elderly who are particularly vulnerable to the loss of self-esteem that is associated with independence and adequacy and is a fundamental ingredient in adequate social functioning, the self-help approach takes on additional meaning. This model is directed to organizing older people to achieving some change in their relationship with one another and in their relationships with the social institutions in their environment. From the standpoint of level of expectations about the participants' self-motivation and self-reliance in reaching for a desired goal, this model calls for greater sophistication among the group's members than would be practical in many advocacy model groups or social action groups.

The self-help model seeks to achieve either short- or long-range objectives. The first undertakes to improve an immediate condition and to help people develop skills and procedures for sustained activity in working out solutions to problems. Outside resources

---

[13] In the course of evaluative research into the effectiveness of a community development activity that had involved the use of the advocacy model in a group of Alaska Eskimo villages, one of the authors asked the paraprofessional community organizer how he judged the success of his advocacy. He replied that when villagers began to make demands of the village council, without his knowledge, and only later told him casually what they had done, he knew they now could "fend for themselves."

may be needed for effective correction of the issue at hand, but primary emphasis is on the efforts of the people themselves and on the educational process involved in their self-help undertaking. Many of the concepts and principles that govern the social action model also are present in self-help, but the purpose is different. Many of the concepts that are present in the advocacy model also are present in the self-help approach but, again, the purpose is different. The purpose of the social action model activity is in the change being sought. The purpose of the advocacy model is that an agent takes action in behalf of the elderly persons and seeks in the process to mobilize them around an issue that will lead them toward action they can take, either with help or alone, in problem-solving. The self-help model geared toward a short-range objective revolves around the problem-solving process and the activity of the participants in their own interests.

The self-help model is applicable not to explicit and direct problem-solving but to organizing a given population toward obtaining resources and power it did not have before. The efforts might center around bringing pressures on existing social institutions. They might be designed to develop new channels of representation whereby previously excluded voices can be heard in the decision-making process. Or they might focus on creating new political-economic arrangements that actually would result in a transfer of resources to them. This self-help model likewise has elements in common with the social action and advocacy models. It also bears some resemblance to the social planning model. Again, however, the purpose is different; namely, in the self-help model there is not just the defined long-range goal to be attained: the *process* of involvement and participation that involves *self* is also part of the *purpose*.

There are numerous examples of the self-help model, many of them located in housing projects or neighborhood concentrations of elderly persons and set into motion by people from various callings or professions. Three with somewhat different aspects will be described here. One is self-generated, two are externally generated. One of these can be characterized as a long-term version, and one as the short-term version of the self-model. The third contains both short- and long-term dimensions.

The first example is to be found in a client-organized group of recipients of Aid to the Totally Disabled (Title XIV of the Social Security Act) and General Relief: The Committee for the Rights of the Disabled. Wrote the president of this organization.

> The Disabled Adult and all of those on General Assistance (General Relief) and Social Security did not have anywhere to go and call for help, or tell us our rights. We were full of fear and frightened as it seemed that no one cared.
>
> That is why C.R.D. was organized—so that all these groups will have a place to go and associate with their own peers who understand the problems, and help alleviate some of the fears that society has leveled on us.[14]

Organized in 1966 by a group of older disabled public assistance recipients, the organization has grown to more than 2,000 members. A panel of volunteer workers, mostly disabled recipients among whom some are bedfast, assists individuals through counseling about welfare eligibility and appeals. They represent the recipient or applicant in any difficulty he has with the health and welfare system, at any level of the bureaucratic hierarchy from the front line eligibility worker at the county level to the state director of the welfare agency. But the Committee has not confined its activities to serving as advocate for troubled and needy individuals. Committee members attend and represent the organization at various public hearings, including those of utilities boards, state legislative committees, county and state welfare agencies. Topics have ranged from housing to Medicaid and attendent care, and to relative responsibility in the adult aids. Committee members have appeared before the United States Senate Committee on the national study of hunger and nutrition and have advocated vocally and strongly the federalization of the adult aids. The Committee has influenced change in some rules and regulations governing state programs to the aged and disabled, and has successfully pressed several class actions to insure rights of

14 Piontkowski, Molly in Ogren, Evelyn H.: *Organized Client Efforts in Welfare Services*. Regional Research Institute in Social Welfare, School of Social Work, University of Southern California, December 1970, p. ii.

eligible public assistance clients. They have received financial help from some church groups, social work and legal groups. They have turned to the latter two for consultation about organizational and strategy matters when they have felt need for such assistance. And they have joined with other organizations to form coalitions when these would serve a useful social action or social planning function. But their objective is to help themselves (1) through individual service by their members to any person needing their help, and (2) through bringing pressure to bear on administration officials and legislative bodies to effect specific and general changes that will benefit those designated by the Committee as disabled.

The second illustration is still in an early stage of development; namely, a proposal to reverse both the despair and the desperate conditions of the nation's elderly in nursing homes by organizing nursing home patients to offset the institutional dominance of the home by an aggregate of countervailing power. The proposal, outlined by the Health Law Project of the University of Pennsylvania Law School,[15] contemplates that an organizer assuming the role of the friendly visitor will walk into a nursing home and begin to establish personal confidences and contacts. The first goal is identified as one of establishing this communication in a setting where communication often does not exist even among the patients themselves. It is anticipated, however, that (1) during the initial contact period, patients' opinions and problems would gradually be elicited and a pattern of common concerns identified, and (2) at an appropriate time, a meeting of patients would take place—probably under the ambience of some social activity such as a bingo party, and the meetings could then be established on a regular basis and a patients' advocacy mechanism established.

To this point, of course, the proposal is to move through an advocacy approach to the purpose of self-help. One self-help objective is to assure that the nursing home patient can exercise his right and access to, and knowledge about, state regulations and other information. With such a base of knowledge about his rights, he can expect to be involved in decision-making in his own behalf,

---

[15] Legal Problems Inherent in Organizing Nursing Home Occupants, in *Clearinghouse Rev,* op. cit., pp. 203-211.

despite conclusions of the state, and question the home's administration or contribute to new decisions as they are made by the
facility's administrators.

Another objective is to enable patients to provide their fellow
patients with support and protection against untimely discharge
or other arbitrary actions inimical to their well-being. Such support would obtain from the organized efforts of knowledgeable
patients who can—through the organization and their knowledge—
help themselves and their fellow patients. The Health Law Project
recognizes and cites many legal implications for patients, organizer,
facility, and government involved, but regards this self-help model
through organization into self-governing groups as a viable undertaking.

The third example is the Older Volunteer Training Program
developed by the Ethel Percy Andrus Gerontology Center of the
University of Southern California.[16] This program, just getting
under way, has two target groups with a different goal for each.

The utilization of the knowledge, skills, experience and maturity of the older adult in a meaningful volunteer role is a stra-
tegic and useful means for enabling him to retain his sense of
self-fulfillment and adequacy. Simultaneously, his contribution
to the society of which he is a productive part is enhanced. Thus,
one goal of the volunteer program is to generate opportunity for
these older persons to serve as volunteers and to motivate and
encourage them to do so. Toward this end, the self-help model is
employed. Based on available knowledge about the population
60 years of age and older, the program assumes the capacity of
most older persons to serve as competent volunteers. Concurrently
there is awareness, also derived from available facts, that motivation is not a characteristic which the older person brings with
him; rather, it is the result of an interaction of the older person
with the situation.

Certainly literature on voluntarism has noted with frequency

16 The project is aided by a grant from the National Retired Teachers Association and American Association of Retired Persons. See Seguin, Mary M.: Older
volunteer training program, a position paper. Ethel Percy Andrus Gerontology
Center, University of Southern California, 1972.

that older adult volunteers are underutilized,[17] especially when cognizance is taken of their numbers and the resources they offer. During the last several years, new and creative volunteer activities such as Retired Seniors Volunteer Program (RSVP) and Foster Grandparents have been influential in linking older citizens with volunteer activities and in providing supports that enable these older persons to gain satisfactions from their volunteer positions. But relatively little has been undertaken to design productive volunteer assignments for elderly volunteers, and this is one of the purposes of the Volunteer program—a self-help purpose.

A companion to the goal of generating opportunities for utilization of older volunteers is to use them optimally in positions of leadership and service. This has the dual objective to benefit the volunteer by reason of his personally satisfying activities, and to benefit consumers of the voluntary service. Although the volunteer services would not be limited to elderly consumers, they are regarded as a major recipient-group of the services.

Staff of the Volunteer Training Program will (1) seek out concentrations of older people; (2) inform them of volunteer needs and positions; (3) arrange for responders to visit volunteer job sites; (4) organize groups of older volunteers; (5) induct them into volunteer positions recruited by the Program staff, (6) train the volunteers to assume the new responsibilities comfortably and competently, and (7) support these elderly persons in their volunteer roles. While the Program has other dimensions relevant to community organization—locating and involving organizations that might use volunteers, for example, and coordinating and evaluating these efforts—the self-help model that involves systematic and planned recruitment, training and placement of older persons as volunteers is the thrust of special interest here.

The application or disregard of certain community organization principles in all likelihood is predictive of the potential for success or failure of the three self-help situations described above. The size of the target group and the size of the community organi-

[17] Schindler-Rainman, Eva and Lippitt, Ronald: *The Volunteer Community: Creative Use of Human Resources,* Washington, D. C., Center for a Voluntary Society, 1971, p. 45.

zation team or staff appear to have little effect, except to the extent that sufficient manpower has to be available from the outset to carry out the prescribed program. The compelling considerations are (1) the relationship of the goal to be achieved with the personal interests and desires of the target persons around whom the self-help undertaking is to be organized; (2) the preliminary and continuous assessment of the elderly capacity and motivation to engage effectively in the contemplated activity; (3) and the probability that the goal will be at least partially if not fully attained. Although each of these must be taken into account before any of the community organization approaches is implemented, they are crucial with regard to the self-help model.

The Committee for the Rights of the Disabled, for example, provides its disabled members with opportunity to channel their otherwise untapped energies (including fears, frustrations, and hostilities) into direct or indirect help to others with whose problems and interests they are identified. Often the help takes place after confrontation with some authority figure or organization, and the outcome of the demand for individual redress or policy change may affect many. This situation contains elements of (1) power derived from the membership in, and strength of, the organization; (2) personal gratification that obtains both from being engaged in a personal satisfying, productive activity that helps others, and demonstrating mastery over a monolithic organization; and (3) enabling the group member to undertake a task that is within his individual capacity to fulfill, whether it be helping a client to file a request for a fair hearing, or insisting by telephone that an agency reexamine a decision relative to eligibility for assistance or the amount of a grant, or appearing before a hearing body either as a presenter or as a supporter of the presenter.

Likewise, the Volunteer Training Program is predicated on knowledge (1) about the general needs, wishes and capabilities of elderly persons for constructive activity and about the personal meanings of work and leisure to well-functioning adults (of any age); (2) of self-determination and of retention of control over one's own affairs as essential components of continued adequate social functioning; and (3) of the impact on older adults when they must cope with a reduction in power, and ways of giving them reassurance and support so they can be successful in their new roles as volunteers. Here, too, taken into early consideration are factors of personal interest and satisfaction, ability to be a volunteer, and the prospect of successful service by the elderly volunteer in a setting in which he is comfortable and confident that he can perform reasonably well in accordance with his individual talents.

In contrast, the nursing home proposal is geared less to the immediate interests and capabilities of the patients than to assuring that certain principles and value of law and equity are exercised *in their* interests. As a matter of fact, some questions require resolution before this undertaking could move from an advocacy model to a self-help model. There is considerable knowledge available about the meaning of illness and the dynamics of behavior in the presence of illness. The relationship of physical and emotional dependency to the source of the illness and its treatment would necessitate consideration of the way the patient perceives himself as an invalid who must rely on the nursing home staff. Would he risk—or be too frightened by its possibility—alienating the facility's caretaking personnel, thereby either impeding his progress toward health or finding himself without some of the attentions he might otherwise have received in his relative isolation as a person sufficiently incapacitated to require nursing home care? How much support could he count on from other equally-dependent persons in an environment in which he has become an antagonist? Can the nursing home resident muster the physical as well as psychological strength to participate in the forming of an organization not necessarily sanctioned by the institution?

These questions address the necessity for advance consideration of (1) who the patients are, (2) their role as patients, (3) whether anxiety and/or satisfaction might be a consequence of the proposed participation, and (4) the impact of such negative or positive feelings on their health status or on their capacity to relate to others in the ways suggested. Irrespective of the merits or demerits of the legal questions and implications for the patient in the nursing home setting, the device proposed for organizing the patients to protect their own and their fellow-patients' interests would appear to skirt some of the basic community organization principles that heretofore have been found important to the success of specific community approaches to problem-solving.

Educational model

Many fields and professions engage in community organization interventions to achieve changes in human relationships and social institutions. Other than social work, probably no profession has devoted more time and effort to developing methodology for this purpose than adult education, and the educational model has particular relevance for effecting change in the arena of aging. For the essence of the educational model is the dissemination of knowledge through which awareness of social problems and possible answers is enlarged, community and individual attitudes modified, and changes in human relationships and social institutions effected.

The efficacy of the educational model lies in (1) the scale and diversity of the targets to which it can reach out, (2) the rational expectation that the current knowledge will be utilized in the curriculum developed to achieve the educational objectives specific to the particular undertaking, (3) the array of methods that can be drawn on for effective imparting of knowledge, and (4) the general accepting attitude in our culture about the value of education and the prestige of an educational facility and/or its faculty. This is not to say that an academic facility must be the setting for the educational model, nor even that it be under the auspices of an educational institution. Rather, the employment of educational techniques in concert with reaching out to engage the interest and activities of specific groups for goal-achievement characterizes and differentiates this model from other community organization approaches in the arena of aging.

The educational model may incorporate components and objectives of any of the other models described, but its two-fold purpose is specific: (1) to broaden the population base which can become sensitized to and sophisticated about the nature and range of problems affecting the older persons; and (2) can be mobilized into an effective force for improvement of these conditions, regardless of the organizations of which they become a part or the strategies in which they become involved toward accomplishment of such improvements.

The 1971 White House Conference on Aging is an example of a gigantic educational model that sought to convey information about many aspects of aging to many groups. The process began at local community levels and was focused on *gathering* information about the needs and problems of the elderly that could be *exchanged* with other local communities as well as at state and national levels. This educational model calls for *feedback* rearding the outcomes of use of the learnings, thus both adding to the information available to those who participated at any level in this pyramidal process and reinforcing their sense of satisfaction gained from self-investment in community service.

The White House Conference process involved many of the elderly themselves as well as other interested citizens, legislators, educators, and representatives from the broad spectrum of professions, industry, government and others with concern about and interest in the aging sector of the population. In the course of preparation for this conference in the nation's capital, and also as a consequence, many who participated devoted energy and time to effecting change through the use of any of the five models described in this chapter.

The process and products of the White House Conference are now common knowledge. Some attention therefore will be directed instead to the many-faceted educational model established in the Ethel Percy Andrus Gerontology Center of the University of Southern California—a model that utilizes a variety of community organization strategies to accomplish an array of subgoals within the purpose previously described.

This multi-disciplinary Center established its Community Projects Program[18] with this rationale: a university traditionally has the triple function of educating, of gaining new knowledge and

18 Originally established in 1968 with the aid of a grant from the National Institute of Mental Health, this Program has had increasing support from other public and private sources as well, not the least of which has come from the University itself.

insights through research, and of channeling this knowledge and these insights to the educational community as well as the community at large. An urban university which lies in the heart of a teeming, complex, constantly-changing metropolis with a sizeable proportion of senior citizens, has a special opportunity and responsibility to translate its educational expertise and its research findings into community service to enhance the quality of life of these elderly and those associated with them. This, then, became the primary task of the Community Projects Program. It would bridge the community and the University to assure that training relevant to the needs of the older adult is available, and that the knowledge learned through research is utilized in the community on behalf of the older adult. To insure effectiveness in accomplishing the ends for which the Community Projects Program was created, its director was selected because of long commitment to improvement of mental health of the aging through the community organization method.

The activities of Community Projects have been addressed to three distinct, yet often overlapping groups. One comprises persons who, in their professional roles, help the elderly directly or indirectly: psychiatrists or other physicians, social workers, nurses, psychologists, clergy or others whose work brings them into direct contact with older adults as counselors, protectors, healers, or in other service relationships. They may be administrators of nursing facilities or service relationships or hospital programs. They may be social planners or designers or administrators of programs concerned with the economic, recreational, social, health or mental health or other service needs of older citizens. Some devote substantial interest, time and energy to the task of alleviating the stress and distress of older adults. They are committed to this undertaking and seek ways to usefully expand their knowledge and enhance the skills they bring to their work. Others have had little prior exposure to the needs and problems of the older citizen, and the staff tries to help them find in the community activities a stimulus for acquiring insights and techniques useful and rewarding in their work with this segment of the population.

Another target group includes educators whose teaching responsibilities can encompass opportunities to acquaint their students with knowledge and understanding of the roles and needs of older members of our society and to prepare these students for effective careers in the area of work with older persons. These educators are in such fields as social work, psychology, religion, nursing, administration, adult education and recreation, law.

The third group consists of the older adults themselves. There are two purposes in reaching out to this group. One is that they do not need to learn about the social, emotional, enocomic, biologic, and other dynamics relevant to the older person; they have first-hand knowledge. Their knowledge may be striated with misconceptions or distorting personal experiences or opinions. Nevertheless, the Center needs even this knowledge—including the attitudinal and mythical aspects, for their existence has implications for the nature of barriers to social and community changes that might be contemplated. The involvement and participation of these older adults are needed in the overall program as an aid to sensitizing the *staff* (and through the staff, others in the community) to areas of special program needs and services that may call for special research or demonstration undertakings, and in assisting staff in compiling insights that can be transformed into teaching materials of value in the work with the other target groups.

The other purpose with this group is to sensitize these *older persons* to the values both for themselves and the community of becoming volunteer providers of services to others, of engaging in self-help approaches like the Volunteer Training Program described earlier, as leaders in an advocacy experience in community organization, and as participants in a social planning or social action undertaking.

Five general categories of activities are pursued toward fulfillment of the program purposes. Within each category are to be found examples of community organization approaches chosen to carry out a particular objective; several will be mentioned here illustratively.

One category is research and demonstration of community services. Included among these activities is an action-research program designed to develop a training model aiming to improve the quality of care for, and the quality of life of, residents of nursing care facilities. The process includes the selection of nursing home administrators for participation in a training program that incorporates both content about older persons and their needs, and consultation and supervision in the application of training techniques in communicating this knowledge to the administrators as trainers of personnel in their own institutions. This project's recruitment of key nursing home adminstrators as planners, consumers, and evaluators of the training and demonstration aspects of the undertaking possesses elements of the advocacy and self-help models. The former pertains largely to the elderly patients and the latter to the personnel, with indirect benefits accruing to the patients. The self-help model in this category of the Program's activities also is illustrated by the volunteer training program already described. A social planning model within the rubric of the educational model was a successfully completed community study by neighborhood residents who sought to identify the needs of elderly disadvantaged minority group members in a Model Cities area and to assist them in formulating a plan for meeting these needs.

A second category comprised a wide range of continuing education activities: community-oriented institutes, workshops, and symposia and longer offerings. These have been addressed to direct and indirect providers of care or service, including planners, administrators, educators, and others. Some have developed on the initiative of the project staff, some at the request of groups or associations of professionals in the community. In all instances, content and format have been the result of the planning of specially designed and developed advisory committees. In some instances these offerings have been sponsored jointly with other units in the University: the Schools of Medicine, Social Work, Law, Architecture, to name a few. Some of the activities have been for special groups such as nurses or clergy or city planners. But certain strategies have been observed throughout: (1) the goal of transmitting knowledge as a step in stimulating responsiveness to the needs of the aged has been foremost in every undertaking; (2) the development and conduct of an institute invariably has been highly dependent on community participation in all aspects and has served many as an experience in social planning that sometimes has led to social action; and (3) coalitions of various kinds have been developed to permit expansion of the content base and the target groups for any given offering. The collaborative programs that emerged from these coalitions contain evidence of a spreading power base as well as heightened interest in the acquisition of further understanding for use with and in the interest of the aged. As a consequence, the interests of some groups have been channeled into specific long-range programs. The clergy, for example, have started projects to aid their aged parishioners.

Another category of the Program's activities may be described as community development; that is, persons in the community— Black or Asian or Mexican-American aged facing retirement —share their experiences and knowledge with the Center's staff. They thus add to the knowkledge which can be utilized in the Center's own educational activities and shared with other institutions and groups desirous of using the teaching aids developed from these experiences. For example, early in the life of the Community Projects Program it became apparent that there was a paucity of information about the life styles and service needs of elderly of various ethnic minorities. If community and professional attention were to be directed to filling the service gaps and providing these groups of elderly with needed services delivered with requisite understanding and effectiveness, there should be some outreach to actual and potential providers of service. Community advisory committees, each focused on the interests of a different ethnic minority, were established.

Accordingly, the Advisory Committee on Continuing Education for Services to the Mexican-American Aged was created. It was started with a small nucleus group of Chicano social workers and others active in the community who proposed members for a larger committee comprising lay citizens and professionals who either were or might be working with elderly of this minority group. A series of institutes then was conducted in which elderly members of the Mexican-American community shared with the professionals information about their needs and their perceptions of limitations of available services and delivery of services. The accessibility and availability of community resources and the scope of their services with regard to this population group were surveyed, and efforts initiated both to expand the available services and to improve the attitudinal and tangible quality of services on which the Mexican American elderly person—or his family for him—could call. The papers published as part of the proceedings of the several institutes have been widely disseminated and used for teaching purposes.[19]

A similarly formed Advisory Committee on Continuing Education for Services to the Black Elderly has served the Program and the community. In addition, this continuing Advisory Committee has taken an active and vital role in counseling Center staff with respect to various research and other activities undertaken or contemplated.

The approach used by Program staff in working with each of these committees has differed. In each instance there has been cognizance of the target group's different interests, aims and ways of relating to their own communities and the community at large. However, the purposes in organizing each were the same, and the objectives and functions of the committees created are essentially alike. Also similar is their initial patterning on the advocacy model, and a transition to a self-help model, with occasional experiences in social planning and/or social action.

The thread that ties together the various community projects developed in the Gerontology Center is continuing education in the area of the aging. The community organization strategies in formulating and conducting the wide range of activities under this rubric incorporate principles already noted with regard to other community organization models.

The New and the Old

The five models described for community approaches to meeting the needs of the elderly have demonstrated that they have actual or potential utility for effectively producing changes in societal attitudes, human relationships, and social institutions purporting to serve the elderly. This is not intended to mean that all activities conforming to any of these models will be successful in improving the conditions of the elderly. However, singly or in

---

[19] For example, *Community Services and the Black Elderly* was released in 1972, and *Health Services and the Mexican American Elderly* in 1973.

tandem, they can make a positive impact on community problem-solving if several factors are observed and applied. (1) The goals must be clear and the tasks for achieving these must be rational and practical, capable of serving as a basis for concerted action even though differences may persist about the tasks or goals. (2) The community organizer must be alert to the demographic, economic, social, political, and emotional factors that contribute at any particular time to the community climate that will positively or negatively affect efforts undertaken toward a social goal. In accordance with the elements that constitute the community climate, the community organizer must selectively involve in the planning for the contemplated activity persons who have interest in the process or objectives of the undertaking and who represent the power base important to the given project. Inherent in the selection considerations would be whether the *interest* the potential participant has in the subject of concern is matched by motivation to work in this area. It is not inconceivable that motivation would need to be stimulated by the community organizer. (3) The power base may be different for each undertaking. However, it devolves on the community organizer—with or without an advisory committee—to exercise judgment as to the parties that should be involved in forming a coalition of power that holds promise for achieveing the objective of the project.

All of the above are predicated on *planning* by the community organizer as to the strategies to be used in the initiation of an activity, and on continuing planning by those subsequently involved in the undertaking. They are predicated also on the *participation* and *involvement* of persons with an interest in the activity's purpose or process as supporter, provider, or consumer. Changes in policy, attitudes or social institutions can occur without the intervention of a community organization person or mechanism. But the extent to which citizen participation is present in any social reform movement profoundly affects the extent to which the related values become imbedded in our culture and in the expectations about what constitutes an appropriate answer to a social problem. Moreover, assurance that the level of participation will be sustained is largely and vitally dependent on the kind of leadership role the person staffing the activity chooses to assume, including the *feedback* he provides those involved in the project with regard to outcomes of their efforts.[20]

There certainly is no single answer to the questions posed at the outset of this chapter regarding where the initiative must rest for developing new approaches for resolution of problems associated with the older population. Nor can there be a single answer for coping with the hopelessness, poverty and other stresses so prevalent among the elderly. Some examples of innovative efforts in this regard have been presented, and some examples of long-established efforts also have been noted. It should be evident that the gargantuan size of the composite of social problems in the field of aging warrants a variety of approaches of intervention by many diverse groups and professions. Essential, of course, is the need for a total integrated community approach that takes cognizance —and appropriate action—of the spectrum of problems touching the aged in that community. A strong and clear national commitment supporting such community action is fundamental for the success of such a local endeavor. The community organization effort now should be addressed to social planning, advocacy, and action aimed at the formulation and implementation of such a national commitment to the nation's elderly.

[20] The person undertaking the community organization activity must decide at the outset, based on the objectives to be achieved and the persons and strategies involved, whether his role will be passive or active, the form his guidance will take, whether he possesses sufficient content knowledge about the given subject or should muster resources of his leadership should be open to modification as circumstances and change, as participants' sophistication and capabilities alter, and as the activity progresses from one stage to the next.

Chapter VIII

THE CONTEXT OF CONTINUING EDUCATION FOR THE LATER YEARS

Marion G. Marshall

THE CONCEPT OF education as a continuing process is not new. What is important is that today we apply this concept to older people, formally educated or not. Continuing education is the right and the privilege of everyone. It is, at the same time, a necessity if we are to keep up with the rapidly changing world around us. If we accept the idea that everyone has a stake in education, if we believe that education means learning, and that learning means change, then older people must continue to receive education—learning—as their lives change.

Through discussion, reading, and listening to experts in the various phases of aging problems, older adults learn to cope with changes. They learn to adjust their thoughts so that they can understand other seniors as well as the younger people in the community. Both physical and psychological problems are often magnified, and adjustments must be made.

Education is no longer a luxury, to be enjoyed only by the very wealthy or the very few who deem it a part of their living patterns. In today's society, education is a vital component of our daily lives. If we are to understand the full implication of the news, if we are to read magazines intelligently and view television with critical judgment, if we would truly like to communicate with younger generations, we must continue to take part in educational pursuits.

Fear of the unknown, memories of frustration, or the dislike of the "establishment," may keep Senior Citizens from the schoolroom. Some older people, especially those who lived in rural areas where schools were far from their homes, may never have had any education. For these people, the thought of going into the school, or classroom, may loom frighteningly.

EDUCATION IS MORE THAN LEARNING

As important as the education itself is the sociability that takes place in the classroom. Friendships develop and some have resulted in marriage. Students enjoy the comradeship and the active discussions that keep each one involved. Everyone is invited to join general classes and hundreds of folks do. They fill music appreciation and choral classes, they join art and ceramic activities, they try to better their English or learn new languages, and they enter public speaking and drama groups. They often fulfill desires that have been denied during years of working or family rearing. Most civic and social science classes, literature, math, psychology or communication classes will find older people enrolled. Some older adults have gone to school to learn typing or brush up on other skills.

At the White House Conference on Aging, John Martin admonished the large group of delegates to "think new." The group listening to him was made up of delegates from all over the United States, young and old, well-educated and poorly educated, rich and not-so-rich. They came from every ethnic group, every persuasion. All were asked to "think new." The delegates did think new. For example, they suggested ways of providing higher education for senior citizens with or without credit. For many older people, getting a college or university degree is an almost forgotten objective, a dream pushed into the unconscious because it could not be fulfilled. Delegates asked WHY? Why couldn't the dream of a lifetime be made into reality? Surely the affluence of this country can provide for its older citizens who want to go to school.

Education can help the Older American fulfill this dream. It can offer new ways of thinking, new ideas to consider, new contacts among classmates and teachers, new outreach. Structured but flexible educational classes will help the older person arrange his time, be conscious of time patterns, find focus each day so that time does not seem to flow endlessly without reason. University administrators must be made to view educational possibilities outside of the traditional methods of achievement. Why not off-campus degrees—external degrees? Why not encourage learning via television classes, or newspaper classes?

Notable for their lack of attention to the aged are the churches. Those who helped to build the churches are neglected by them while emphasis is put upon reaching the young people. But that is being changed. Conscious efforts now are being made to get the aged involved by offering facilities for recreational and educational activities. Rooms that once stood empty all day are now filled with older people, bringing life and warmth into dreary corridors. And activity breeds activity! If one church in a community starts, others follow. A consortium or cluster of churches, for example, can offer a rotating nutrition class, so that older people feel wanted, yet no one group is expected to furnish the meal each week. One church in Los Angeles has built an excellent educational program for adults of all ages by cooperating with the school system. Labeled a "Friendship Center," the church has developed a reputation for community involvement and is constantly buzzing with active people. Even though the young families have moved away from the area, the chapel is filled and the church is prospering.

Just as gerontology classes, that is, education geared to older students, are taken into the areas of high concentration of older people, other classes, even at the university level, can be offered through extension services. Residency requirements baffle many older people, for they cannot afford to live on campus, and may not want to do so.

Can older people learn? Educators are often afraid of this question. For so long we have heard, and many have maintained, that the learning process is slowed if older adults are involved. Wonderment is expressed when anyone over 45 years of age earns a degree. Many schools will not permit work on higher degrees to be started after the age of 40. Yet, research carried on at several gerontology and learning centers have shown that older people can learn, though at a slower rate than their younger counterparts. So long as they can pace themselves they can learn JUST AS WELL. Retention is often better in later years and, certainly, motivation is stronger. Older people go to school voluntarily and this makes a great difference in their acceptance of the rigors of advanced learning. Competition is lessened, too, so the older person, who does not need to look for work or compete for grades is a more relaxed, confident student. If his imagination is captured, he will work hard. Being able to draw from years of experience in living, he can often make the class more interesting and realistic in approach. If the class involves a skill that he has used, the older individual is eager to pass along his techniques to classmates or to help younger people improve.

Each old person is an individual. Some researchers tell us that "as you age you become more of whatever you were when you were younger." People do change, however, and since learning implies change, older students change as learning takes place. Ask any older student why he continues to attend school and he will tell you that he enjoys learning, having a place to go and making friends with other students. He enjoys the stimulation, the mind-stretching, the exploring and study.

Many among our 20 million older Americans reside in clubs, retirement homes, special villages and "ghettos." They have been categorized into income levels, educational levels and social classes. They band together for outings, legislative lobbies, insurance and medical buying clubs. The elderly fill our convalescent homes, converted hotels, chartered planes, and park benches.

What are they looking for, these people who either sit dejectedly or rush into every possible activity? Why haven't the many programs aimed at helping the aged succeeded in making the vast group of retirees happy and contented? This country has achieved an outstanding goal, that of giving man added years in which to live at leisure. Theoretically, each older person should be enriched by the knowledge that he has helped humanity build this world. He has reared his family, lived according to his values, worked hard, made friends, established a place for himself in society. Why, then, should there be such concern about the older about? Why isn't a retired person revered, proud of his achievements, happy in the leisure years?

Perhaps it is because the one ingredient that has been missing has been education. Education *in* living and *for* living. During the working, "productive" years, energy was used in making a living. Any education was primarily geared to helping the individual reach this goal. From the time the young person considers his educational pattern—college, vocational school, apprenticeship, or just job after job—he is conscious that the major goal is a successful career. He is measured and respected by the kind of work he does, the amount of money he earns, his visible contributions to society. Looking at the problem practically, however, the realization comes that there has been no education for living those longer years that are now possible. Instead, these added years stretch before him in vast bareness. Time is no longer important, and many old people find that making segments of time meaningful is quite difficult.

All the ills of aging were to be eased in 1935 when President Franklin D. Roosevelt signed the Social Security Act as "the cornerstone in a structure . . . by no means complete." The structure may never be complete, and even its beginnings may be toppled by our rapidly growing numbers of elderly people. Problems now considered difficult will be magnified. Advance planning must somehow help meet these anticipated problems. Solutions must begin before crises set in. Education is one answer if the current thinking of educators is correct. Continuing education implies the assimilation of information and knowledge, and the setting of values and priorities which change as life progresses through the years. What is needed at infancy is not the same as the education needed during the school years. Even the time one spends in elementary grades differs from time spent in secondary school. Although these educational levels present many superficial similarities, as in the instance of mathematics and reading, expectations with respect to the levels of competence required are obviously quite different. Again, childhood years differ greatly from that time when a young person reaches college where independent research and higher forms of education are necessary ingredients for success.

Once out of college and engaged in a job, formal education is no longer expected unless you are in "people-related" work; for example, teaching, sociology, medicine, psychology. Even in the young adult years there is little education available for parenthood, leisure, human relations, or consumerism. Growing numbers of senior adults means growing needs and growing demand. This has been estimated at a forty billion dollar market. This is a most impressive market and, from this standpoint alone, would justify considerable attention to appropriate educational model programs for the old.

As the population of the old grows larger with an expanding number of "younger" retirees who are increasingly affluent and willing to spend their money on satisfying their more modern consumer desires, the impact of this older generation on the market place is more noticeable. Older people are demanding adequate and attractive housing, clothing that doesn't ape the teenager, medications that relieve pain and allow for greater physical and mental activity, and recreational and educational facilities and programs suitable to their years. In response, national, state and local commissions and committees on aging are employing full-time staffs. Legislators are being educated to the needs of their older constituents by lobbyists.

Gerontology, the study of aging, has been accepted by scientists as a discipline. Universities have introduced the study of aging into their departments concerned with human growth and development. The widespread range of professions interested in the aging process demonstrates the emergence of the aged as a viable segment of the population and points to the need for better understanding of these later years.

But what of the older adult himself? Nothing much has been done to insure his continued education. There is a dearth of true education for senior citizens. Colleges and universities are primarily interested in people who want to earn degrees and train for careers. Most adult schools are geared to turning out elementary or high school diplomas for the young person who needs some formal education in order to obtain and retain his job. Organizations, such as the American Association for Retired Persons, do a good job in offering educational opportunities to its members, but thousands of older people are not members and do not live near enough to educational centers to attend classes.

It is difficult to separate education from recreation or leisure-time pursuits. Such separation is not important if the goals are the same; namely, that of increasing the awareness and activity of the older adult. Usually the separation is far more important to the professionals in the field than to the recipients. Quality recreation and/or education is to be the goal, not who gets credit for conducting the activity. Television is one medium that can and should offer educational programs for the elderly which would provide recreation at the same time. Studies have shown that 70 percent of older adults own television sets and watch, on an average, three hours per day. The higher their educational achievement, the more older people watch news and commentary. If only new ideas in television were offered! Programs could offer learning in exciting, stimulating education.

Characteristics of Older Students

Who goes to school? What is the older student like? He may be a retired teacher, engineer, minister, dentist. On the other hand, he may be like the gentleman who said he wanted to learn to write his name before he died. Asked what his occupation was before retirement he said he had been a chauffeur for a wealthy family. In reply to questions of how he read traffic signs and street names, he said, "When you took me somewhere, or showed me something, I never forgot it." Though he never learned to write his name, he loved coming to class because he had never had a chance at any kind of formal education before.

Those people who were active in organizations, had many friends, or went to lectures or concerts find it easy to go to school. They will seek out the types of educational groups they want to join, and will usually make very good students. It is more difficult to interest the people who worked or kept house but seldom went to PTA or neighborhood clubs. These are the people who need education, need to be helped to expand their spheres of contacts, but who often shy away from such urgings.

A recent Model Cities Program involved the delivery of hot meals to home shut-ins along with a lesson in nutrition and health. These were delivered by senior citizen aides, with lessons prepared by professional teachers. Aides also distributed materials on arthritis, simple exercises that recipients could do alone, easy-to-do recipes for one and two persons. Important, too, were the visits that encouraged shut-ins to try some self-help, that told them there were other older people who cared about them. At the beginning of the project, several of the shut-ins would neither open their doors nor accept any form of education, though they were eager to have the meals. After only a few months, aides were cordially invited into homes. Neighbors of older persons needing help waited at delivery times to inform the aides; the shut-ins began to set places for the meals, to have paper and pencils and lessons ready for work, and two of them were able to join the ambulatory class.

LEARNING DEVELOPMENTS

What results can a teacher expect of older students? Does any actual learning take place or is the classroom just someplace to go? These are questions often heard when discussions of continuing education arises. As mentioned before, among adult educators, stress today is not on gerontology but on job training and placement, with much of education geared to young people just starting their vocational careers. Older people who want to work are somehow expected to already know their jobs. Second careers need to be learned, however, just as in other jobs. Retirement employment often involves service types of work, such as home-maker, transportation, or community aide, crisis intervention worker, or tutor. An earlier career as a mechanic does not equip one to become a competent hospital assistant. A new language pattern may be needed as well as job operational skills.

It is indeed remarkable to watch the development of students in a class for senior adults. If they have been education-oriented and have attended other classes there is an immediate acceptance and active participation. If the student is new to the classroom, the adjustment is slower and sometimes a bit painful. Like other adults, older people will "shop around," joining a class to try it out. If the group is not what they want, they will not return, and may then be lost to any attempt the teacher may make. If a student attends a few times, chances are he will stay in the class. He may become a real booster, recruiting and encouraging other

Senior Citizens to join.

Some older people are afraid of the authority—the establishment—that a teacher and formal education represent. Some find the travel involved in getting to class just too much to undertake. Still others are afraid of being ridiculed for their lack of education, for their untutored language or "silly ideas." There are some who even fear their families will think them "senile" for going back to more formal education. What actually happens is quite the contrary. Families are generally pleased that the older person has found wider interests, expanded his sphere of friendships. They find conversations easier because there are now new subjects to discuss, new viewpoints to explore. The older adult can assert himself again, quoting his teacher and classmates. He has logical, legitimate arguments and references that are current.

Financially, the older adult often has serious problems for, on retirement, earnings are usually cut, insurance rates go up, more medical bills may appear, and the loss of a driver's license often involves added bus and cab fares. Physical inconveniences, differing time schedules and new life styles must be dealt with in realistic terms. Coupled with the cost of transportation and the need to dress up, the obstacles of getting to a class are enormous. Leaving home involves normally getting dressed, being ready at a certain time, being expected, hearing your name called or writing it on a roll sheet. Older people who may not have anyone to talk with, whose only outside contact for a week at a time may be a radio, find themselves, in this instance, important. They are again individuals in their own right.

Taking the class to the student is one method of meeting some of these obstacles. For many older citizens, "outreach" is necessary. This may involve actual pick-up and delivery to class and home, reminder telephone calls or post cards, or a buddy system for help in getting to class. Slowly, however, results will be seen. Greater interest and participation, social growth, stimulating ideas, and an urgent need to attend every meeting develop. Leadership in the class setting often carries over into other activities, and the stimulation received in the classroom provides enough motivation for further community and/or family participation.

Educators have noted that coping skills needed for aging losses may result indirectly from exposure to the class setting. This is not to say that indirect learning can replace formal education in such things as lip reading or braille but, indirectly, one can learn to listen critically to newscasts, or become aware of the thoughts of younger people. Students learn how to become politically active, not necessarily in party support, but in legislative determination. This may lead to learning how and where to write letters to community and political leaders, as well as learning the importance of planning club and community support.

Learning to read newspapers critically and evaluate the work of elected officials, and knowing that he will be discussing issues of the times, makes education relevant. Government officials urge older people to get involved. Actually, older voters are more conscientious when it comes to going to the polls than are younger voters. The older population in the United States is 10 percent of the total, yet 20 percent of those who vote are 65 years of age and older. This is a very sizable group and can produce a political majority on any issue. Politicians and legislators expressed this repeatedly at the White House Conference on Aging, urging older adults to use political "clout" to make their demands known. Delegates were admonished to vote for those things that are good for the older people, and to educate other seniors to the importance of voting. "Don't be afraid of pressure. It is not a dirty word," they said.

What happens when older adults join a class? Are there any positive "results" that can be anticipated? The answer to the last question is an unequivocal "Yes"! Mere attendance provides an opportunity to see other people, to talk and socialize. The class structure provides for communication, hearing and, most important, being heard. Instruction and discussion impart learning, increase the scope of interest, and offer opportunities for mental growth. It is very gratifying and exciting to see students develop personally and intellectually. They walk more rapidly, stand more erect, look alive and buoyant. Family members remark about the changes and usually encourage the older person to continue his schooling.

Older people are often intolerant of their peers. They resent hearing a student repeat over and over an incident that occurred to him. They are sometimes intolerant of the person who wanders in and out of a classroom. The teacher must be sensitive to all the class members, helping them to get the education for which they ostensibly come to class, and to find the satisfactions inherent in good group activity. An enthusiastic student will bring others, will keep the class alert, will provide the support the adult education department may need.

Education has different meanings, depending on the semantics you enjoy. Education can be formal, taking place in traditional classrooms, involving traditional curricula, as in a math or literature class with formal grading of tests, where skills of performance are verified before advancement is permitted. Such classes usually involve textbooks, memorization of facts, ability to write or add or recite these facts. Or, education can be informal and freewheeling, with open discussions, challenging projects, exploration. The English Open School is one form of this latter type of education. It is becoming more popular in the United States as parents seek alternative educational systems for their children. Open "rap" sessions, group counseling for high school students, has been introduced into regular school programs in the hope of providing opportunities for self-expression in a nonthreatening environment.

This open, warm, friendly discussion format, where older students are free to come and go, where there are no exams or tests, no formal homework, are most popular with the elderly. This does not imply dull, unstimulating subjects, but rather a setting conducive to thinking, to exploration of a subject. Exercise, for example, can be formal drills to a precise count, or can be done to pleasant music in an informal, relaxed environment with fun considered a vital part of the class time. Intergenerational understanding is a topic that can arouse concern, anger and deep feeling of resentment. But if the subject is approached as an open exploration of a common problem, understandingly handled by a skilled teacher, older adults can gain insight and develop tolerance.

In another model, education may be carried on alone in library, school or home, church, senior citizen center, a hospital or as part of advanced study in a university, or a small project carried on in the student's yard. Independent study has become an accepted form of education so that individual interests can be part of a degree program. A senior volunteer in a Senior Citizen Center often can use his work as independent study by writing a report or research project. A visit to a large library will reveal many older people reading or studying alone. The quiet solitude of a library can be very reassuring to some people. Others enjoy the sense of action, the feeling of belonging to a class in an active, busy senior center.

Another format is education conducted as a group activity in either large or small groups at any location where older people find it possible to congregate. Churches, Community Centers, parks, meeting rooms in banks, retirement homes, even restaurants or cafeterias are potentially good educational settings. The greatest prerequisite to choosing a classroom is transportation—the ability of the old person to reach the classroom. Many community organizations will give rooms free or for small maintenance fees. Cheerfulness, adequate lighting and ventilation are, of course, important.

Another popular medium is by means of "traveling by armchair" or in actuality to places of interest and/or nostalgia. An evening of slides or films showing beautiful and interesting pictures of other countries will always draw a large group of people. Students will often talk knowingly about a country they have never visited except by armchair. Teachers who have traveled and bring back slides find it relatively easy to build classes of older adults.

Other group educational experiences provide vehicles for enjoying conversations with peers, making new friends, and social contacts. Perhaps one of the most important products of class sessions is the social contact a student is able to make. A study of a nutrition class showed that the meal eaten together was remembered because it provided an opportunity for interaction with others. Also remembered, however, were the educational lessons offered in the class session. After a year, following a series of classes, the elderly students were still using information learned in the nutrition class.

In their educational efforts the older students may also be creating a role model for younger generations to follow. By attending school, older people are showing that education is important and that young people would do well to follow their example. If education continues to be a vital part of retirement years, certainly it will tell younger people that they must be educated for the years ahead. More directly, for many older persons, fulfillment of a lifelong dream of obtaining a college degree may be an important goal. Following the emphasis on education during the White House Conference on Aging, colleges have begun to encourage older adults to take advantage of classes being offered. Even knowing that by so doing there will be no monetary returns, older people may, nevertheless, pursue higher degrees.

Education also may mean training in new skills which one never had time to practice. Learning typing, creative writing, public speaking, painting and ceramics are among the skills many people learn in retirement. When job and family no longer fill available time, older people discover and develop many talents and hobbies. One man, who had never taught before, tutors youngsters in a low-income area school. His teaching methods may be unorthodox and frowned upon by educators, but the children learn. Further, gaining information and using community facilities and agencies add scope to living. Included in most classes, particularly those teaching older people to cope, is information on utilizing both private and public community agencies. Such information deals with welfare agencies, libraries, recreation and similar service organizations.

Education may provide learning to cope with encroaching deafness, with painful arthritis, with fears of the deteriorating aspects of approaching old age. Perhaps the hardest thing to come to grips with is the physical changes that occur in the aging process. For example, lip reading can help with the problem of deafness; learning to shop and cook for one person can help when left alone in the context of solitary living; and appropriate exercise may reduce pain.

Finally, there is learning for the sake of learning, a reaching out to new experiences; and volunteering for community work.

It has been said that "volunteering is the price you pay for the space you occupy." For many older people, this is a compelling reason to serve as a volunteer. They are needed again, with a place to be and with meaningful work waiting. They are appreciated, are making substantial contributions to society, can function as a whole person. Orientation to the job, inservice training, good supervision, all can be gratifying experiences.

Perhaps most significant to the older adult himself is the discussion and formulation of a philosophy of living in today's world, accepting changes, finding a proper, comfortable place for himself. No longer just "an old person," he has status as a student or as a volunteer or in a new career. His opinions are listened to, he is sought out for committee work and reports.

A WORKING MODEL

Is such an educational format actually in operation? The Los Angeles Unified School District has a geronotology specialist in a full-time position with the Division of Career and Continuing Education. This specialist supervises 25-part-time, certified teachers who conduct some 50 ongoing class series, plus another 50 short-term series. At least one city-wide conference is held each year, so that students understand the scope of the program. Here, classes mingle so that south side meets north side; they hear speakers on subjects of general interest; they participate in discussions.

Each gerontology class is under the direct administration of a Community Adult School Principal and is included in the general budget of each school. Since older people prefer classes held during the daytime, "Branch Locations" are used. Churches senior centers, parks, libraries, and recreation centers become classrooms. Of course, all general classes are open to older students but these are often held during evening hours, making continuous attendance more difficult. Interesting is the fact that a 1965 survey of attendance showed that 52 percent of all community adult school classes have large numbers of older students. This statistic should lay to rest the myths that there is no market, that older people do not want to learn, or that "you can't teach an old dog new tricks." Several years ago, when federal programming was just starting, one elderly couple heard of a gerontology class starting in the recreation center of the housing project in which they lived. "I can't tell you how happy that makes me," said the woman. Then she added, "After all, how many paper flowers can you make!"

Organizing Classes

Techniques successful in forming classes in one area may not work in another. The writer once started a class in a community consisting of people familiar with education and community organization. With just a one-page flier announcing the class, 63 people enrolled at the first meeting. Obviously, the flier had piqued the desire to learn, therefore, it was a good piece of publicity. However, when used in another area of the city, the attendance totaled zero! No one came, even though a great deal of preliminary groundwork had been done.

Why? What was learned from this experience? The second area is in a crowded part of the city. No one had asked the-elderly people in that community what kind of classes they wanted, nor were there previous experiences by which to plan. No committees were formed to help recruit students. Assumptions made were based on successes in other, totally different areas of the city. The second area, now five years later, supports several classes, Senior Citizen Clubs, nutrition projects and volunteer programs. Each has been carefully planned by cooperating agencies and community people. Leadership is encouraged and taught. Advisory committees reflect the growing community concerns and involvement. Gerontology classes in this area draw attendances of 25 to 100 students at each class each week.

The Mott Foundation in Detroit, has been innovative enough to establish learning centers in public school buildings. In a program titled "Lighted Schools," the Foundation conducted classes and groups for all members of the family. Adult classes encompass gardening skills as well as mathematics, parent education and physical education. Activities are provided for children ranging from basketball to study labs. More of this type of community facility is needed, allowing parents to enjoy continuing educational opportunities while their children take part in recreation or pursue their own studies. Rather than bemoaning the lack of family and community facilities and the high cost of maintaining public school buildings, a relaxing of bureaucratic controls can give most areas ready access to community-based and financed programming. Cooperation rather than competition, partnership rather than possessiveness, will make these moves possible.

Curriculum

What kind of education are older people concerned with? Keeping body and mind limber is the goal. This means keeping interests alive, making the education both relevant and fun. (Depending on their previous exposure to schooling, and upon the kind of work in which they engaged, the amount and kind of classes will vary.) Most teachers combine subjects in one session, a little physical exercise along with something for mental stimulation. For example, a class may begin traditionally with the Pledge of Allegience, some community singing or a poem or story of interest, followed by 15 minutes of exercise. If students are new, or quite elderly, these exercises may be done while sitting in chairs—even wheelchairs. When they become more capable of limber movements, teachers encourage their students to move out of the chairs into more active exercise.

The remainder of the class time will be devoted to the main subject, such as consumer protection, problems and issues of the times, nutrition and health, community leadership, pre-retirement planning, literature and related subjects. Some classes are designed especially for physical exercise (Los Angeles lists these as The Aging Process—Body Dynamics) and the total class time is devoted to such movement. Approved class titles include: Nutrition and Health, with often a hot meal eaten together after class; Planning for Retirement; The Aging Process—Body Dynamics; Consumer Protection; The Older Adult As Depicted in Literature; Community Leadership Training; Understanding the Aged; and Gerontology—a general category which is described as "Topics of interest to older adults." Lip reading, public speaking, issues and problems, philosophy, social sciences, comparative religion, world geography all are taught under this broad heading. This definition allows for new, experimental subjects to be tried. If successful, a separate subject category is listed in the catalog. For example, lip reading was first tried on an experimental basis. It is now in such demand that it may be listed under its own title. This means that a course outline will be approved and become part of the gerontology curriculum. Certificated teachers skilled in the subject become staff members.

CHOOSING THE RIGHT TEACHERS

Anyone who plans on teaching classes that are geared to older people needs certain characteristics and should make an honest self-assessment to assure himself that this is what he wants to do. Some of the personal traits that help are (1) knowledge of the subject matter; (2) a real interest in other people; (3) a willingness to listen and communicate; (4) stick-to-it-iveness that will help him return time and again; (5) an ability to accept the pace of the older person; (6) good diction and a strong voice; (7) enough self-assurance so that it is easy to enter into exercises, dances, informal drama and other creative efforts; (8) a variety of interests so that subject matter can be pertinent and timely; and (9) an understanding of the aged that includes acceptance of each individual.

Specific training for becoming a teacher of older adults is yet to be offered. Schools and Institutes of Gerontology are for the students who will specialize in medicine, psychology, sociology, architecture and other related fields. But, for the classroom teacher, there has been little direct education. Studies of how older people learn are available in large numbers, but too few apply their findings to the classroom. Yet, adult learners are different from young learners, and older adults are a little different than younger adults. This chapter has tried to point out some of these differences, with the hope that those who want to enter the field will find the courage to do so. Many older students write poetry or eassys to express their gratitude to teacher and school. These are read to appreciative class members and instructors. One teacher wrote, "It's great to be a gerontology teacher! When students tell me how happy they are and how important the class is, I feel ten feet tall!"

But these are only the beginnings. An innovative teacher can discover other avenues of interest and good subject matter. Students will request subjects, suggest ideas for additional classes, buzz groups or brain storming sessions given the topic of "new classes" will develop whole new fields of interest. Here is an area for innovation and some of the older students will enjoy the challenge.

The trend in educational units is to eliminate class fees for those 65 years of age or older, or for those on any form of Social Security or welfare. In Los Angeles, a special "Golden Age Pass" is presented all who register for a class. This lets the older person know that he is welcome at any class of his local community adult school, and gives phone numbers to call for information. Such a card also serves as identification for special school events, most of which are also free for older adults.

Community Colleges are beginning to open their doors to older students, encouraging them to attend classes with other students. Some of these colleges advertise "no degrees or previous educational achievement needed; just a desire to be educated." A few older people are taking advantage of these offers, but again, many of the elderly find distances, transportation, and the fear of failure too much to overcome.

REACHING OUT

What about the "shut-in" or "hidden" older persons? Should we try to find them and encourage their attendance at classes? Very often the "hidden elderly" are not ready to take advantage of the many educational opportunities. They find it hard to join any kind of group, are fearful of new friendships, and seem to be at ease only when they are alone, enclosed in their own "cocoon." Reaching these older people is difficult and discouraging. It can be done, however, if one takes the time and patience to nurture friendship slowly. Two young women studying at a local university in a sociology class, termed "The Older Adult in Today's Society," took as a project the interviewing of older people, mostly men, at a park. Day after day these older people sit around the park lake, feed the pigeons occasionally, or stare out in space. Little animated conversation takes place, and little exchange of friendly relations is noticeable. The two students sat down and began to talk with some of the oldsters. They had planned to use a tape recorder, but wisely refrained when they understood the situation. The girls were delighted to find that, after a half-hour or so of careful and polite approach, the old people sitting on the benches began to talk. "Before we left they were standing in line wanting to be interviewed," one girl later reported. The young women had planned on spending an hour in the park; they stayed all day, foregoing lunch and leaving only when it began to get dark and the old people started leaving. If this pattern could be repeated every day for a period of time, many of these "bench sitters" might become interested in doing more with their time and their minds. Knowing someone wants to talk with you can give the necessary stimulation. Discovering that you are interesting enough to keep someone else listening is especially motivating.

DREAM A BIT

If money were no object, what might one evision as the ultimate in education for the senior citizen? A school that could double as a recreation center? Classrooms with kitchens for experimenting with special menus for those who cook for one or two, for consumer education, for learning to prepare nutritious foods? Maybe a laboratory, where sciences can be studied, or art rooms for painting and ceramics? How about a lounge where students can talk informally, or rest when tired? What about busses that transport people to school, including those who need special busses because of wheelchairs and braces?

There are educational programs that senior citizens can take part in that will serve others. Volunteer tutors, for example, help younger people with their studies. Volunteer grandparents can help teachers and provide intriguing information and stories about their own school days in this or foreign countries. Panels of older adults will help high school students understand some of the problems encountered during other eras that relate to today's world. Many senior citizens are willing to become research data, cooperating with students in various studies of gerontology.

It may seem a little presumptuous, perhaps, for teachers to

try and educate older people in some areas. Nutrition, for instance. When someone has lived for 75 or 80 years it becomes a little unnecessary to explain the "Basic Four" of nutrition and to try to get him to eat with this in mind. If you consider the subject as one of special interest to everyone as a consumer, as a cook, and homemaker, it takes on new dimensions. Add to that the information about today's methods of food processing and the need to add nutrients for vigor and health, and the older person may become interested and eager to learn.

Motivation for education, then, becomes an important consideration in planning an educational program. It can be the difference between successful participation in class, group, or community; or indifferent attendance. Even if the class becomes only "someplace to go" it has value. Some of the discussion will be absorbed, and new friendships can lead to new interests. Again, indirect learning is often as important as directed education.

There are now a few Colleges for Senior Citizens throughout the country, especially for the well-educated older person who finds he would like to renew or continue his education after retirement. Several universities have "Emeriti" groups, made up of retired professors who organize for sociability and educational pursuits. Members of the Emeriti become the instructors in the Colleges. Usually, they receive no payment for their work, but are rewarded by the appreciative students involved in the classroom. Many more such colleges are needed. Funding becomes a major issue, and many institutions of higher education are looking for money to keep their current programs operating.

Still, older people do bring a new dimension to the campus. Many can pay the fees necessary to help the college treasury. Some can add immeasurably to the learning enviroment. Most have the time for special research and are pleased to be asked to help with such studies. There has been some debate over the placement of a college for Senior Citizens. Should it be on campus where the generations can mix, or at least see each other? Or should it be in an easily available area, where much walking is not necessary, and where the older student can feel more secure, reacting to just his own peer group?

Like the "Lady and the Tiger," there is no single, correct

answer. Certainly, interaction between age groups is always important and often desirable. There is also much to be said for the comfortable feelings that come when one is with his own peer group. Posing the question to older people brings many interesting answers. One man who had completed only three grades in elementary school, but who had educated himself quite well, said, "I don't want to go to school with all those old people." Another indicated that he, too, would prefer younger classmates, because "I get tired of hearing old folks complain. I can offer the same complaints myself." On the other hand, an elderly lady confided that she likes the group to be dynamic, and felt that young people "are so far out of touch with reality, they really can't be dynamic." Several older students said that they would like the opportunity to meet with younger people, but were not sure about doing so at each class session.

Teachers have noted that many old people feel better with other old people making up the class; younger students lend an excitement they may not get with just older people. The learning expectation level is higher when the class consists of both young graduate students and older students, but does not appear to be as high when the group is made up of young under-graduates and older people. Much more experimentation and re-search is necessary before any firm conclusions can be drawn. Until such time as more colleges establish special classes and/or open their doors to senior citizens answers to such questions will remain unanswered.

A few years ago, the Social Security Administration introduced Medicare and Medical Insurance. The deadline for signing up for the insurance plan came and officials were amazed at the small number of older citizens who had registered and paid the nominal fee required. A massive campaign was organized at the suggestion of the leaders of senior citizen groups. Older people were hired to go from door to door telling about the plan and signing up eligible residents. The results were phenomenal. Within weeks, thousands of old people had signed up for the insurance plan. Why the success now when earlier public rela-tion attempts had failed? Perhaps because the door-to-door cam-paign involved old people educating old people; neighbors helping neighbors understand the system and fill in the necessary papers; maybe because the old people felt that their government really cared about them—enough to send someone to teach them, to their very door. Here is a parable of our times. Bring education to the people, in understandable and palatable form and they will accept it gratefully. Bring it to them where they can feel comfortable, where they can make actual use of the information, where they can act when it is necessary.

The Senior Citizen today is changing from passive to active; from resignation to his lot in life, to determination of what he wants that life to be; from uneducated or undereducated, to well-informed, eager-to-learn retirees; from the uninvolved who feels his life is over, to the much involved who feels that life begins with retirement. Education must keep pace, encouraging people to become active, become well-informed, become involved. The retirement years can, indeed, be the Golden Years of one's lifetime. And education can help make the dream of a satisfying, fulfilling, old age a reality.

BIBLIOGRAPHY

Birren, James: *Psychology of Aging.* Englewood Cliffs, N. J., Prentice-Hall, 1964.

Buford, Thomas O.: *Toward A Philosophy of Education.* New York, Holt, Rinehart and Winston, 1969.

Busse, Ewald W. and Pfeiffer, Eric (Eds.): *Behavior and Adaptation in Late Life.* Boston, Little, Brown, 1969.

California Commission on Aging: *Delivery and Administration of Services for the Elderly.* Los Angeles, University of Southern California, 1968-69.

———: *Statewide Education and Training Program in Gerontology.* San Jose, Calif., San Jose State College, 1969-70.

Donahue, Wilma and Tibbetts, Clark (Eds.): *Politics of Age.* Ann Arbor, University of Michigan Gerontology Center, 1962.

Knowles, Malcolm S.: *The Modern Practice of Adult Education.* New York, Association Press, 1970.

Neugarten, Bernice: *Personality in Middle and Late Life.* New York, Atherton Press, 1964.

Petersen, James A.: *A Time for Work, A Time for Leisure.* Los Angeles, Andus Gerontology Center, University of Southern California, 1971.

Riley, M. W., Riley, J. W. and Johanson, M. E. (Eds.): *Aging and Society,* two vols. New York, Russell Sage Foundation, 1968-69.

Chapter IX

THERAPEUTIC INTERVENTION IN MARITAL AND FAMILY PROBLEMS OF AGING PERSONS

James A. Peterson

A RECENT PRESS dispatch reported a meeting of psychiatrists where the keynote address focused on a discussion of possible alternatives to the family because of the growing toll that marital breakdown exacted on family members. As usual, nothing was said of the implications of mobility and divorce on the emotional lives of parents and grandparents. This paper has as its goal an understanding of family changes in structure, function and durability as these influence its older members, and of the areas of stress which invite therapeutic intervention.

THE FAMILY AND ITS OLDER MEMBERS

The major controversy in family sociology during the last ten years has been conflicting descriptions of the structure of the family. Hill, Liwak, Sussman and others have argued against the Parsonian formulation of the nuclear family. (Sussman, 1959) They claim that research indicates viable and meaningful relationships between generations. Parsons, Peterson and others have insisted that while there are such relationships they do not have the consistent or intimate emotional meanings that characterized the extended family of half a century ago. The actual number of contacts depends, of course, on the ecology of the family and on social class variables. The primary question is whether or not this "semi-extended" family meets the basic needs of its older members. Not much research has been done on this point. Some studies have asked older persons about the problem but this research has been plagued by its obvious distortion by social desirability factors. Few case studies supplement in depth our information.

Shifts in basic attitudes toward family obligations have been indicated by some studies of the family and its older members. The following table compares attitudes discovered in a study at Cornell University (Streib and Thompson, 1960) with a California study utilizing the same scale (Peterson, Hadwen and Larsen, 1969).

TABLE IX-1

PARENTAL NORMS CONCERNING ACHIEVEMENT, CONTACT
AND LIVING ARRANGEMENTS OF CHILDREN

	Agreement with Statement	
		Peterson, Hadwen
	Streib-Thompson	& Larsen
Statement	%	%
Getting ahead in the world may be a bad thing if it keeps your family from being close.	49	67
When children are unmarried adults it is nice to have them live at home with their parents.	45	46
Children should not move away from their parents because of better financial opportunities elsewhere.	10	5
When parents get older and need help, they should be asked to move in with their married children.	8	14
Even when children are married, it is nice to to have them living with parents.	5	2

The data from the east and west coast indicates that, despite the implied deprivations, older persons are socialized to the achievement motivation process. In one sense this is acceptance of the inevitability of mobility in our society. Only 17 persons of 400 in the California sample had ever lived with their children but 14 of these indicated that this experience was a temporary one during a transitional period in their lives. Further, when asked under what conditions they would consider moving in with their children, the vast majority of the 400 replied that under no circumstances would they ever consent to such a move. These findings led the authors to generalize that, at least for these two populations, the norms associated with the extended family had been abandoned. A further statistical analysis was made of the relationship between *familism* and *life satisfaction*. The reason for the inquiry was to determine whether those who hold familistic attitudes would be so frustrated by contemporary attitudes and mobility that they would show a lower life satisfaction score. Analysis of Table IX-2 indicates that hypothesis is sustained.

TABLE IX-2

FAMILISM AND LIFE SATISFACTION

Familism								
				Life Satisfaction				
	High		*Medium*		*Low*		*Total*	
	N	%	N	%	N	%	N	%
High	36	33.3	47	34.8	26	51.0	109	
Medium	25	23.2	34	25.2	7	13.7	66	
Low	47	43.5	54	40.0	18	35.3	119	
Total	108	100.0	135	100.0	51	100.0	294	

The data indicates that for this population familistic attitudes associated with the extended family are gone. About one half of the children of this sample live in other parts of California or in other states. The inference is that those who held familistic expectations would be frustrated because distance made family contact impossible. The data on familism and life satisfaction seem to support this hypothesis. But there is a further adaptation on the part of parents to the present social situation. A recent investigation of family relationships (Solomon, 1968) in lower class groups indicates that most parents in this group accept separation and lack of contact as the norm, providing that there is enough interaction by letter and telephone so that the children remain as security for future exigencies. The children are not expected to play a major part in the lives of their parents but they are expected to be insurance against disaster. This is un-doubtably a major and significant function but it is a neglible barrier against loneliness. If this expectation is true of any significant number of older persons then we can add another implication to the psychiatrists' concern for family substitutes. Something must take the place of family for the older generation or they will be socially and emotionally deprived.

Lowenthal (1968) has well established the necessity of intimacy as a crucial variable in understanding trauma and illness of the older generation. There has been a response to this need in England where in a great many smaller towns and suburbs an organization called CRUSE brings widows together who share their problems and sorrows. We have nothing like this in America although the National Retired Teachers Organization and the American Association of Retired Persons are beginning to conduct pilot programs to find an American model of the British organization.

But British older persons do not face the pain that many American older persons do in seeing the marriages and families of their sons and daughters disrupted by conflict and divorce. No one in the literature has commented about the emotional dislocations that divorce brings to older parents who must suffer in silence as they see their children go through divorce trauma or share the alienation of grandchildren who are separated from them by divorce. All parents have high expectations for their offspring and a divorce of their child is seen against a different moral background than that of today. To many of them, the divorce of their child is not only a moral failure but is interpreted as *their* failure. In this sense, their loneliness is exacerbated by their vague feelings of failure in not giving their children stronger characters or personalities. This frustration is often expressed in hostility which further divides the generations.

THE QUALITY OF OLDER PERSONS' MARRIAGES

It was something of a shock to family sociologists to discover that the divorce process was beginning to characterize not only young but middle-age marriages. But this was an inevitable consequence of the failure of many middle-aged marital partners to adjust to the phenomenon of longer marriages. Marriages have always been broken in middle age but in past generations the decisive factor was death. Today, with longer life, marriages are doing little better with either psychological or legal separation taking the place of death as the crucial factor. The major studies of middle-age marriage document this. Pineo's careful study of a Chicago sample found that by the time Burgess and Wallin's couples had been married for fifteen or twenty years he could best describe their psychological relationship as that of *Disenchantment.* (Pineo, 1961) Blood and Wolfe, using a cross-sectional model in their Detroit study, found that only one out of seven wives were still "very satisfied" with the marriage to their mates. Their descriptive term was that time was *corrosive* to marriage (Blood and Wolfe, 1960). Cuber and Harroff, studying a highly successful sample of significant Americans, describes many of the marriages as either "habitually conflicted" or "devitalized" (Cuber and Harroff, 1965). Birren, in an intensive study of men, found that almost half of his subjects were part of a family situation that was fragmented and unhappy. (Birren, 1967). The consequence of this inability to find adjustment after the children leave home has been a general increase in both marital maladjustment and divorce. If present gradients continue, a growing volume of divorced men and women will come to retirement as single and lonely persons.

With this kind of marital instability at middle age as the foundation for adjustment of marriage in the last years, the question must inevitably be raised as to adjustment in the retirement years: does it continue on the low level of middle age or is there a new integration later on? One observation is clear, by age 65 and after, about two-thirds of men but only one-third of women are living with spouses. Most of the two-thirds without spouses are widows but an increasing number are divorcees. One-fourth of these widows live alone. They report greater worry, unhappiness and anticipation of death than do married persons. Some of the studies to date indicate that older persons accept their marital roles but are seen to have lost both the zest that characterizes early marriage and the poignancy of problems that lead to divorce. They report a slightly higher degree of marital satisfaction than do middle-aged couples. Other studies stress the problems that arise from role inversion for older people. Neugarten and Gutman (1957), in their description of marriage of older persons, suggest that there is a growing conflict between husband and wife.

The male is characterized as an "Old Man" stripped of power because he has lost his instrumental role as the supporter of the family. They picture the wife as growing moralistic and autocratic and in search of the former power the husband held. In our study (Peterson, Hadwen and Larsen, 1968), we found that in making decisions the husband did tend to give in more than the wife but we had no previous history to indicate whether or not this represented a major or minor shift in power. While the Neugarten study would indicate that the conflict incidental to role inversion affected satisfaction, our study indicated that there was little or no relationship between marital adjustment and life satisfaction. This finding is in line with that of Cuber and Harroff who found that, although later marriages were "devitalized," the husband and wife were having significant and creative experiences in their other pursuits and in other human contacts. Both the Cuber and Harroff studies and the Peterson, Hadwen and Larsen studies seem to indicate that couples just accept their marriages and tone down their disagreements and love-expectations.

PROBLEM AREAS WITH MARRIAGE AND FAMILY DURING THE LATER YEARS

This part of the chapter deals with the major problems that stem from the tension areas implied in the theoretical description furnished above. The problems will be presented through short vignettes of case histories. No attempt is made to ascertain the incidence of these problems because this field is almost virginal as far as research is concerned. No one has tried to catalogue these problems in the sense of their relative importance but any therapist who deals in this area has encountered these difficulties many times. Future research must not only detail their significance statistically but also measure the utility of differential modes of intervention.

Role Inversions

If middle-aged sons or daughters feel that their aging parents no longer are capable of making decisions the children often become "Parents to their parents." This action is often taken with intense resentment by the parent and guilt on the part of the son or daughter. The following case illustrates this problem:

> John Broadus and his wife presented themselves to the therapist as prosperous, competent and generous middle-aged persons. John went to great pains to explain that his eighty-year-old father and mother could no longer take care of themselves and he had gone to great pains to discover a high quality medical facility for them. But, much to his chagrin, they would have nothing to do with such a move even though he was going to pay for it. The intensity of his voice as he described what happened indicated that he had a very great investment in this plan. In a sense, it developed, what he was doing now compensated for years in which he had spent little time with his parents. Their vehemence of rejection also reflected a bitterness born of neglect. John's wife took the side of the parents but revealed later that she resented the money John would spend on his parents. As it developed, the issue of the parents giving up their home was only the arena in which was played out all of the resentments which had accumulated during the last twenty-five years in which the parents felt neglected and scorned by both John and his wife. Because dealing with a housing move was the superficial aspect of this case it was handled as family therapy and all four persons were invited to work out a totally different way of dealing with each other.

In other cases, the role shift of the younger man or woman suddenly becoming the authority figure for those who had been their authorities so long engendered such anxiety that this proved to be the focus of intervention. In many cases like this the intervention will fail utterly if the therapist is not aware that this role shift precipitates long-defended hostilities and yearnings.

The therapist who knows the field of aging knows very well that placing a parent in a medical facility is fraught with emotional overtones. In many cases, where the son or daughter is forever plaguing the administration of the facility with complaints, the true etiological situation has nothing whatsoever to do with the facility, good or bad as it may be. The complaints of the son or daughter reflect their guilt over not taking the parent into their home but rather, placing them in the care of strangers. Administrators who want to deal with this issue need to have the help of social workers or psychologists who can help the son or daughter locate the real source of their discomfort. In some blatant cases a daughter seems very anxious to prove that the home is not competent because she feels deeply that her own care was not adequate. So she says to mother: "They are not feeding you well, are they, mother?" What she is really asking for is reassurance that she has not abandoned mother, that mother will understand that she loves her, or that her significant others will not think badly about her over her treatment of mother. All of these comments are not meant in any way to impugn those sons and daughters who make careful inquiries about retirement homes and nursing homes before they place their parents in them. The literature abounds with enough horror stories (and they are horrid) about facilities so that caution and care in placement is certainly indicated. But the wise therapist needs to ascertain whether complaints and accusations stem from a normal anxiety or represent a displacement of more personal awareness of failure.

A second role shift is that described by Neugarten which involves the shift of roles between husband and wife. As indicated earlier there is no question but that such shifts do occur because they have been mentioned in other studies. However, the incidence of that role inversion may be somewhat less than universal. The following case from the author's file is just such a case:

> Jim Baxton did not want to retire when he did. But a severe arthritic shoulder caused him to give up his work at age 59. This occasioned considerable anxiety about financial matters on the part of his wife who had always had deep worry about finances due in part to the problems of her family during the depression. She plagued her husband to go back to work but his pain was such that he could not. She decided that she would resume her own secretarial career. He objected to this as unnecessary and demeaning and she told him that if he could not work she could. He attempted unsuccessfully to find other work that he could do. He felt that her anxiety was unnecessary because they had a tidy savings account and that her working was done to shame him back to work. Arguments and psychological distance resulted. When questions regarding the purchase of a new car and their vacation came up she took a determined stance and reminded Jim that *she* was now earning the money. She carried the same kind of authoritarian attitude to work and eventually had to change jobs because her employer found her somewhat obnoxious. Her husband grew in-

creasingly unhappy with her dominance and role shift. Their efforts at solution at the clinic were not successful. The therapist was not able to help the husband modify his bitterness or the wife to change her new-found joy in trying to rule the house and the relationship.

In other cases, the problem has been a wife who was patently much more insightful and rational than her husband and as they passed the middle years she felt that her superior intelligence ought to protect them during their last years. But her husband was used to the role of decision-maker and he resented her intrusion in policy-making. That case ended in divorce. In still other cases, what had been occasional criticism on the part of either the husband or the wife became pure nagging as the couple grew older. This, too, is difficult for intervention because lifelong trends seem to be exaggerated in the sixties.

The last mentioned series of cases also illustrates some of the problems encountered in dealing either pre-or post-maritally with "retirement marriages." These are fraught with several difficulties. Those encountered by the author center around memories or rigidities. In the first case, both the husband and wife have a tendency to compare the husband in a late marriage with the first mate. Sometimes the wife or husband is unkind enough to make an overt comparison but generally it is either an unspoken comparison or a defended one. In other instances, the eccentricities of individuals that were not so troublesome in younger years sometimes grow more pronounced in the later years and become sources of tension to these retirement marriages. However, despite the lack of study of such marriages, those that have been made are in agreement that marriages contracted in retirement have about the same degree of satisfaction that characterizes younger unions. Those who have the opportunity to see couples before such marriages do well in investigating both the idealization of dead partners and the degree of rigidity they manifest in terms of attitudes and living styles. It is obviously better to deal with such threats to consensus before marriage than later.

Sexual Adjustment

A further problem for older married couples has to do with

sexual adjustment. The following case illustrates a number of etiological vectors in understanding older persons. It shows among other things (1) the losses, described by Burgess and Wallin, Blood and Wolfe and others, sustained by a couple during middle-age and often carried into retirement years; (2) the threat to an achievement-oriented male which retirement represents; (3) the reinforcement of sexual anxiety by even a few episodes of impotence; (4) the possibility of help for such problems; and (5) the phenomenon that is known as the "life review":

Mr. Ben Hurtz presented himself as a neat, intelligent, achieving man of 64 years of age. He was anxious and agitated and had difficulty in staying in his chair during the first interview. His presenting complaint was complete and somewhat sudden impotence. This had been going on for nine months and his incapacity had now become an obsession . . . he could think of little else. The condition, however, was constantly referred to as "growing old." He was a highly successful business man who had built a business and raised a family of four who were now gone.

His marriage had been more than rewarding and, until the previous year, he had enjoyed a long and good erotic relationship with an ardent wife. She was still ardent but he could not satisfy her, in fact, he could not achieve an erection with her. Questioning revealed that the onset of his impotence had coincided with a somewhat formal meeting of his superiors at which time his retirement at sixty-five was anticipated. He saw no relationship between these events but he had reacted to this conference with some degree of hypochrondriacal response and a strenuous career of dieting, exercise and planning for his retirement. It was not a surprise that during this regime he had experienced an episode which confirmed his diagnosis that he was in fact "growing old." He reacted to the impotence with extreme anxiety and was not able to achieve erection in a further sexual attempt. He immediately visited his doctor who after examination pronounced him fit and found nothing to account for the impotence except that Ben was in fact growing old. His secretary had been divorced the year before and made no secret of her attachment to Ben. He was sure that he could have an affair with her but he desisted because as he said, "If I failed with her, I would know for sure that I was through." His impotence preyed on his mind and he had thought of little else until he came to see the clinic. The wife was immediately involved, further physiological tests were made, and treatment began. Treatment consisted of a great deal of confrontation about Ben's fears of aging. His reactions to his impending retirement and to some of his myths about sexuality in older persons. In the meantime, his wife was most understanding and a period of rather gentle sexual exploration was initiated between them. The results were totally positive because Ben dealt with his trauma regarding retirement and its threat to his ego and status, because he learned once more to trust his wife enough to communicate with her, and because he learned a great deal about the values and limits of sex during the later years.[1]

Masters and Johnson have long ago waylaid the myth about the loss of sexual capacity or enjoyment during the later years. However, the threat to a male's ego by episodes of sexual impotence are still a major factor in cases of this kind. They lay major stress on the importance of physiological factors such as the restoration of hormonal balance to compensate for tissue changes during and following the menopause. Here the psychological therapist must work with his counterpart in physical medicine. They also stress both for the male and female the critical importance of continuity in sexual expression. In all of their studies those who had had successful and continuous sexual encounters through the years had far less difficulty in sexual adjustment and response than those who had interrupted their sexual lives. (Masters and Johnson, 1966).

But this recalls our past analysis that, while two-thirds of men past sixty-five are married, only one-third of the women at this age have a partner. There seems to be no way in which marriage can bring physical intimacy with its rewards to older women unless the institution of marriage is modified, to permit some form of polygamy. Recent authors, pointing to the disproportionate number of women past the age of sixty, have asked the question as to any solution to this problem under present norms. Of course, affairs outside of marriage might meet the needs of some women but it is doubtful if many women at this age and

---

[1] James A. Peterson: *Marital and Family Therapy Involving the Aged*. Paper delivered for the symposium, Strategies for Intervention in Old Age, Gerontology Society Meeting, Houston, October 1971.

with their training could tolerate such arrangements. It is rather indicated that most of these women will live celibate lives until society, recognizing the problem, makes alternate solutions socially permissable. It is possible to overstress this problem because a great many of these women were conditioned in days when a Victorian approach was current and their menopause and widowhood were occasions for them of relief because they never had had a rewarding physical interaction with any man. But with more permissive attitudes growing in society such a condition is not likely to characterize the next generation. It is also true that a great many widows who had a splendid relationship with their husbands have no wish to find a sexual relationship with another man. They are content to live with the afterglow of their marriages. Whether or not this solution is optimal for their physical and psychological health has not been investigated.

Widowhood

There is a very special problem with widowhood both for men and women in this country. Heads of retirement housing facilities have noted the problem such persons create for others living in such communities. Psychiatrists deal daily with their depression. They do not remarry in the numbers or as soon as do divorcees. In some cases they feel that they cannot find anyone the equal to their mate's memory to contract another marriage and in still other cases because of plurality of women it is simply not possible to find another mate. The following vignette illustrates some of these problems:

> Mary came into the office melancholy and depressed. She only came because friends insisted on the visit. She was visibly depressed. Two years had passed since the death of her husband and she seemed to be in permanent "grief work." She had found no compensations for his absence. She told how she sat in a chair and there was no one there to speak with her. She had little financial resources so that the effort to find new interests was beyond her resources. Her children had ceased, after the funeral, to have much interest in her and they lived far away. She had been primarily a housewife and had never developed outside interests. Her main focus had always been on her husband and now there was nothing left of her life.

She said quite honestly that she wanted to die and would do so but her friends kept insisting that she try to find a new life and she had been unable to do so. She had no appetite and had been consistently losing weight. She only brightened when the therapist began to sympathize with her condition. What became apparent was her need to feel sad and martyred. The case was handled by refusing to permit her a single moment of martyrdom. She was not permitted to become reminiscent or lugubrious. In fact, the therapist walked out of the room when she began to extol the extent of her suffering. Perhaps the therapist took a chance but he saw early that to play into her need to expiate past wrongs by extreme sadness and even suicidal depression was to lose any hope of helping her. She began to come alive when she became very angry with the therapist as a heartless and unfriendly fellow. From then on her visits were bitter but animated and ultimately she began to have other interests.

Depression is often a vehicle for repressed anger or frustration and it must be handled very carefully. We no longer believe that when a person suggests suicide that it is not a very real threat. In this case, as in many cases, Mary's apathy was her only way to cry for help to escape the vicious cycle she inhabited. She escaped that cycle but others who are not fortunate in finding some understanding person are not so fortunate and often just wither away. But whether or not a widow withers away is really not as large a problem as those who shrivel away. Their lives become so constricted and limited that it may be true that they are in the grave at least as far as their creativity and spirit are concerned. Expert therapeutic intervention often is essential but, many times, friends, churches or other groups can mobilize a "social blanket" to help such persons. There certainly has been little concentration on this problem but it may be that the effort of the American Association of Retired Persons in their organizational pilot studies may find ways of organizing groups which can at least ameliorate the sadness and isolation or millions of widows in this country. Wide research is essential to denote the degree and type of problems widows encounter.

Facing Death

In the area of helping individuals face their eventual demise we are doing more research and more therapy than in any other area facing older persons. However, even in this area most of the research is limited to helping the individual look at his or her attitudes. Often older persons say that they long to talk with their mate or their families about their death but they are met by rejection or denial. Nevertheless, a great deal of the mythology about death and dying is being overcome and we can be a good deal more direct and helping in this area than before. In a recent research study the author discovered that older persons need to discuss death with their families, be with their families at death, and feel the warmth of primary persons rather than that of medical personnel. But there are a great many areas such as that of arranging for last rites, making wills and settling old conflicts which are basically important to the elderly which have gone almost unnoticed. The following vignette illustrates this problem:

> Mrs. Smith was almost apologetic for taking the time of a "busy man" to listen to her difficulty. She thought that perhaps she should not have come. She had all the diffidence of the aged person who has been socialized to believe that she really didn't count for much and it was an imposition on her part to want to talk with anyone. When she finally came to the point her request was simple enough. She said her minister, her doctor, and her family would not talk to her about dying. She was 82, not in good health, and she wanted to discuss some things. It turned out that she needed referal to a funeral director, to her minister and to a lawyer to deal with some unsettled aspects of her death. But beyond that she was concerned with a long-standing conflict which she had had with one daughter. That daughter had left home after a quarrel and had lived a life of which the mother disapproved. Now, after both had lived apart many years, the mother had mellowed and wondered if there was some possibility of reconciliation with the daughter before she died. She did not want to go to her grave with alienation between them. Her daughter lived in a community a hundred miles away. She was encouraged to call her daughter and see if they could meet. This proved unsuccessful. The therapist then called the daughter and asked to see her. She would not come but she consented to see the therapist if he came to her home. He felt that this matter meant enough to his client so that he made the trip. What he discovered was a daughter who needed even more than the mother to feel for-

given and accepted. A meeting was arranged and it was meaningful to both parties. The mother actually did die soon after that but with a much more peaceful heart. The daughter's life was also changed.

Raising a family is not easy in this generation. The ebbs and tides of emotional interaction often leave older parents with much "unfinished business." The therapist who is prepared to do family therapy can often smooth the death trajectory and eliminate childrens' guilt if he knows the necessity for and appropriate ways to intervene in such situations.

More Commonplace Problems

If the therapist is preparing himself to intervene in the lives of older persons there are a great many commonplace problems which may seem mundane to him but which are exceptionally important to the client. The few that follow are only mentioned to indicate something of the need of older persons for informed and competent guidance on a great variety of subjects which they face in "a world they never made."

The problem of finance is a critical one. We are not referring here to the fact that the last census indicated that 25 percent of the twenty-one million aged in this country have income which is less than the minimum level outlined by the Labor department as essential to a bare existence. The fact is stark and a shame to this affluent country. We are referring rather to the need for any counselor to have some passing awareness of the provisions of Social Security and Old Age Assistance, and of all the programs designed to supplement the budget of elderly persons. The minimum requirement would be a knowledge of those persons in the community who were experts and who could give dependable information to clients. In our complex society there are sources of help at hand for elderly persons, but not available because the older person does not know how to find or use the agencies which are there.

We have suggested that a great many older persons need help in legal matters such as making wills and disposing of their property. The aware therapist can be of great help to the elderly person to have on file individuals who not only understand but feel kindly to such persons. Often their financial situation is marginal and the referral must be made to individuals with conscience about money. Sadly, not all counseling agencies or individuals keep such files.

The problems of housing and nursing homes is monumental. Much of my mail deals with requests from individuals to help them find a suitable home or situation in which to spend their last years. This is specialized knowledge and few counselors would have this information. Again, the American Association of Retired Persons does try to keep abreast of such housing resources in their communities and this is a good referral. Often such requests masks a trend towards greater dependency and anxiety about the future. This anxiety is the proper concern of the therapist while the listing of housing resources is not. Still the counselor ought to have referral sources at hand so that he could direct the aged person to them. If they need help in making choices he may stand for them as an alter ego of the son they do not have or who is too far away to help.

The selection of suitable medical help is important to an older person and any counselor who has shown that he will listen to older persons will have requests for a "doctor who understands older persons." While such a request indicates often that the person has anxiety about his health, it is often a sincere request for a referral to adequate medical resources. The therapist can soon discover if his client is a "doctor hopper" or one who is never satisfied with the diagnosis and wants constant attention instead of treatment. Such persons need to come to understand their needs and act accordingly. A great many visits to doctors' offices by older people have nothing to do with illness and everything to do with loneliness.

It may not be as exciting for the therapist to deal with the uncertainty and anxiety of an older person trying to make a decision about his future housing as it would be to deal with his full-blown depression but it probably is more important. Far more individuals are beset in their last year by *situational* rather than deeply *psychological* probems. We know about the incidence of the more severe mental problems of older persons. While crime seems to decrease after retirement, mental illness increases. And suicide also increases but only for men; women suffer but they do not end the suffering by taking their lives. Two factors influence the increase in mental illness. In the first place, the older person has had a longer time to experience the "pangs of outrageous fortune" and to develop irrational response patterns. In the second place, tissue and organ impairment predisposes the old more than the young to brain damage, degeneration of the nervous system, etc. Elderly persons with physical disabilities are more likely to demonstrate correlated mental disturbances for both physical and psychological reasons. But, granting the reduced resistance of older persons to mental illness, still less than 10 percent are afflicted by only one of the various forms of such illness. Furthermore only 3 percent of older persons are in institutions. These persons who have such dramatic symptomotology that society focuses on them are probably receiving far better attention than those suffering the kinds of problems detailed in this chapter. We are not unsympathetic to them nor wishing to depreciate their need for treatment. But they do receive treatment because of the very urgency of their conditions. It is the vast residue of older persons who have relatively good mental health that occupies our attention. Their personal, marital and family crises invite the help of a therapeutic community that has largely overlooked them.

THE TRAUMA OF RETIREMENT

Retirement is a major crisis in the lives of both husbands and wives. The problem for wives is sometimes summarized by the trenchant comment of one wife that "I married him for dinner but not for the lunch hour." By the time a couple reaches retirement age they both have deeply-set patterns of activity. It does not include being together during the whole day or trying to find ways of entertaining each other twenty-four hours a day. They have not been socialized to a new relationship in which the husband watches and sometimes tries to bring new efficiency into the wife's home-making habits. If we are to take the statistics on the miseries of middle-age marriage seriously we might suggest that it is all that the average couple can do to adjust well to each other for ten hours, not twenty-four. At any rate, we know that there are a great many new difficulties that arise when a man comes home for good.

Of course there are considerably more basic problems for the male at the termination of his life work. It is in that work that he has felt useful and creative. It is in working that he finds ego-sustenance. When he retires he loses not only the order and habits of a lifetime but, more profoundly, the very basic justification of his being. He enters into a period of aimless hours, of spiritual wandering. This feeling of anomie is reinforced by the general point-of-view of a youth-oriented culture that he is now *useless.* He loses also the camaraderies, the fellowship, the closeness of fellow-workers. His life space contracts in about every way it could. He shrivels in stimulation and in socialization.

The following case illustrates some of the typical reactions of men who are given a watch upon retirement to listen to the seconds tick off his meaningless existence and his movement toward the end of it all:

Jim Harkness had been a popular foreman at his plant. Although he was in exuberant health, company policy dictated retirement at age 65. He had pleaded his ability, his health, his long commitment to the company but all of this meant nothing to the personnel of his company. The day of his sixty-fifth birthday came and the vice-president came to his section, congratulated him, and gave him his gold watch. The other men reacted with sorrow that he was leaving but a few of them remarked on leaving the meeting that "maybe now there would be a few promotions around here."

Jim was mature enough to know that he could not finally change the decision of the company. At first he looked for other jobs but he was told that other companies wanted men no older than forty. He thought he might set up his own consultant firm but he was told politely that his skills were passé and companies were interested in young men from the universities who could bring new ideas of "systems and technology."

Jim never had developed many hobbies. He enjoyed fishing and hiking but he knew that these could never occupy him fulltime. After a time he came to a type of resignation to his chair in front of the TV and to rather welcoming long rests during the day and early evening in bed. Rather than think disquieting thoughts he repressed them along with his questions regarding a society that had suddenly "dumped him."

Jim grew quieter and quieter. He did not have the zest he had had two years earlier and his friends found him a bore. His wife after a time became alarmed and talked with their doctor. He was induced to see a counselor who judged that Jim was in a deep depression and would need extensive treatment to escape. Jim reacted negatively to the suggestions and asked, "But what's the use? I'm on the shelf for good."

The problems of retiring at 65 are going to be compounded for those who are now retiring at 55. Major industries such as steel, auto manufacturing, and electrical maintenance have now set retirement after 30 years of work or at 55. This means that at least one-quarter of their life will be before these men as they step out of the factory for the last time. They will be in the prime of health and ability. How will society handle their feelings of anomie? Certainly the social consequences of vast technological advances have not been imaginatively considered.

It is possible that a totally new and large area of counseling procedure is involved in these changes. A few universities, such as Cornell and the University of Oregon, have been experimenting with various forms of group pre-retirement counseling practices to discover some norms for facing these role crises. They have had some success in modifying depression and anomie. But they have discovered that such counseling requires more than giving information about pension plans or Medicare; it involves a profound investigation of the anxieties and ego structures of their counselees. Most so-called pre-retirement counseling sessions have focused on situational and not personality factors. This level of treatment insures mediocre results. These experimental programs have also discovered that it is almost impossible to make headway unless both the husband and the wife join in the counseling process. There is no record that the total family of the retiree has ever been involved in such therapeutic sessions but in many cases total family involvement is indicated. Furthermore, it is probably that the tentative nature of the group process utilized thus far by even these experiments is too brief and too tangential to have far-reaching results. As in many other areas of our society, the lack of attention to this particular crisis phase indicates the lack of imagination of the whole therapeutic community.

It is not necessary to be a prophet to predict that, as earlier retirement becomes a fact of life, industrial companies and social agencies will begin to take quite seriously their obligations to help individuals surmount the traumas of this crisis. The task of the therapist who looks at pre-retirement counseling in the broad sense will be a comprehensive one. In some cases he will deal with the problems retirement brings to a marriage; in others to the disturbed relationship with children and other relatives; certainly to the problem of helping both the man and the wife find meaning in the time when the children are no longer home and the husband is home but without meaningful occupation. The counselor ought to know something about agencies so that if situational problems regarding income, pensions, Medicare and Medical come up he knows where answers may be found. But, beyond this, the therapist needs to have much association with other persons so that he becomes familiar with their problems, their propensities and their potentialities. He ought to have divested himself of the old myths regarding the inevitable failure of older persons' minds, health and sexual capacities. He will probably have to deal sooner or later with nurses in nursing homes who are shocked to find evidence of sexuality in "dirty old men" and hostility and guilt pervading the approach of middle-age children to their parents.

Gerontology Centers about the country would do well to provide at least two services to the clinician. They should provide basic training for new clinicians in understanding older persons and their problems as well as numerous institutes in mental health for all those who associate with the older person. The first task would be to provide a new discipline of clinical personnel for the aging. The second task would be to upgrade the understanding and skills of present therapists. But, beyond these training tasks, every center would do well to initiate functional research to develop models of treatment. We need to ascertain what modes of approach are best. Is it better to involve a group of older persons in group process or does one-to-one counseling bring better results? Is confrontive, "realistic" therapy superior to non-directive? What problems of the older person can be best faced, as in terms of pre-retirement counseling, by the husband and wife together and what areas seem to dictate individual treatment? When should the family of the older person be involved? Which auxiliary agents, such as doctors, ministers, undertakers, nurses, and social workers, are especially valuable as allies in facing crisis with older persons? There are a host of pivotal questions regarding therapy with the aged individual and his family that are unanswered because we have neither case analyses or empirical research on which to base answers. As the sheer numbers of retired individuals increase, the need for skilled intervention increases. Training Centers are the logical places in which to find answers. However, in many instances this will involve a close interaction with existing clinics or agencies. *There is at present no program in the nation directed* at research clinical training or mental health objectives. However, at the University of Southern California such a program is proposed and is seeking funding. It may well provide models for other schools.

CONCLUSION

The psychiatrists may be correct in reporting that, as we move away from the extended and now from the semi-extended family, new means of human interaction must be provided for children and, we add, for older persons. The twenty-one million persons over 65 who have lost many significant contacts with their brothers and sisters and their children, whose marriages have lost a great many emotional rewards, whose income in many cases is not sufficient to enable them to substitute social groups for their families, constitute a huge and needy sector of our population. To date, this sector has been ignored both in research and in treatment by family experts, psychologists and psychiatrists. Social workers have done better, but their numbers are limited. Every large community needs a specialized agency dealing specifically with the problems of older persons particularly as these relate to the multiplicity of family problems, some of which have been detailed in this report. Just as basic is research to provide the cognitive base on which to base intervention. As the retirement age lowers and the number of retired increases in our society this need becomes overwhelming, as a challenge to established persons in the professional fields who might be expected to pioneer in this new arena of human need.

BIBLIOGRAPHY

Birren, J. E. and Associates: *Human Aging.* Bethesda, Maryland, U. S. Department of Health, Education and Welfare, 1967.

Blood, R. O., Jr., and Wolfe, D. M.: *Husbands and Wives: The Dynamics of Married Living.* Glencoe, Ill., The Free Press, 1960.

Cuber, J. F. and Harroff, P. B.: *The Significant Americans.* New York, Appleton Century, 1965.

Duval, E. M.: *Family Development.* New York, J. B. Lippincott, 1962.

Farber, B.: A Model for the Study of the Family as mutually contingent Careers. Urbana, University of Illinois, 1956, (Mimeographed).

Glick, P. C.: *American Families.* New York, John Wiley and Sons, 1957.

Kinsey, A. C., Pomeroy, W. B., Martin, C. E., and Gebhardt, P. H.: *Sexual Behavior in the Human Female.* Philadelphia, W. B. Saunders Company, 1953.

Kutner, B., Fanishel, D., Togo, A. M., and Langner, T. S.: *Five Hundred Over Sixty.* New York, Russel Sage Foundation, 1956.

Lowenthal, M. F. and Clayton, H.: Interaction and adaption: intimacy as a crucial variable. *Am Sociol Rev, 33*:1, 1968.

Masters, W. and Johnson, V. E.: *Human Sexual Response.* Boston, Little, Brown and Company, 1966.

Peterson, J. A., Hadwen, T., and Larson, A. E.: *A Time for Work, A Time for Leisure: A Study of Retirement Community In-Movers.* Los Angeles, Gerontology Center, University of Southern California, 1969.

Pineo, P. C.: Disenchantment in the later years of marriage. *Marriage Fam Liv, 23*:00, 1961.

Rubin, I.: *Sexual Life After Sixty.* New York, Basic Books, Inc. 1965.

Sussman, M.: The isolated nuclear family: fact or fiction. *Social Problems, 6*: 1959.

Part IV

MULTIDISCIPLINARY STRATEGIES

Chapter X

TRAINING FOR PROFESSIONALS IN THE FIELD OF AGING: NEEDS, GOALS, MODELS, AND MEANS

Diana S. Woodruff and James E. Birren

THE MOST IMPRESSIVE fact about professional training in the field of aging is that there has been so little of it. This conclusion has been well documented in the White House Conference technical report on training (Birren, Gribbin, & Woodruff, 1971) and supported by surveys on academic and professional training (U.S.D.H.E.W., 1968, 1969). The purpose of this chapter is to stimulate professional training in the field of aging by providing a realistic picture of the present situation, and the prospects and opportunities. An analysis will be made of the needs, goals, models and means of training. In addition to presenting specific information about training programs, prospects for implementing such programs will be discussed. Not only do we wish to intrigue educators and professionals with the opportunities for new careers, but also to offer suggestions to education about innovative programs, courses, and alternatives to class instruction.

NEEDS AND GOALS
The Great Gap

Tremendous social changes have taken place in the twentieth century and the rate of social and technological change continues to accelerate (Toffler, 1970). One of the results of such change has been the continued growth of the population of aged. The number of the retired elderly in the United States exceeds the entire population of many nations. The rapid growth of the numbers of aged will be documented along with predictions of the size of future cohorts of elderly. Such statistics, when compared to the amount of training and research currently underway in Gerontology, provide a startling contrast between demand and supply. In short, such statistics point out a great gap.

Changes in Age Structure in the Population

Since 1900, about thirty years have been added to the life expectancy of the average American. Advances in medicine and health care delivery have made large inroads in infant mortality rates and in mortality resulting from infectious diseases. The net effect of these advances has resulted in the fact that many more individuals are surviving to reach retirement and old age. In addition to the declining mortality rate there has been a decline in immigration rate and, more recently, a decline in birth rate. One effect of these combined forces is that the number of aged in the population has continued to increase faster than the population as a whole. Figure X-1 depicts this change in the age structure of the population. Until around 1900, less than 4 percent of the population of the United States was over the age of 65. By 1970, the percentage of individuals over 65 had increased to nearly 10 percent and, at the present rate of growth, demographers predict that, by the year 2000, there will be 28 million people over 65, 11 percent of the population.

Several factors led demographers to revise these predictions upwards. First, the birth rate is declining and attempts are being made to achieve zero population growth. If zero population growth is achieved by the next century the over-age-65 cohorts might constitute 16 percent of the population. These estimates assume that no further increases in life expectancy after age 65 will occur, but life expectancy after age 65 could be altered by technological advances in medicine, by biochemical modifications of the aging of human cells or by both. For example, if mortality due to cardiovascular and renal disease is cut in half, it is estimated that three years would be added to the life expect-

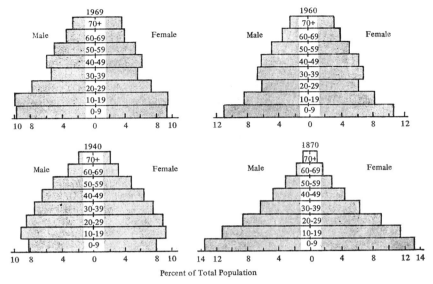

Figure X-1. Distribution of the Population by Age and Sex: 1870 to 1969 (Source: U. S. Bureau of the Census: *Current Population Reports.* P-25, 441, Washington, D. C.: U. S. Government Printing Office, 1970.)

ancy at the age of 65. Life expectancy might also be extended if the standard of living and health services were improved for the economically handicapped segments of the population. Hence, it is conceivable that the aged could account for as much as 25 percent of the population in the Twenty-first Century. Considering the tremendous surge of growth of this aged segment of the population since 1900, there are great gaps in the amount of knowledge available on aging and the amount of training which has been undertaken to fill these knowledge gaps and to serve the elderly.

The Need for Training

A point that was clearly documented in the source paper on training for the 1971 White House Conference on Aging (Birren, Gribbin & Woodruff, 1971) was that, in relation to the surveyed and demonstrated need, the amount of training and educational activities in the field of aging is astonishingly low. While there has been some progress and there are high quality programs in a few institutions, most states have not had appreciable training of any type related to problems of aging. The need for education and training exists for many types of persons and for many kinds of subject matter at different levels: professional, scientific, graduate, undergraduate, high school, and elementary school. Now is the time to put into effect major plans for training and to evaluate alternatives so the following decades of this century will be marked by a notably higher level of training.

In a report to the United States Congress by the Secretary of the Department of Health, Education and Welfare, it was stated that, while there were 350,000 professional and technical workers employed solely or primarily in the service of the elderly, only 10 to 20 percent of these workers had any formal training (U. S. Congress, 1969). Projections based on this report suggest that by 1980 almost a million professionals and technicians specializing in aging must be trained. An analysis of the numbers and types of professional and technical workers needed to serve the aging is presented in the White House Conference source paper on training (Birren, Gribbin & Woodruff, 1971). Some of the categories in which additional professionals and technicians must be trained to serve the elderly are administrators (e.g., for institutions, community organizations, federal and state agencies), architects, personnel to staff housing developments for the aged, dieticians, homemakers and home health aides, licensed practical and registered nurses, occupational therapists, physical therapists, clinical psychologists, dentists, podiatrists, medical and psychiatric social workers, physicians, nursing home aides, social workers and comunity aides, teachers (to teach both to and about the aged), recreation supervisors and program leaders, pastors, pastoral counselors, librarians, social insurance workers, speech pathologists and audiologists. The aged have a variety of needs and, to meet such needs, a wide range of specialists must be trained.

While it would be desirable to immediately undertake the training of professionals and technicians to work with the elderly, such a goal in many instances is difficult because experienced personnel required to train professionals are not available. Additionally, much of the information which would be useful to professionals working with the aged is simply not available or is not being translated for application. To cope with such issues it is imperative to train additional Ph.D. level teachers and researchers and M.A. level teachers and translators of research.

There are currently no precise estimates of the number of teachers and researchers involved in gerontology, but a recent survey of doctoral dissertations in aging indicated that, of 262,151 dissertations produced in the period 1934 to 1968, only 667 were on problems of aging. This represents 0.25 percent of the total dissertations, indicating an extremely limited emphasis on academic study and training in aging (Moore and Birren, 1971). In view of this small amount of gerontological research and training, increased effort must be made to develop academic career potential in aging by expanding recruitment, teaching, research facilities and opportunities for graduate students. An appropriate ten-year goal for the sciences proposed by Kleemeier and Birren (1967) was the training of 5,000 doctoral-level personnel in gerontology. It was proposed that by 1976 there should be between 1500-2000 active trained researchers in each of the areas of biological sciences, physiological and medical sciences and behavioral and social sciences. However, teaching and research programs must be enlarged to meet such goals. The estimated increase in support research and training grants by 1968-1973 was 230 percent (U.S.D.H.E.W., 1968). While encouraging, it is doubtful whether this dollar increase will result in training even the conservatively estimated number of 5,000 PhD's proposed by Kleemeier and Birren (1967).

Two thirds of the training currently offered in gerontology is at the graduate level, and a priority must be given to training at this level to develop the personnel who will provide the impetus for gerontological training at all levels. Two broad types of graduate education were identified by an AoA survey (U.S.D.H.E.W., 1969).

1. Long-term career training leading to the doctorate, designed to produce teachers and researchers in the biological, behavioral and social sciences; and teachers, researchers, administrators and planners in the professional fields serving the older population.

2. Long-term training leading to the masters degree, designed to produce skilled practitioners, supervisors, consultants, administrators, and instructors in junior college and short course programs, designed to train individuals for employment in agencies serving older people.

A third category of training, summer institute and short-term courses, is usually administered at the graduate level. This type of training is especially useful to reach professionals working with the elderly.

The number of trainees in doctoral degree programs is small, but the contribution of doctoral candidates to manpower resources in the field cannot be measured by numbers alone. Doctoral candidates become the professors, researchers and authors of text books. These highly trained individuals account for much of the new knowledge being accumulated and provide a large measure of the leadership in program planning and strategy. Because so much rests on so few, it is desirable to increase the support to levels more appropriate to current needs.

In a survey undertaken by AoA, specific needs were identified for training at the doctoral level. It is necessary to: (1) increase the number of faculty members engaged in teaching along with the number of trainees, (2) make higher stipends available to attract applicants from among promising practitioners, supervisory and managerial staff in operating agencies, and (3) develop interdisciplinary training centers in biological, social, and applied gerontology (U.S.D.H.E.W., 1969).

Programs at the masters degree level are essential for the delivery of high quality services for the elderly. Masters programs involve a shorter training period than do doctoral programs, and emphasize preparation for actual practice in service programs. Personnel trained at this level are in great demand for tasks such as program planning and administration, administration of facilities for the aged, provision of direct services, supervision of semiprofessional and technical personnel engaged in service provision, and teaching in vocational education programs. In an AoA survey it was found that there was a ratio of 1 to 7 between the number of persons working in aging programs and the total manpower pool in the same occupation (U.S.D.H.E.W., 1969), but only 1/100 of the total masters degree output are accounted for by federal programs. This gap between demand and supply is enormous.

The survey undertaken by the AoA pointed out eight needs for training at the masters level. These needs were: (1) to draw attention to special problems posed by the elderly and to the special skills found useful in the administration and practice of programs serving the aged, (2) to point out the limitations of generic training in fields such as social work, public health and nursing in contrast with some of the newer and more important professional-administrative careers in aging (nursing home administration, retirement housing management, senior center administration), (3) to use agencies and programs now serving older persons for effecting field training, (4) to train enough individuals at the masters level to fill the need for skilled services, (5) to emphasize leadership and supervision in training rather than the delivery of skilled individual service, (6) to increase the dollar level of available stipends, (7) to equalize the dollar level of federal training program stipends, and (8) to raise to a competitive level the salaries in senior centers, retirement housing, state and community coordination programs, public welfare and other fields serving the aged and into which holders of masters degrees can go (U.S.D.H.E.W., 1969).

In addition to the actual programs of training at the doctorate and masters degree level, graduate training in gerontology involves measures designed to establish university centers and ancillary facilities for training and research. Creation of multidisciplinary institutes of gerontology increases the visibility of the field of aging, affords faculty and students an opportunity for exposure to greater competence, and facilitates interaction between disciplines.

The technical paper on training for the White House Conference on aging listed other potential functions of centers. In addition to meeting training needs, university-based multidisciplinary gerontology centers could:

1. Recruit personnel at the professional and subprofessional levels.

2. Conduct basic and applied research.

3. Provide consultation to public and voluntary organizations in assessing the needs of the elderly and in planning and developing services for them.

4. Serve as a repository of information and knowledge on the subject.

5. Stimulate the incorporation of content matter in aging into the teaching of the biological, behavioral, and social sciences.

6. Urge the development of training programs in aging in the university schools of social work, public health, health care administration, and education.

7. Afford opportunities for innovative multidisciplinary efforts in teaching, research and demonstration projects (Birren, Gribbin & Woodruff, 1971, pp. 6-7).

While most of the training effort in the past decade has been directed at the graduate level, one survey indicated that 71 of the 335 courses in gerontology offered in 1955-66 were at the undergraduate level, and there was one baccalaureate program in gerontology (U.S.D.H.E.W., 1968). As it has been urgent to attend to graduate training in the sixties, it is important to develop other education and training in gerontology at undergraduate and high school levels in the seventies.

Many benefits would accrue from introducing the subject matter of aging at the undergraduate level. Negative and unrealistic stereotypes about aging and the aged might be modified with better public understanding of aging as a human biological and social phenomenon. General undergraduate courses open to all undergraduate students regardless of major could change both the image of the aged and the status of the study of aging. Considerable potential for awakening interest in aging as a career is another benefit to be gained from introducing the subject at the undergraduate level. Post-high school training at the community college and vocational education level also is an area where the introduction of courses on aging in recruitment to the field of aging could be accomplished. Occupational and vocational education programs are growing in number and variety, including several in fields applicable to aging. Nursing, hospital management, social work, recreation and education are fields where individuals at this level could be trained for careers in aging. Four potential trainee groups might be introduced to careers in aging through post-high school training (U.S.D.H.E.W., 1969, p. 62):

1. Young people, just out of high school, who do not want or cannot afford a 4-year collegiate program and are seeking training to prepare for beginning technical or sub-professional positions in a specific occupation.

2. Medical corpsmen discharged from the armed forces, equipped with a high school education and interested in converting their military occupation specialty to civilian uses.

3. Housewives with grown children, retired military personnel, and others in their middle years looking for specialized training to take on a new career.

4. Older people who wish to develop a retirement career in service to the older population.

Curricula for these four groups would differ, but individuals in all groups can be considered as potential trainees for sub-professional and lower level professional positions in agencies serving the aged. A program in curriculum development and recruitment in these areas should be undertaken.

The career-decision process frequently begins at the elementary and high school levels, so it is extremely important to expose students at these levels to some of the facts and issues in gerontology. The desirability of introducing content on the human life cycle and the biological and social aspects of aging at this level is obvious, but the occurrence of such education at this level is undoubtedly rare.

Materials for Training

For the development and maintenance of high quality training programs, curricula, course syllabi, textbooks, films, case study materials, teaching guides and short course models are essential. There is a paucity of texts and other materials available for such training and, when the materials do exist, they are scattered and difficult to find and do not present an organized and systematic body of easily available information. It has been recommended that, before new materials are developed, a survey of existing materials should be undertaken to distinguish major gaps in current materials and to discern desirable trends in organization (Birren, Gribbin and Woodruff, 1971). Since most of the materials currently available are directed to training at the graduate level, there is a need to develop instructional materials at the under-graduate and high school levels. Updating of materials also is necessary.

There is a crucial need for dissemination of current research information in the field of gerontology. *The Adult Development and Aging Abstracts* published for a brief period by the NICHD was a useful innovation for researchers and scholars. Its discontinuance for economic reasons was a loss to the field. Frequently, valuable information is neglected because it appears in an obscure journal or because it is shelved in an institutional report. Practitioners and researchers read and publish in different journals and they approach problems of aging and the aged in different ways, dictated by the conventions of their profession. If teachers in academic and professional training programs had access to an organized literature in aging which reviewed both research data and applied information, student trainees in research and applied areas might be better trained to bridge the gap between research and practice (cf. Chapt. XII).

Training of the many types discussed will have to be planned and extended to meet not only the presently recognized needs but also important emergent ones. In this time of accelerating change, the content, techniques and goals of training programs cannot remain fixed. At the same time, changes must first occur within institutions having long-range commitments and competent personnel, to insure that the changes will be rational rather than quick or opportunistic responses.

The Need for Applied and Basic Knowledge

A training program can be no better than the knowledge on which it is based. Often the best training programs are conducted in institutions that also have active research programs. There seems to be in fact a relationship of the vitality of a profession to its support of research. The view of the authors is that the quality of training and the support and quality of research go hand-in-hand. Thus, those who would do training in aging should lend their support to the organization and utilization of research. To adequately serve the aged and to train individuals for such tasks, applied and basic knowledge on aging must be available.

One clear implication of the recommendations of the White House Conference of 1971 is that the physical, mental and social well-being of the older population have not been adequately surveyed (Maddox and Bierman, 1971). This fact suggests the need for social indicators (cf. Chapt. II). Since business and industrial activity can be summarized with reasonable accuracy with economic indicators, perhaps social indicators can be used to monitor societal activities such as health status, standard of living, social integration and perceived well-being. Social gerontologists have been interested in the specific application of social indicators to older persons, and they have suggested that this application is significant inasmuch as the welfare of especially vulnerable members of society, the aged, may be a sensitive indication of the operation of societal institutions generally (Birren, Woodruff and Bergman, 1972).

In addition to the development of social indicators is the need for information about how to change the level of well-being of the older population. This information is typically called applied or proximal in that it lies close to the needs of aged individuals in society. More remote is the kind of information called for by the scientist who seeks what is usually called basic knowledge. Social gerontologists recently have given attention to basic knowledge gaps which exist in the field of aging. Immediately following the White House Conference on Aging, the Gerontological Society convened an International conference of social scientists to examine the results of the White House Conference. One of the main tasks undertaken by this group was to identify knowledge gaps in six different areas which represented a grouping of the major problems addressed by the White House Conference: Housing, Transportation, Income, Health and Nutrition, Employment and Retirement, Planning, and Research, Demonstration and Training. The work of this group was recently published in a special volume of the *Gerontologist* (Eisdorfer & Taves, 1972), and we refer the interested reader to this volume for a rather extensive presentation of basic knowledge gaps in social gerontology.

Both applied and basic knowledge are essential if individuals are trained to improve the quality of life for the elderly. Birren, Woodruff and Bergman (1972) used the analogy of the needs for information to develop and provide prosthetic devices for the disabled elderly and the need for information to reduce the occurrence of disability. The need for knowledge covers a wide range from that which can be used now to that which will be of use in future generations. While these types of information are not incompatible, the pressure for immediate gains often overshadows the desirability of basic research even though it is a small but valuable investment in the future. The dominant opinion of the delegates to the White House Conference appeared to be that priority should be given to applying existing knowledge to present needs of the aged. To realize such application, large-scale training efforts must be undertaken to increase the numbers of teachers and researchers in gerontology and to provide communication channels among the professionals, paraprofessionals and volunteers working with the aged and with the social scientists doing research.

Training and Intervention

It has become evident that certain segments of the population are deprived, and large-scale intervention programs such as Project Head Start have been devised to accelerate or alter development. In the case of Head Start, the aim was to alleviate intellectual and linguistic deprivation in disadvantaged children. Intervention has been conceived as the introduction of planned programming deliberately timed to accelerate, decelerate or otherwise alter projected age functions. Most intervention activity has focused on the early stages of the life-span, but intervention can and should be aimed at any age level or circumstance where inequity exists.

This section is concerned with training as a large-scale intervention strategy to alleviate deprivation in contemporary cohorts of aging, to enrich the lives of present and future cohorts of elderly and to prevent deprivation, poverty, suffering and alienation in future cohorts of aged. The goals of training in the field of aging must be long-ranged as well as short-ranged and, in this sense, planners must think in terms of enrichment and prevention as well as in terms of alleviation. In addition to meeting current demands for services by merely reacting to problems as they arise, attempts must be undertaken to predict future problem areas and prevent them. Also, rather than focusing only on deficiencies, attempts to enrich the quality of life should be considered. The following paragraphs present some long- and short-range goals for training and intervention in terms of alleviation, enrichment and prevention.

Alleviation

In the report of President Nixon's task force on aging (Meyer, 1970) it was stated, "The Task Force recognizes as a major aspect of the manpower and research problem the extent to which indifference and negative attitudes toward serving or studying the aging exist on the part of some members of the professions." (p. 51). Achieving the goal of alleviating negative attitudes toward the elderly would facilitate recruitment and training of personnel in the field of gerontology, and it would undoubtedly improve the competence and life satisfaction of the aged themselves. Contemporary attitudes and orientations to aging and the aged involve misperceptions and negative stereotypes accepted by young and old alike. Several extensive reviews of the scientific literature on attitudes toward aging present documentation for the negative stereotype (Peterson and Peters, 1971; Riley, Johnson and Foner, 1971). It has been suggested, however, that most negative stereotypes of the aged are invalid either because the deficient behavior attributed to the elderly does not occur in great frequency or because it results from social expectations rather than normal development (e.g., Schaie, 1972; Bengtson, 1969). Regardless of the validity of negative stereotypes of the aged, old and young alike have a negative attitude toward aging and the aged. Since perceived rather than real age differences are of great significance in determining behavior (e.g., Ahamme and Baltes, 1972; Bengtson and Kuypers, 1971; Thomas, 1970; Woodruff and Birren,

1972), it is crucial to change negative attitudes in order to improve the status and well-being of the aged. The aged accept the perception that they are inferior and behave accordingly—thus the negative stereotype becomes a self-fulfilling prophecy.

Intervention in the form of training and education could help to reverse this cycle. If individuals of all ages were provided with factual information about adult development and aging, misunderstanding would decrease. Education about the life cycle needs to be incorporated into elementary and high school curricula, and such information should also be offered in adult education courses so the aged themselves will regain their self-respect.

Another problem which intervention through training of professionals (in this case, teachers) in gerontology could alleviate is the educational deprivation in the elderly. About 67 percent of the aged over 65 have not gone beyond eighth grade while only 17 percent of the individuals aged 25-29 in 1960 had this level of schooling (U. S. Bureau of the Census, 1960). Additionally, most individuals in the aged cohort were educated in the early 1900's. Clearly, their eighth grade education is not comparable to an eighth grade education in the 1970's. While they are able to read, write and perform simple skills in arithmetic, in every other sense many of the aged are scholastically handicapped (Eklund, 1969). Remedial education at the elementary and high school levels is essential to alleviate educational deprivation in the elderly.

Remedial education also might facilitate understanding between cohorts and improve the status of the elderly. (cf. Chapt. VIII). Granick and Friedman (1970) suggested that education may play a role in enabling the aged to maintain their intellectual effectiveness. A number of years ago, investigators called attention to the fact that the relatively lower educational status of older cohorts could account for the apparent decline in intellectual functioning with age, (e.g., Birren and Morrison, 1971; Granick and Friedman, 1967; Lorge, 1955). Coupled with the longitudinal data on well-educated adults who showed little or no intellectual decline in many aspects of intellectual functioning (e.g. Owens, 1953, 1966; Bayley and Oden, 1955), it became apparent that intelligence shows little evidence of decline over most of the adult life-span. There is clear evidence that the elderly can perform well on intelliectual measures (see Baltes and Labouvie, 1972; Jarvik, Eisdorfer, and Blum, 1972), and they have considerable potential to benefit from education. Hence, by providing the elderly with educational opportunities equal to that of younger cohorts, harmful stereotypes about intellectual deterioration with age could be shattered.

Enrichment

It has become increasingly clear that there is a general state of economic and social deprivation in a majority of the aged and, to enrich the lives of these individuals, training and education must be undertaken for the goal of raising the quality of life in the elderly. This goal was given first priority by the Committee for Training at an International Symposium to evaluate the White House Conference (Birren, Woodruff and Bergman, 1972). This group recommended that, in the next ten years, training should be oriented to raising the quality of life for older persons whose incomes are below the median income of the population.

Because of economic factors the emphasis in American society on elevating the quality services available to individuals in the upper income brackets has not filtered down to those below the median income. In areas such as health, education and housing, many elderly individuals remain outside the stream of society's benefits. Hence, improvements in the quality of life for those in the population below the median income can probably be achieved more rapidly and less expensively if programs are aimed directly at this group rather than investing in top levels and expecting the investment to flow downwards through society. The gains to be made with investments aimed at individuals below the median income are much greater than the gains that might be made in economically advantaged groups.

In line with the recommendation to raise the quality of life for the elderly poor, the International Symposium Training Committee emphasized that a priority should be given to training of persons who will be in direct contact with those segments of the population exhibiting the greater need. Since many professionals in contact with the aged have no training in gerontology or geriatrics, an important priority must be given to alleviate this situation and "gerontologize" the professions. This would involve introducing the content of the field to existing professionals (e.g., physicians, social workers, educators, nurses) rather than creating an entirely new profession or discipline. Concurrent with such an emphasis there is a need to retain, improve, and expand high-quality academic training programs so that the orderly development of new knowledge based on research can proceed. Research is vital. To suggest that a major goal is to raise the average level of life in this country by initially relying on knowledge already available does not conflict with the need to insure high-quality training programs for the development of new knowledge.

The great expansion of effort should lie in the training of persons who give service to the older population, but personnel to train the servers must also be trained.

Prevention

In addition to alleviating problems, training and education must focus on the prevention of suffering in future cohorts of elderly. One means to meet this goal would be to train a sufficient number of professionals and technicians in the field of aging to serve and attend the needs of the increasing population of elderly. Some projections on the number of trained personnel required to serve the aged have been presented previously.

Education and training also might prevent suffering in late life as a result of early experiences. For example, adjustment to retirement is difficult for many individuals who lose their self-image as productive members of society. President Nixon's Task Force on Aging asserted that the elderly would be less dependent on society if they were provided during middle-age with opportunities to prepare for subsequent years. This Task Force supported the proposition of education as a lifelong process and stated: "We, therefore, recommend that the Office of Education in cooperation with the Administration on Aging establish a new program to conduct research on, promote, and provide technical assistance to communities concerning education for continued living for life" (Meyer, 1970, p. 46). To achieve this goal of preventing a decline in adaptive capacity with retirement, several thrusts in training must be undertaken. Educators capable of stimulating middle-aged adults and helping them to prepare for retirement must be trained as well as pre-retirement and retirement counselors. Birren and Woodruff (1972) suggested that psychology is one discipline in which professionals must be especially prepared to help the aging in minimizing problems and maximizing life satisfactions. Training psychologists and educators to counsel and teach the middle-aged and aging about the developmental tasks they will face will help countless individuals to enjoy greater fulfillment throughout their lives.

Requisites for Implementation

Funding

In a survey undertaken in 1968 by the Gerontological Society for the NICHD, funding was cited as the number one need for programs of training and research (U.S.D.H.E.W., 1968). The shortage of adequate funding is a typical complaint in academic and applied settings alike, but the shortage of funds has been acute in gerontology where the need is so great. A major source of academic training in gerontology is funded by the Adult Development and Aging Branch of NICHD; yet, of the five branches at NICHD, the aging branch has by far the lowest budget. Hence, an urgent recommendation of the Gerontological Society survey was to increase present appropriations for training and research in aging by a minimum of 100 percent over the years 1968-1973. It was also stated in this report that more crucial than the amount of funds is the manner in which funds are spent. More and different ways to extend and diversify research and training monies must be sought.

Current and expanded efforts in training will enhance the quality of life for future generations of retired Americans. Costs of present training and that required over the next decade have to be viewed partly in terms of the reduced costs to the nation as they will insure that a greater proportion of the retired will be healthy, independently living adults. The contemporary cohort of aged have earned a right to finish their lives in dignity, and training costs can be viewed as an investment in the lives of these individuals and future generations of aged. Hence, efforts must be made to increase the share of money for training in aging in national, local, and private budgets.

Government Organizations

Delegates to the 1971 White House Conference on Aging placed a high priority on the establishment of a National Institute of Gerontology which would consolidate the currently scattered thrusts at training and research in aging. It seems likely that this goal will be attained as the House of Representatives passed a bill, by a vote of 380 to 10, which would establish the National Institute of Aging in the National Institutes of Health. Combining the resources of the various federal agencies which have provided support for training and research in gerontology could improve the quality of training by making a directed impact with broad national goals for training and by increasing the level of funding of training.

Indeed, most long-range goals concerned with government institutions deal primarily with funding (Birren, Gribbin and Woodruff, 1971). Recommendations for new and enlarged facilities for research and training are typically cited in government reports, and there are also calls for government funding for gerontological curricula in colleges and professional schools, for short-term training of professionals, paraprofessionals and subprofessionals and for volunteers.

One government report included the recommendation that the Administration on Aging, in cooperation with the Office of Education, the Public Health Service, the Office of Economic Opportunity, the Department of Labor and other units of the Social and Rehabilitation Service become involved in training personnel including the middle-aged and aged themselves to serve as aides and technicians in a wide range of programs for the aged (U.S.D.H.E.W., 1969). Included in the effort should be:

1. Development and testing of model short courses by federal agencies, colleges, universities, and professional organizations;
2. Strong efforts to encourage widespread offering of such courses by educational and other appropriate agencies;
3. Greater utilization of funds available under Titles III, IV,

and V of the Older Americans Act, the Vocational Education Act, the Manpower Training and Development Act, Title 1 of the Higher Education Act, relevant provisions of the Public Health Service Act and of the Social Security Act, and other appropriate funding programs;

4. Experiment and innovation in the use of field experience as a training device; and

5. Testing the effectiveness of various devices for attracting trainees to short courses, including payment of stipends. (U.S.D.H.E.W., 1969, p. 68).

To adequately train researchers and teachers in the field of aging, modern and well-equipped facilities for the training programs must be provided. There are no federal funds available to support the construction of university centers for training, research and related purposes in aging. It has been recommended that AoA, the Public Health Service, the Office of Education, the Department of Housing and Urban Development, and other federal agencies, as appropriate to their objectives and programs, should be authorized to provide financial assistance for the construction of model multi-service senior centers, housing projects, and personal care and nursing homes, to be operated in conjunction with training and research programs in universities and professional schools (U.S.D.H.E.W., 1968). Without such facilities, the funds invested in personnel and students will not be most efficiently spent.

Goals for geographical planning of gerontology centers must also be considered by government organizations. Gerontology centers or institutes within universities can provide leadership to a State and region. It was recommended in the technical paper on training for the White House Conference (Birren, Gribbin and Woodruff, 1971) that five to six major interdisciplinary regional centers should be established by 1976, and nine or ten should be in operation by 1982. Such centers could provide the leadership for training in gerontology. Without the establishment of such centers, it is doubtful that a high quality training effort can be sustained over the next ten years.

Universities and Colleges

At the level of universities and colleges, implementation of training in gerontology requires the development of new curricula and research and teaching facilities as well as the recruitment of high quality faculty and students. The question of how best to implement the goals of universities in order to serve the greatest number of interested persons in the most effective manner is of great concern. Kleemeier and Birren (1967) and Birren and Woodruff (1972) emphasized the need for the establishment of major training programs in selected graduate schools. This strategy would concentrate key people at central locations. Centralization is considered more desirable than the less efficient process of introducing scattered courses in aging into each of many schools. There is evidence which suggests that the work of individual professors who are without administrative support tends to get diluted (U.S.D.H.E.W., 1968). Academic departments in the social sciences of direct concern to the field of aging are psychology, sociology, and anthropology, and at least one program in economics and political science should be established. Training and research in the biological sciences is an essential component of a Gerontology Center. In addition, such fields as social work, education, psychiatry, public administration and public health and the professional schools should have training programs with goals of twice the enrollment of the sciences.

As rapidly as resources permit, universities and colleges must be stimulated to introduce aging as a subject field for study and research at the masters and doctoral degree level. Such training will provide increased numbers of qualified persons who are needed to train the future practitioners and researchers to keep up with the projected demand. At the same time, universities and colleges must provide more field training opportunities to acquaint the trainees with the applied problems they will be encountering. One issue which has been frequently discussed is whether universities and colleges should produce generalists or specialists. Both types of professionals need to be trained. There cannot be good general training in gerontology unless there exist training and research centers that have competent teachers within the specialties. For example, a good physician is a generalist and must know anatomy, physiology, pharmacology and the knowledge from other special disciplines. Similarly, a generalist in gerontology will have to know some elements of biology, psychology, sociology, economics, social work and government policy. The best manner in which to teach these subjects appears to be in institutions that have senior staff who have devoted their careers to research and teaching on aging within an academic discipline. On the other hand, it seems unreasonable to expect that good generalists are produced solely from classroom teaching of academic topics. Field experience is essential for these professionals. Hence, good training, good research and good service go hand in hand, as do qualified generalists and specialists.

In addition to training at the masters and doctoral degree level, colleges and schools of education should be encouraged to provide short-term training in gerontology to primary and secondary school teachers who, in turn, may incorporate appropriate material into courses in the elementary and high school curriculum. Eventually, the aim should be to include content on aging in career preparation for teachers at the primary and secondary school levels. Vocational educational facilities need to develop curricula designed to prepare trainees for employment as community aides, senior center aides, housing, and other program aides in aging programs. Along this same line, it is important for local vocational schools and junior and community colleges to offer courses and recruit students for training in technical occupations which are essential to the provision of services for the older population.

Professional and Scientific Societies

It has been proposed that a consortium of societies for the aged and retired (CONSAR) could be organized which would have committees to establish goals and programs for research, training, services, products, and public policy (Birren, Gribbin and Woodruff, 1971). Constituent societies could be those in the relevant professions, sciences, and associations of retired persons. By facilitating communication in this manner, such organizations could lend their collective efforts to catalyze mutually desired goals, including an increase in the amount and quality of training. While the major goals and activities of the three types of organizations are very different, their purposes are complementary. The associations for the retired represent millions of older persons who are concerned with the quality of life in retirement, and these associations are spokesmen for their constituents' needs when public policy is discussed. Interaction between scientific, professional and retirement organizations will tend to insure that planning and training in the sciences and professions will reflect compassion for the individual and concern for the needs of society. From the viewpoint of the retired person the consortium approach would insure that the benefits of science and professional advances would be directed toward improving the circumstances of life in the later years. Public support of the programs of the sciences and professions by the millions of retired persons can only be brought about by greater mutual understanding. A consortium of scientific, professional and retirement organizations might facilitate such understanding.

Educational and Information Technology

Only advanced technological nations provide the basis for successful survival to the later years and it is only with technology that the support and care of large populations of retired persons can be accomplished. Technological advances have been adapted for educational purposes and such advances should be adapted for use in training in gerontology. For example, programmed instruction, biofeedback training, communications media programming, and counseling methods may be especially useful in the field of aging. A number of proposals have been made for the use of such techniques for training and education (e.g., Birren and Woodruff, 1973; Davis, 1971, 1972; Hoyer, 1972; Woodruff, 1971).

There are other aspects of training in gerontology which require technology. In a multidisciplinary field such as gerontology, the exchange of ideas is often hampered by the inaccessability of information. Information management is an especially problematic issue in training in gerontology because gerontology is relevant to many disciplines within academia, as well as many professions. This issue, however, is not unsolvable. A relatively small amount of money would provide sufficient access to equipment and personnel who already have the skills needed to organize

information. Academics as well as professionals working in applied settings must learn to take advantage of technological advances as they occur rather than continuing to meet new problems
with outdated equipment and organization.

Professional Standards and Quality Control

Pressures have been created by retired persons and by government groups for quality control measures in the form of certification or licensing. A well-known example of such pressure is
President Nixon's assault on inadequate conditions in nursing
homes. Such action leads to calls for instant training programs
and there are few social institutions or government agencies prepared to respond to these demands. Preparation for future demands for licensing and certification is also lacking. At the
present time, few of the major professions are requiring any time
in the curriculum for the subject matter of aging. It is possible
for many professional persons to render services to the aged without having had any formal training for the role and without any
supervised graduate or postgraduate experience in dealing with
the special problems of later life. Inadvertently, professional and
institutional rigidities may be contributing to a failure to advance
the quality of service to the aged. Often the justification is used
that there are inadequate numbers of trained personnel available
and to insist on higher personnel standards will only result in
making fewer personnel available. This circle of events can be
broken up by the interjection of training at many levels.

Quality control implies a goal of a greater degree of institutionalization and centralization of the effort in training. Lack
of public standards for personnel and institutions is regarded as
being accompanied by low quality of services, while increasing
institutionalization of standards can lead to improvements in the
quality of institutions, services and products. At the same time,
institutions are frequently rigid and adverse to change. Avoiding
rigidities in institutions warrants discussion. Means should be
built into formal quality control measures to keep institutions
contemporary and abreast of advances in the sciences and professions, and also for a balanced representation of constituent groups

on policy-making and enforcement bodies, thus providing for public response.

MODELS AND MEANS

Advanced Degree Programs

The significance of advanced degree programs has been stressed previously, and it has been stated that Ph.D. and master's level academicians and professionals are the leaders and planners upon which new direction and continued vitality rest. Basic to a long-range concern with the quality of training is the strength of the scientists, educators and administrators. Application of knowledge must rest upon a base of scientific and educational excellence and it is for this reason attention must be given to the amount and quality of training in advanced degree programs.

It seems clear that grouping scientists and educators in large multidisciplinary centers accelerates the progress of the field of gerontology and multiply the effect of funds invested in training (Birren, Woodruff and Bergman, 1972; U.S.D.H.E.W., 1968, 1969). Once such centers are established, questions arise as to whether degree-granting capacity should be within single disciplines or if the center itself should offer degrees in gerontology. Questions also arise as to how much training should involve specialization within one discipline and how much interdisciplinary training should take place. The issue of the "single-discipline" versus the "multi-discipline" approach to graduate education in aging will be an important topic to follow over the next decade, and various organizational structures for carrying out both types of programs are in existence. No single training technique is offered as the best and final word since the most appropriate program depends on the goals of the training, the special interests of the faculty, and the resources and administrative structure of each university.

Tables X-1, X-2, and X-3 present the major advanced degree programs in gerontology in the United States. Funding for all these programs comes from federal sources. Thirty-eight of the existing programs presented in Tables X-1, X-2, and X-3 involve training in one discipline administered through one department.

Such programs might become multidisciplinary if they were joined by other departments in the institution in which they are located. Thirteen of the programs award degrees in a number of specialized disciplines so that students from different disciplines are brought together in one setting to study aging. This multidisciplinary approach fosters interaction between disciplines and produces specialists with depth in one area coupled with a broad perspective of the field of aging. There are five programs designed to train individuals in concepts and methodologies of a number of disciplines. One of these programs leads to a degree in aging, another to a degree in gerontology, while the rest of the interdisciplinary programs lead to more traditional degrees in areas such as public administration and social work. Individuals graduating from these programs are well-suited for administrative or practice and service positions.

Some of the strategies used in existing training programs have proved viable and might be incorporated into new or expanding training programs in aging. For example, to bridge the gap between theory, research and application, the Human Development Program at the University of Chicago requires students to devote three quarters a year to course work and a fourth quarter in a field or action setting. To facilitate communication between researchers, educators and practitioners, the Ethel Percy Andrus Gerontology Center at the University of Southern California sponsors a summer institute to which personnel working in academic and those in applied settings are invited to work and study together. The College of Human Development at Pennsylvania State University facilitates interdisciplinary communication by offering courses team-taught by academicians representing several disciplines. The Life-span Developmental Program at West Virginia University emphasizes the importance of understanding human behavior in the aged as a consequence of life-long processes and this program has been instrumental in unifying the field of developmental psychology. At Duke University, the Center for the Study of Aging and Human Development attracts trained Ph.D's into the field of gerontology by providing a program of postdoctoral training. These and many other programs have provided the means for facilitating communication and recruitment

TABLE X-1. RESEARCH TRAINING GRANTS FUNDED BY THE ADULT DEVELOPMENT AND AGING BRANCH, NICHD

Institution	Training Objective	Degree or Program Level	First Year Enrolled	Total Enrolled Through Academic Year 1968-1969	Traineeships Alloted for Academic Year 1969-1970	First Year of Graduation	Number of Graduates Through 8/31/69
Associated Universities, Inc. Brookhaven National Laboratory	Gerontology—biological	Postdoctoral	1967	5	6	NA	NA
Boston University	Training for research in the biochemistry of aging	PhD	1967	5	6	1969	1
California, University of (Berkeley)	Developmental physiology and aging	PhD	1965	8	10	1966	11
California, University of (Los Angeles)	Gerontology, behavioral	PhD	1964	3	4	1967	2
California, University of (San Francisco)	Training program in adult development and aging, sociological and psychological	PhD	1968	12	18	1970	—
California, University of (Santa Barbara)	The physiology of stress and exercise	PhD	1967	2	3	1968	2
Case Western Reserve University	Sociology and gerontology	PhD	1966	6	6	1969	2
Chicago, University of	Adult development and aging and human development	PhD	1963 (transfer)	20	22	1963	17
Community Studies, Inc. Kansas City, Mo.	Social gerontology	PhD	1966	20	22	1968	11
Duke University Medical Center	Behavior and physiology in aging and human development	PhD Postdoctoral	1966	15	20	1969	7
Gerontological Society	Research in aging, sociological and psychological	PhD Postdoctoral	1969	—	summer students	1970	—

Institution	Program	Degree	Year			Year	
Maryland, University of	Physiology of gerontology	PhD	1966	4	8	1970	—
Miami, University of	Training in gerontology, biological	PhD	1966	9	12	1968	2
Nebraska, University of	Biochemistry of aging	PhD	1966	3	4	1968	1
New York University Downstate Medical Center	Aging in relation to the reproductive and endocrine system	MD-PhD	1968	2	3	1970	—
Pennsylvania State University	Adult development and aging, sociological	PhD	1967	8	12	1969	1
Pennsylvania, University of	Social gerontology	PhD	1967	4	6	1971	—
Pittsburgh, University of	Cell biology and aging	PhD	1963 (transfer)	13	15	1963	13
Retina Foundation Boston, Mass.	Biochemical and biophysical basis of aging	PhD Postdoctoral	1969	3	6	1970	—
Rochester, University of	Biological aspects of aging		1968		5	1968	2
Southern California, University of	Multidisciplinary approach to gerontology	PhD	1966	27	28	1968	8
Syracuse University	Developmental psychology-development and aging, sociological and psychological	PhD	1966	7	8	1967	8
Tennessee, University of	Training in aging, biological	PhD Postdoctoral	1969	—	4	1970	—
Washington University	Research in psychology—geriatrics	PhD	1964 (transfer)	12	12	1963	14
West Virginia, University of	Life-span developmental psychology	PhD	1965	6	6	1969	3
Wisconsin, University of	Social gerontology	PhD	1966	5	6	1969	2

Source: *The Gerontologist*. "Education and Training in Gerontology—1970," 10(1), Part 1, p. 63.

TABLE X-2. TRAINING GRANTS AWARDED OR CONTINUING IN FY 1969 CONCERNING THE AGING, NIMH

Institution	Training Objective	Degree Granted or Program Level	First Year Enrolled	NIMH Trainee Stipends 1969-1970	First Year of Graduation
Schools of Social Work					
Boston University	To improve and expand social work training relevant to mental health of the aged and their families through case work, community organization, and group work	MSW	1961-1962	5	1962-1963
California, University of		MSW	1966-1967	3	1967-1968
Connecticut, University of		MSW	1960-1961	4	1961-1962
Florida State University		MSW	1960-1961	4	1961-1962
Howard University		MSW	1961-1962	6	1962-1963
Iowa, University of		MSW	1961-1962	5	1962-1963
Michigan, University of		MSW	1962-1963	3	1963-1964
Missouri, University of		MSW	1961-1962	4	1962-1963
New York University		MSW	1963-1964	7	1964-1965
Pennsylvania, University of		MSW	1964-1965	5	1965-1966
Pittsburgh, University of		MSW	1966-1967	3	1967-1968
Tennessee, University of		MSW	1961-1962	5	1962-1963
Western Reserve		MSW	1962-1963	5	1963-1964
Wisconsin, University of		MSW	1964-1965	6	1965-1966
Medical Schools					
Duke University Medical Center	To learn how to treat aged psychiatric patients	2-year geriatric psychiatric residency	1965-1966	2	1966-1967
Nursing Schools					
Duke University School of Nursing	To meet psychiatric nursing needs of aged people	1-year post-master	1967-1968	5	1967-1968

Institution	Training Objective	Persons to be Trained	Date Funding Began	No. of Person to be Trained
Continuing Education Grants Gerontological Society	1) To assess need for continuing education 2) To design and carry out training programs	Various agencies and professional groups	1969-1970	
University of Southern California Gerontology Center	To educate professional personnel in mental health problems of the aging through postgraduate courses, colloquia, and conferences	Professionals: 1) counsellors in direct service to the aged 2) administrators and planners 3) persons whose knowledge of mental health problems of the aged will help them in supervisory functions of others	1968-1969	590
Inservice Training *Hospital Staff Development* *Hospital Improvement Program* Craft-Farrow State Hospital Columbia, S.C.	To prepare psychiatric aides to assume more effective role in care of long-term and geriatric patients	Attendants	1965-1966	17-20 yearly
Cushing Hospital, Framingham, Mass.	To teach staff how to remotivate and socially activate geriatric patients	Attendants, practical nurses, registered nurses, etc.	1964-1965	578 (entire staff)
Kerrville State Hospital, Kerrville, Tex.	To develop skills in the attendants' care of geriatric patients	Attendants	1967-1968	40 yearly
Northern State Hospital, Sedro-Wooley, Wash.	To improve interpersonal and leadership skills in personnel to give more effective patient service	Hospital personnel of leadership ability	1969-1970	20 yearly
Yankton State Hospital, Yankton, S.D.	To conduct courses or workshops in geriatric nursing (part of overall HSD program—53% of patients at Yankton are over 60)	Total service staff	1969-1970	412
Big Spring State Hospital, Big Spring, Tex.	To motivate attendants to upgrade care of chronic schizophrenic and geriatric patients for greater self-care	Attendants	1965-1966	70 attendants yearly

Source: *The Gerontologist.* "Education and Training in Gerontology—1970," 10(2), Part 2, p. 154.

TABLE X-3. LONG-TERM TRAINING PROGRAMS FUNDED BY THE ADMINISTRATION ON AGING UNDER TITLE V OF THE OLDER AMERICANS ACT

Institution	Training Objective	Degree or Program Level	Students by Academic Years				
			First Year Enrolled	Total Enrolled Through Academic Year 1968-1969	Trainee-ship Alotted for Academic Year 1969-1970	First Year of Gradua-tion	Number of Graduates Through 8/31/69
Arizona, University of (College of Business and Public Administration)	Retirement housing management, administration of homes for the aged and related facilities	MPA	1969-70	—	10	1970-71	—
Brandeis University (Florence Heller Graduate School for Advanced Studies in Social Welfare)	Applied social gerontology (Planning, administration, teaching, research)	MSW DSW PhD	1967-68	15	15	1967-68	1
California, University of (Berkeley) (School of Social Welfare)	Community planning and development	MSW	1968-69	6	14	1969-70	—
Chicago, University of (School of Social Service Administration)	Community planning and development	MSW	1968-69	4	6	1969-70	—
Columbia University (Teachers College)	Recreation leadership, senior center direction, programming	MA, MS, EdD, Prof. Dipl.	1967-68	27	40	1967-68	10
Michigan, University of and Wayne State University (Institute of Gerontology)	Federal-State planning and admn., community planning and develop't, retirement housing management, senior center direction, environment design (Arch.), adult education, counseling, undergraduate majors	MPA, MEd., MSW, MArchitect PhD, EdD, Bacc.	1967-68 1968-69 1968-69 1968-69 1968-69	41	58	1968-69	18

Institution	Description	Degree	Year			Year	
Minnesota, University of (Public Administration Center)	Federal-State planning and administration	MA in Pub. Admn.	1966-67	47	40	1967-68	9
North Carolina, University of (Curriculum in Recreation Administration, School of Education)	Recreation leadership, senior center direction and programming, adult education	MS in Rec. Admn. MS in Ed.	1967-68 1969-70	19	27	1968-69	6
North Texas State University (Center for Studies in Aging)	Administration of homes for the aged and related institutions, Federal-State planning and administration, library science, speech correction	MS in aging MA in aging	1968-69 1969-70	18	36	1969-70	—
Oregon, University of (Center for Gerontology) Portland State University	Undergrad, practitioners, business administration, communication, counseling, urban planning, dental hygiene, health education, recreation leadership	Bacc. Various Master's degrees PhD	1968-69 1968-69 1969-70	18	51	1968-69	2
California State University, San Diego (School of Social Work)	Community planning and development	MSW	1967-68	12	10	1967-68	8
South Florida, University of (Institute on Aging)	Social gerontology	MA in Ger.	1968-69	17	36	1969-70	—
Southern California, University of (Gerontology Center)	Environmental design (Architecture)	MArchitect	1968-69	2	6	1970-71	—
Washington, University of (School of Social Work)	Community planning and development	MSW	1968-69	4	6	1968-69	4
Wisconsin, University of (School of Social Work)	Social work generalists	MSW	1967-68	13	8	1967-68	5
Total			—	243	363	—	63

Source: *The Gerontologist*, "Education and Training in Gerontology—1970," 10(1), Part 1, p. 55.

and have strengthened the field of gerontology. Efforts should be made to encourage the exchange of ideas among the various institutions so that more successful strategies can be adopted by many programs.

As a result of negative attitudes toward applied topics and toward aging and the aged, the leadership of universities and colleges have given relatively little attention to the development of gerontology (U.S.D.H.E.W., 1968). One mechanism for improving the atmosphere for administrative support in universities is to conduct one- or two-day regional briefing sessions for university and college administrators. Such briefing sessions should present the picture of the needs of society and individuals, the requirements for training and research, and ways in which training can be supported by Federal and private agencies.

More persons need to be exchanged for short intervals between universities, colleges, research institutes, professional centers, governmental groups and other activities to provide a rounded education in gerontology to selected persons. Such training exchanges should also include institutions abroad where values and program emphases may be quite different and thereby offer training and opportunities for insight that will later be useful. Personal and institutional flexibility comes from insight into alternative ways of approaching the same problem. Institutional exchanges should appropriately include associations for retired persons since they offer unusual opportunities to study and work with large and important organizations of older persons. In this view, the goal of a program of student exchange would involve visiting associates in the sciences, in the professions and in administrative roles.

A Visiting Scientist Program has been suggested (U.S.D.H.E.W., 1968), in which distinguished gerontologists would be recruited to give a limited number of days to visiting other campuses where there is a potential for development of interests and activities in aging. The visiting scientists and lecturers would be available for lectures to undergraduate and graduate students, and for consultations with students interested in the possibilities in the field of aging and with faculty interested in exploring teaching and research possibilities. Moreover, they would help to upgrade existing research in aging by their advice and by the moral support they would give to the one or two persons on campus working in aging but who feel isolated. Another suggestion to eliminate this feeling of isolation among the "lone" gerontologists is the development and sponsorship, by present training centers, of short-term training seminars (not less than two weeks) addressed primarily to faculty.

An extension of the Visiting Scientist Program, the Resident Visiting Program (U.S.D.H.E.W., 1968), has all the benefits of the former, but the impact would be greater because it would extend over a longer period of time. Such a program would necessitate the universities be given financial assistance in order to invite scientists to spend periods of as much as six months to a year as resident visiting scientists in the field of aging.

An additional recommendation in the NICHD report (U.S.D.-H.E.W., 1968) concerns what it terms town-gown collaboration. It suggests that universities should seek collaboration with non-academic institutions in the field of aging. The report notes that the problem of standards will exist, but could be met by increasing the support for research to non-academic institutions and by encouraging their affiliation with local academic institutions.

Integration of national training resources is also a goal to be considered. Many national institutions such as the Veterans' Administration, Atomic Energy Commission, Public Health Service and other organizations have facilities and populations that offer excellent training opportunities. Perhaps these could be approached and made more available to scholarship students and trainees who are pursuing research training or professional training. If not an integrated plan, at least a national roster of such facilities would seem to be in order. In particular, the Veterans' Administration is a key institution needing more personnel specifically trained in aging and one that has facilities for providng better training in collaboration with universities.

Continuing Education

Because little content in aging is taught in medical schools and university departments where professionals are trained, most professionals—both new and experienced practitioners—are introduced to the field of aging through the use of continuing education.

Short term extension courses are a means of introducing students, practitioners and, occasionally, researchers, to the field of aging. They also serve to retrain and update available knowledge for individuals who are already established in gerontology. One of the main goals of continuing education is to indoctrinate ("gerontologize") members of existing professions who extend service to the aged in various areas of care with greater knowledge and understanding of the problems of older people.

Some strategies designed to produce the desired change in the attitudes of professionals were presented by Birren, Woodruff and Bergman (1972, pp. 77-78). These suggestions included:

1. Selecting, for the first stage of penetration, those professional groups which probably lend themselves more to such a penetration (e.g., social workers and nurses) and working out differential approaches.
2. Setting up model field training units for comprehensive services and using them for placement of trainees from different professions.
3. Providing the necessary inducements to professional educational facilities to establish demonstration programs, develop curricula containing the gerontological components, etc.
4. Providing the means for training teachers from within the given professions themselves to teach the gerontological components.
5. Using existing gerontological organizations, centers, or other foci of gerontological excellence and orientation, to act as change agents in the areas of their influence and to aid older persons to develop and maintain an advocacy role for themselves.
6. Extending the areas of funding agencies (AoA, others) to provide funds for such new activities.

Undergraduate Training

There are two general approaches for baccalaureate degree training in aging which need to be developed: (1) training as part of a broad liberal arts education, and (2) training for a particular occupation. Undergraduate education in aging would expose the student to the biological, behavioral and social aspects of aging as part of his general education. He might then want to pursue the study of aging in depth at the graduate level, or he might consider serving the aged in one of the helping professions. The minimum that would be accomplished by such exposure would be the contribution to our culture through better understanding of aging and the life cycle and the problems of the aged. An introduction of courses at the junior college level would also serve the purpose of creating an aware and informed public about aging and the aged.

Training at the undergraduate level also includes training in community colleges. The educational potential of the community colleges to undertake training in aging must be researched. The possibility of expanding the role of the community college to that of a center offering training programs for aging, or for special crash programs for personnel providing services to the aging in the community, has to be thoroughly studied and evaluated. Studies should be done on those community colleges already involved as to how they became involved. It was thought that the placement of a social gerontologist in the community college would help the development of programs, not that such a person would supply all of the instructional material, but he could be an influencing agent who would help to recruit students and also get persons mobilized with special knowledge to provide the technical training. It is particularly important that the American Association of Community Colleges be contacted and a conference arranged so their role could be developed effectively. Crash programs must be developed now, and problem detector studies should be undertaken so that the curricula of the community college can be directly geared to the needs of the aged in the community.

The placement of a social gerontologist with a B.A. or an M.A. degree in the community college would provide someone to act as a planner and coordinator. The Associate Arts degree given by the college after two years could follow both an academic and practical program. Suggestions have been offered such as having a survey course on aging as well as some specialized courses in the areas of psychology, sociology, and health. Such a first year could be accompanied by a wide spectrum of opportunities for half-day field placement. The second year could be devoted to specializing in some area that would bring direct skills to older persons such as nursing home aides, homemakers, recreation aides, and others.

Courses

More than ever before, undergraduates are demanding that course material be relevant to them personally and to society in general, and the subject matter of adult development and aging opens for them a field that fulfills these needs. Contemporary undergraduates are motivated to seek out and work for neglected minority groups, and many volunteer to spend long hours interacting with and studying the elderly in setting such as senior centers, extended care facilities and retirement communities. Undergraduates have responded well to programmed texts, and *Basic Concepts of Aging: A Programmed Manual* (Rich & Gilmore, 1969) was received with great enthusiasm by undergraduates at the University of Southern California. Other techniques which have worked well in undergraduate courses are field trips to applied settings, panels of older people who interact with the class, panels of professionals who work with the aged, and "Task Forces" of students who undertake basic or field research on topics relevant to gerontology.

Coordinated Semester Programs

Frequently, college or university courses are relatively uncoordinated with the student left wondering about the relatedness of material even in courses taught within the same department. In response to the feeling that undergraduate courses don't integrate enough, schools have shown interest in a total semester group of courses around a single topic or theme. Thus there have been "Biology Semesters" and "Urban Semesters." Relevant here is a Human Development Semester organized at the University of Southern California in which the human life-span, from conception to death, was looked at from the vantage points of four fields. The semester was regarded as giving students a comprehensive grasp of the main determinants and characteristics of human life at all stages in the life cycle. In this semester students take a total of 5 full courses: Physiology of Human Development; Psychology of Human Development; Sociology of Human Development; and Crises of Human Development. The fifth academic credit activity was a one-day per week field exposure to institutions dealing with individuals in various phases of the life-span.

Similar semesters could be organized under the theme of "Gerontology Semester," in which the aging of man could be examined from biological, psychological, and sociological viewpoints with additional information provided by social work, economics, political science, and medicine. The gains and losses in separating early development from aging have to be weighed. As a work program in aging, a Gerontology Semester would appear desirable, yet in terms of depth of understanding it would also appear desirable to teach from the perspective of the whole life-span.

Taking an undergraduate Human Development Semester or a Gerontology Semester would be excellent preparation for a student headed for a subsequent professional career in medicine, social work, education, nursing or, in brief, all professions that must serve the needs of an aging population.

Academic Majors in Gerontology

An even more concentrated preparation for a professional career in aging than the specialized semester would be a specialized baccalaureate program. As yet, to the authors' knowledge, only one such program exists (Mt. Angel College, Oregon). Development of such programs seems but a limited extension of present thinking. One strategy would be to have the degree(s) as a specialized extension of existing degree programs, e.g., B.A. in biological, psychological, and social gerontology. In these instances, the degree program would qualify the individual as a major in his area, i.e., biology, psychology, or sociology. One advantage to this approach would be that the individual could apply to graduate school in his major science.

Another pattern could be created in which the biological, psychological, and social elements of aging would be combined in a sequence of courses leading to a bachelor's degree in gerontology. This would offer the opportunity for cohesiveness in planning and provide for a greater breadth of background.

Baccalaureate programs are also needed which would teach and develop skills for a particular occupation serving the aged. Such programs would be directed to the large number of college students who, when they graduate with a bachelor's degree, enter the labor force and take a beginning position of a technical or professional or sub-professional character, including positions in programs serving the elderly. Individuals interested in entering the labor force with a bachelor's degree often find themselves handicapped by lack of specialized training and some, but by no means a majority, return to the university for graduate study or professional training. Introduction of training in gerontology into the curriculum in the third and fourth years of undergraduate study would also be of great benefit to students majoring in health or community service fields.

High School Education

An NICHD (U.S.D.H.E.W., 1969b) survey indicated that there were three basic needs for training in aging at the high school level. To introduce concepts of aging at this level it is necessary to develop:

1. Institutes for teachers to project concepts of aging within the particular framework of their respective area, i.e., biology, social studies, etc.
2. Institutes for students to provide opportunities to observe and even to participate in research activities, e.g., during summer vacations.
3. Appropriate materials for introducing concepts of aging within the existing high school curricula.

If such approaches to training in aging were adopted in all states, then the prospects and impetus for trainees in gerontology at undergraduate and graduate levels would be greatly improved.

Alternatives to Class Instruction

It is somehow very easy to discuss the characteristics and needs of older adults in a classroom lecture far removed from the environments in which they live. Classroom instruction, unsupported with field experience, tends to encourage in the young student the development of an attitude that compresses the wide range of individual differences among the aged into a single category with stereotypic qualities. There are among the aged many impressive differences that will with exposure defy simplistic attitudes. There are the wealthy and the poor, robust athletic individuals and bed-ridden invalids, the mentally active and the psychologically vegetative, the socially active and the passive rocking-chair types, and the highly ethical as well as the survivors of an amoral skid-row existence. In addition to being trained with respect to the special needs of some particular part of the aged population, the student must become aware of the range of individual differences and see the older adult functioning in his usual environment whether it be in a hospital or cultivating a farm.

Universities often maintain nursery schools and laboratory schools at the elementary and high school levels as training and research facilities for faculty and students. Highly unusual would be a university that maintained a "senior citizens" all-purpose center for professional training and research. The essential point is that universities lack training facilities in aging and do not at present show much inclination to develop them. Many possibilities exist as alternatives or as supplements to class instruction: recreation centers, adult education classes (usually held in community school rooms), retirement communities, housing projects for the aged, nursing homes, community mental health centers, retirement clubs and associations. Brief periods of volunteer service in some of these settings would result in the students having a grasp of the wide range of individual differences as well as an appreciation for some of the social and biological forces that influence the lives of older adults.

Field observational projects for groups of students encourage the exchange of information and evaluation of experiences as does the team research group that may undertake an experiment to manipulate behavior or the social and physical environment.

Evaluation of Training

Universities tend to function without regard to a systematic evaluation of training and few institutions regularly follow their graduates to find out how many of them remain in the primary area of their training. The question which should be asked it: How many persons actually remain within the field in which they were trained? One might establish large training programs at the volunteer, paraprofessional, professional, and academic levels and find out subsequently that the individuals after completing their training did not remain in the field. Hence evaluation components of training programs should be built in and linked to assistance for continuation of the program.

Greater efficiency in training might also be achieved with the development of more flexible funding policies. In this regard the following suggestions are made:

1. Training grants should be given for longer periods of time than presently (certain programs hardly get started when funding terminates.)

2. Special grants of considerable amounts of money should be made to selected universities and gerontological scientists specifically charged with the development of innovative training programs at the intermediate level outside the university, with requirements for the evaluation of the program built in from the outset (curriculum development, counseling to the community, training of trainers, evaluation, cooperation with service facilities, developing applied research, and "research receptivity" in early stages of training, etc.). Experts in the field of gerontology need to be encouraged to widen this influence beyond their own institutions.

The final criterion of progress, of course, should rest on the extent to which our training and research efforts really enter the social system of the country. In respect to the multipurpose community center, the questions requiring answers would include: Has the information available to older persons been elevated in quality and quantity? Has the older person become socialized into a more rewarding interpersonal life? Does the older person have greater access to services than previously? Does he have access to more education and more options to exercise? Thus, for the community resident, one of the functions of social gerontology is to provide increased information and opportunities for choices regarding personal relationships, housing, recreation, and educational activities.

The task for the next decade must be to raise the base level of the quality of life so that every aged person in this country can be provided with a social environment in which he or she may receive no less than good, average care when needed. Trained manpower to provide that care at all required levels of skills and professional knowledge is a major precondition for the success of this challenging task.

PROSPECTS, SHORT AND LONG-RANGE

If one poses the question, "What are the prospects for training of professionals in the field of aging?," a second question immediately comes to mind. The second question is, "prospects for whom?" Does one refer to the prospects for dependent elderly persons receiving needed professional services? Or does one have in mind the prospects of professional persons obtaining training and a position, or the prospects of educational institutions developing training programs?

Underlying any of the above prospects is the basic economic issue of how much of the national economy the government will devote to the well-being of older persons. In a free enterprise society those persons who have the means can buy services and goods. Since most of the aged have low incomes relatively few can compete to purchase goods and buy services at a level of the employed. It is not unexpected, then, that professional services for the aged have not shown a quantitative and qualitative development. Kreps (1971) pointed out that the income of the elderly worsened in the last decade compared with young families; "since 1962 the median income of elderly individuals has risen 16 percent, which is about half the percentage increase for younger persons." (Kreps 1971, p. 138).

Apparently, in recent years, the rises in pensions have done little more than meet rises in prices. Although private pensions and social security benefits are expected to rise in the next decade they will likely rise at a rate equal to inflation and not much more. Thus, there seems little prospect that older persons will be relatively better off in the future. Kreps (1971, p. 138) quotes the results of a projection of income to 1980 as prepared by Schulz (1967). The findings indicate that in 1980 half of the married retirees and more than four-fifths of the single retirees will have $3000 or less in annual pension income from both public and private sources. By 1980, if the income estimates are corrected for price increases, 81 percent of retired couples are estimated to have a real income from pensions and assets of $4000 or less. The income prospects are such that only a small proportion of retired persons will even by 1980 be in a good position to compete with younger employed persons for goods and services.

While there are retired persons of great wealth, the distribution of income among the retired is such that most retirees are and will be poor or relatively poor compared with employed persons. Thus the prospects seem dim for more professional services being purchased by the elderly in the open market.

Political efforts may of course result in legislation and appropriations to put a larger portion of the national economy into the hands of older persons. The White House Conference of 1971 indicated that retired persons were coming to be a more visible political force (Oriol, 1971). There seems to be no evidence, however, that the retired will receive more from the economy relative to other pressure groups during the remainder of the 1970's. Traditional pressures for tax relief to industry to expand our rate of economic growth, pressures for direct expenditures for capital improvement, e.g., transportation, urban development and water and air pollution control, seem more likely to be successful than are efforts to give a substantial rise in retired persons' income. Political views may change but unless there is a wide-spread conviction that raising retirement incomes will be a good way to expand the economy, legislatures will not vote funds to supplement retirement incomes.

Since most older persons will not have incomes to pay for major professional services it would seem that there is not likely to be any larger increase in self-employed professionals serving the retired population. An exception would be professionals serving the aged who are in the upper 5 percent of annual incomes. Where, then, will there be any dramatic gains in professional services to the retired? Probably, the gains will come in institutional efforts and rises will occur in institutional employment of professionals. Immediate prospects seem most encouraging for salaried professionals working in public and private organizations and institutions of all types that serve the older population. As was said before, these and other prospects assume no dramatic change in this decade in the political philosophy about distribution of wealth.

The Politics of Aging

As suggested, the White House Conference of 1971 gave visibility to the retired population and a considerable flurry of legislative activity followed it with pledges of interest from both political parties. Closer attention will likely be given to legislation affecting older persons by legislatures as political action committees of retired persons are beginning to form to monitor legislative actions. The millions of members of retired persons who belong to national organizations seem destined to have an impact on legislative voting, e.g., the American Association of Retired Persons, National Council of Senior Citizens, and National Retired Teachers Association. It would seem that the political views of these organizations represent a cross-section of American opinion and, while legislators may wish to see retired persons gain in their standard of living, it seems unlikely that these legislators would support legislation that departs greatly from the platforms of the major political parties. It should be realized, however, that the greater the rate of economic growth the greater grows the difference between incomes of employed workers and retirement incomes. If the remainder of this decade is accompanied by a high rate of economic growth the tensions between the retired and the employed population will likely grow and retirement organizations may come to adopt political positions independent of the political parties.

Political efforts by the retired seem directed at increasing the benefits to be obtained through existing agencies, e.g., Social and Rehabilitation Services, Administration on Aging, and the Veterans' Administration; and through systems of payment like Medicare. Professional organizations have not, for the most part, exercised leadership in this arena, particularly in concert with the powerful organizations of retired persons. Faced with the fact that professional training in the field of aging has been almost non-existent in some areas, the lethargy of professional organizations is startling. If they can become motivated and can couple their training goals to the political action potentials of retirement organizations some progressive steps could be taken to meet some of the documented needs of the retired population (Birren, Gribbin, and Woodruff, 1971). Prospects seem best at the moment for actions to be taken by existing government agencies.

Government Agencies

Pressures on the government agencies resulting from the White House Conference of 1971 have resulted in more self-examination with regard to their efforts in training. Although the overall picture for professional training is not bright, training in aging seems to be receiving a justified increase in support. In 1972-73, agencies with training in aging—the Administration on Aging, National Institute of Mental Health, National Institute of Child Health and Human Development and others—increased their commitments. Immediate prospects for training appear best for those programs that fit the goals and procedures of these agencies. It seems highly likely that Federal expenditures for training in aging will increase over this decade, offering encouragement to schools and individuals to develop an adequate supply of professional, technical and paraprofessional personnel to provide specialized services to older people. Prospects for financial support seem good to excellent, particularly for support of innovative programs.

Personnel—Recruitment and Visibility

At a time when the void in training is becoming an unavoidable issue, capable persons to exercise leadership are in short supply. At the outset of the present new thrust for training in aging there is a shortage of senior or well-qualified persons to fill positions that are being created. This suggests that some recruitment should be undertaken of personnel from adjacent specialties. Special training programs of a crash nature for cramming facts, theories and techniques relevant to the needs of older persons will be needed. University summer programs for training educators also will be useful in recruiting new personnel with experience in an adjacent professional area. While new job opportunities are in themselves a great recruiting force, and a force leading people to get background training, the status and visibility of the field is itself an issue. How attractive is the prospect of a career in professional services to older people relative to other career options of working with children, youth, or young adults? Since material on aging is rarely found in high school biological or social science texts or curricula or in undergraduate courses, there is little basis for creating a later interest.

The opportunities and rewards for careers in aging need visibility so that individuals will be encouraged to undertake training. At the same time, however, information about aging and related careers can be introduced into high school and elementary school curricula by books, articles, films, and other means. This requires professional effort, and perhaps research on why aging has been so poorly visible should be undertaken. Such information can be extremely useful in this period when a larger portion of the labor force will be elevated to personal services rather than productive labor in the industrial sense. An automated industrial society requires few people in producing consumer goods, the labor not used in industry can and is moving into service jobs. In this arena, services to the aged is a large area for job development. The rapidity of recruiting service personnel and professionals to the field hinges upon its attractiveness.

Questions may be raised about the fact that many of the constituent sciences and professions have grossly undertrained in an area of serving the aged where there are huge social demands. Have individuals selectively not gone into the field? Have the institutions biased the career planning of their students? There is a research issue involved here about how people select their occupations but have not chosen gerontology. Thus, a needed area of research is one of finding out the basic issues and motivations which lead people to choose or not to choose a career in aging. Studies of motivation for selection of aging as an area of career or clinical preference could supply needed insight into the motivation of the learners and might possibly lead to a "typology" of trainees best suited for the area of aging in whom training resources could be more profitably invested.

For professionals and paraprofessionals the question generally is the actual prestige and economic status for those who work with older persons. It is apparent that we have a social-political issue in society, in that the professionals are not developing careers in an area where there are great social pressures. Conceivably, this is partly an out-growth of the attitudes toward aging in a society that is still youth- and pioneering-oriented. Implications here call for research on whether or not there have been changing attitudes toward the aged.

Athough the general state of "gerontological poverty" in professional education is known, more information is needed on the extent of the problem in the various professional fields, e.g., of the nearly one hundred medical schools in the country, half do not include *any* gerontological component; what the extent and content of the component included in the curricula of the other half is, of course, of no less practical importance. Research on professional schools has to be undertaken on such probems as: What is to be taught and by whom? How is the gerontological component to be integrated? How are faculty members to be trained who will teach the subjects? What exposures and clinical/field experiences need to be developed? Success in this area could have considerable positive consequences for better understanding and care of the middle-aged and aged in the community.

The status of aging in our society is to no small extent influenced by the negative image of old age as a period of negligible suitability for investment in training and associated low expectations for reasonable return in satisfaction, treatment results, and personal and professional status. Although some small sample studies among students in various professions (psychology, nursing, etc.) indicate that prejudices remain among them after increased exposure to information and knowledge about aging, there seems to be some decrease in negative stereotypes and greater inclination to relate to work with aged on the professional-instrumental rather than affective-negative dimension. There also seems to be some indication in small sample studies and in other observations that exposure to aging may have a positive effect on the student's perception of aging and his inclination to select this area of interest or practice. However, this requires further exploration in various professional groups and on various levels of learning. The few existing studies of professional curricula of medical schools or social work schools present a rather sad picture of the conscious or unconscious attitude of training institutions to this matter. However, our existing knowledge here is insufficient and further studies on reasons for and strategies for changing these attitudes are of practical urgency if we are to re-orient the professions and achieve an expanded recruitment in this area.

Some research seems to indicate that social regard for the elderly in the United States has actually improved over time. Increased interest in problems of aging and the growing pressure for larger number of "care-givers" make recruitment based on better knowledge imperative; more research in this area is urgent.

It is possible that there is no relationship between the amount of education a person receives on issues of gerontology and his willingness to work in the field of aging. Thus, "gerontologizing" a professional curriculum does not necessarily mean that more graduates will elect to go into the field. A significant feature is the desirability of establishing career ladders in gerontology. These should be such that the younger professional or academic person can see opportunities for further development and promotion. Further factors such as built-in "career potential," financial inducements in the form of stipends and other forms of assistance, availability of later training for higher professional standing, assurance of job opportunities, and affiliation of the training facilities with institutions of higher learning have to be developed and studied for their effectiveness in creating a positive "recruitment climate" for training.

The foregoing discussion points to the prospect that more sophistication is going to be required in the sense that recruitment efforts and attempts to introduce material on aging into professional school curricula will have to be based upon knowledge gained from a wide range of research. The main obligation for those responsible for training is to increase manyfold the amount of training over the next decade. This increased training effort should, however, be based upon research.

Emergent Issues

Training in aging must be undertaken with the view that new issues are emerging and will continue to emerge. For example, as the standard of living in this country has improved in this century, women have gained more in life expectancy than men. This, coupled with a tradition of men marrying women younger than they, results in millions of older women being widows. The huge population of elderly widows presents society with a number of problems ranging from ways to reduce the psychological and social isolation of widows to matters of consumer protection and financial management.

Another emergent issue is the increasing population of the minority elderly. In past generations, life expectancy has been shorter for the non-white population compared with the white. Life expectancy has been improving for the non-white population with the result that there are growing numbers of elderly blacks, for example, with special needs. Little is known about the personal needs and circumstances of many aged in different ethnic groups, e.g., Spanish-speaking, Black, Oriental, or Indian populations. Technological change reaches all groups in society but, unless something is known of the circumstances of the aged members of minority ethnic groups, the conditions of communication cannot be created, consequently such persons will not partake in services to which they are entitled in a changing society. For example, large numbers of elderly Mexican-American persons will require Spanish-speaking professionals in a variety of fields.

The nature of the needs of the minority aged, the types of programs which are required to alleviate their needs, the training called for and the personnel needed to implement programs are all important questions which cannot be answered at this time. Planned efforts should be made to recruit research and service personnel from disadvantaged ethnic groups as those who might best be able to help the elderly in their own ethnic group. Trainees recruited from ethnic and minority groups would help to provide valuable facts about aging in ethnic groups and lead to the improvement of training programs.

Agencies are now becoming more sensitive to evaluation of

training. It can be expected that more evaluations based upon designed research will be required of training programs if supported by public funds. These can best be undertaken if the goals of training are made explicit at the onset of a training program and a plan for follow-up of graduates is made and followed. Thus, the prospects for training in the next decade include an increasing emphasis on evaluation.

Another emergent issue to be faced by educational institutions will be growing numbers of middle-aged and old adults applying for graduate study or professional training. Since training institutions are usually involved with young persons, adaptations will be required in student selection policies and student financial support. The "age-integration" of our training programs will be an issue in some respects similar to admission and support of ethnic persons or representatives from financially disadvantaged groups.

Translation of Research into Use

There has been a rise in suspiciousness on the part of society that research is not always useful or, indeed, that academic persons may not be interested in seeing it put to use. In the field of aging one may expect an increased emphasis on the utilization of research, a function that often is not filled.

The potential contributions to society through research and training in aging require that both society and social gerontologists be realistic in their expectations. The scientists who do research and training, mostly located in our institutions of higher learning, will have to become more sophisticated about the problems of evaluating and translating scientific evidence which may be used as a basis for social policy. Society, on the other hand, must develop a sense of patience. Breakthroughs in research on aging require time and support for the establishment of effective research and training organizations in our universities.

Social indicators of the well-being of an aging population are needed. We have not followed satisfactorily the physical, mental, and social well-being of our older population. Social indicators are needed if planners are to have adequate lead time to develop service programs and required manpower. Implicit in the development of social indicators and surveillance statistics is the ability of scientists to measure what society regards as important and to have the technical skills to construct good indicators. Training to monitor the well-being of the older population should be the concern of at least one training center.

SUMMARY

The purposes of this chapter were to document the need for training of professionals in the field of aging, to establish some goals for such training, and to present concrete plans for the achievement of the goals. Realistic assessment of the short- and long-range prospects of achieving the goals was also considered. The following statements summarize the main points of the chapter.

1. There is a tremendous gap between the amount of existing training in gerontology and the amount which is required to meet the needs of an expanding population of elderly persons.

2. Education on aging should be undertaken at the graduate, undergraduate, junior college and high school levels, with a priority given to graduate training to develop personnel who will provide leadership and give an impetus to training at all levels.

3. To provide for the most effective development of materials for training, a survey of existing materials should be undertaken. With this knowledge, existing materials could be updated and new materials could be developed without duplication of older resources. New teaching methods should be adapted to the field and means for more efficient dissemination of information are also needed.

4. Both applied and basic research programs are essential components of high quality gerontology training programs.

5. Alleviation of negative attitudes towards the elderly would facilitate recruitment and training of personnel in gerontology, and training and education in gerontology might lead to more realistic attitudes toward aging and the aged.

6. To raise the quality of life for the elderly poor, emphasis should be placed on training those professionals, paraprofessionals and technicians who will be in direct contact with them.

7. Rather than creating a new profession or discipline to meet

the needs of the aged, existing professions (e.g., medicine, nuring, social work, education) should include components of training in gerontology and existing professionals should receive additional training in gerontology.

8. Funding is a current primary need for implementing gerontology programs of training and research.

9. The strategy of concentrating major gerontological training and research centers in selected universities is favored over introducing gerontology in a large number of schools and may be accomplished by sending individual gerontologists to different colleges and universities. Centralization of gerontological resources appears to accelerate progress while the work of lone gerontologists tends to get diluted.

10. The organization of a consortium of organizations for the aged and retired (CONSAR), composed of professional and scientific societies and associations of retired persons, would facilitate communication between these groups and might also serve as a catalyst for mutually-desired goals.

11. Efforts should be made to encourage the exchange of ideas among the institutions where gerontology training now exists so that successful strategies at one institution can be used more widely. Exchange of faculty and students for short periods between different universities, colleges, research institutes, professional centers and governmental groups would also facilitate interaction among institutions as well as broadening the education of the selected individuals.

12. A visiting scientist program in which distinguished gerontologists would be recruited to give a limited number of days to visiting campuses where there is a potential for development of interests and activities in aging might accelerate the development of gerontology. Interested faculty and students could attend lectures and consultations with a visiting scientist and, in this manner, individuals might be recruited for the field of aging.

13. Collaboration between universities and non-academic institutions would provide facilities and populations for additional training opportunities.

14. Continuing education is an effective strategy to "gerontologize" the professions by introducing existing professionals

working with the aged to concepts and issues in gerontology. Short-term courses can also be used to update and upgrade professionals who have received training in gerontology.

15. Two general approaches for undergraduate training in aging must be developed: (a) training as a part of a broad liberal arts education, and (b) training for a particular occupation.

16. In addition to undergraduate courses in gerontology, coordinated semester programs and academic majors in gerontology should be developed to stimulate interest and activity at the undergraduate level. Such programs offer tremendous potential for recruitment of personnel for graduate training in gerontology as well as a potential supply of professional, sub-professional and technical workers in the field of aging.

17. Introduction of gerontology at the high school level will involve the development of institutes to train high school teachers, institutes for students to observe and participate in research activities, and appropriate materials for introducing gerontology at the high school level.

18. All levels of classroom instruction in gerontology should be supplemented with field experience and exposure to the elderly. Training facilities developed in cooperation with universities might include recreation centers, adult education classes, retirement communities, housing projects, nursing homes, and retirement clubs. Volunteer service in these settings would provide students with an awareness of the wide range of individual differences in the elderly and an appreciation for some of the biological, psychological and social forces affecting the lives of the aged.

19. As a part of training programs in gerontology there should be provision for the evaluation of the program. Follow-up of graduates to ensure that they are employed and effective at the tasks for which they were trained is an important component absent in many training programs. Such information should be the basis on which additional training funds are supplied.

20. While the prospects seem dim for more professional services being purchased in the open market by the elderly, more professionals must be trained to serve the elderly as gains will come in institutional employment of professionals. Immediate

prospects seem most encouraging for salaried professionals working in public and private organizations and institutions serving the aged.

21. Voting in state legislatures and congress will probably reflect the impact of pressure from large retirement organizations. If professional educators in gerontology can couple their training goals to the retirement organizations' potential for political action, progressive steps in training could be made to meet many needs of the retired population.

22. It seems likely that Federal expenditures for training in aging will increase over this decade. Schools and individuals will be encouraged to develop an adequate supply of professional, technical and paraprofessional personnel to provide specialized services to the elderly.

23. Since persons capable of exercising leadership for training in aging are in short supply, there is a shortage of senior persons to fill new positions which are being created. To meet immediate needs, recruitment of personnel from adjacent specialities should be undertaken. Additionally, visibility of gerontology at all levels from elementary school to working professionals must be increased so that recruitment can be accelerated.

24. Training programs must avoid rigidity and should be designed to meet emergent as well as existing needs.

25. Scientists involved in research and training will have to become more sophisticated about the problems of evaluating and translating scientific evidence to be used to design social policy.

26. Training in gerontology is still in its early pioneering stage. Many kinds of experimental programs will have to be tried in the process of attempting to meet the personnel needs of the present and future. This is an area for long-term investment on the part of institutions of higher learning. Hopefully, many schools will begin to make such investments in this decade.

BIBLIOGRAPHY

Ahamme, I. M. and Baltes, P. B.: Objective versus perceived age differences in personality: How do adolescents, adults, and older people view themselves and each other? *J Gerontol,* 27:46-51, 1972.

Baltes, P. B. and Labouvie, G. V.: Adult development of intellectual performance: Description, explanation, modification. In Eisdorfer, C. and Lawton, M. P., (Eds.): *APA Task Force on Aging.* Washington, D. C., American Psychological Association, in press, 1973.

Bayley, N., and Oden, M. H.: The maintenance of intellectual ability in gifted adults. *J Gerontol, 10*:91-107, 1955.

Bengtson, V. L.: Adult socialization and personality differentiation: The social psychology of aging. In Birren, J. E. (Ed.): *Contemporary Gerontology: Issues and Concepts.* Los Angeles, University of Southern California, 1968.

———— and Kuypers, J. A.: Generational differences: Perception, reality and the developmental stake. *Aging Hum Dev, 2*: in press, 1971.

Birren, J. E., Gribbin, K. J. and Woodruff, D. S.: *Training: Background.* Washington, D. C., White House Conference on Aging, 1971.

———— and Morrison, D. F.: Analysis of the WAIS subtests in relation to age and education. *J Gerontol, 16*:363-369, 1961.

———— and Woodruff, D. S.: Academic and professional training in the psychology of aging. In Eisdorfer, C. and Lawton, M. P. (Eds.): *APA Task Force on Aging.* Washington, D. C.: American Psychological Association, 1973, in press.

————: Human development over the life-span through education. In Baltes, P. B. and Schaie, K. W. (Eds.): *Life-span Developmental Psychology: Personality and Socialization.* New York, Academic Press, 1973, in press.

———— and Bergman, S. (Eds.): Research, demonstration, and training: issues and methodology in social gerontology. *Gerontologist, 12*:49-83, 1972.

Davis, R. H.: Television and the older adult. *J Broadcast, 15*:153-160, 1971.

————: A descriptive study of television in the lives of an elderly population. Unpublished doctoral dissertation, University of Southern California, 1972.

Eisdorfer, C. and Taves M. (Eds.): International research and education in social gerontology: goals and strategies. *Gerontologist, 12*: 2-85, 1972.

Eklund, L.: Aging and the field of education. In Riley, M. W., Riley, J. W. Jr., Johnson, M. E. Forner, A. and Hess, B. (Eds.): *Aging and Society: II. Aging and the Professions,* New York, Russell Sage Foundation, 1969.

Granick, S. and Friedman, A. S.: The effect of education on the decline of psychometric performance with age. *J Gerontol, 22*:191-195, 1967.

————: The influence of education on the maintenance of intellectual functioning in the aged. Paper presented at the 78th Annual Meeting of the American Psychological Association, Miami, September, 1970.

Hoyer, W. J.: Application of operant techniques to the modification of elderly behavior. In Baltes, P. B. (Ed.): Strategies for psychological intervention in old age. *Gerontologist*, Vol. 13, No. 1, 1973.

Jarvik, L. F., Eisdorfer, C. and Blum, J. E. (Eds.): *Intellectual Functioning in Adults*. New York, Springer, 1972.

Kleemeier, R. W. and Birren, J. E.: Society and the study of aging. In Kushner, R. E. and Bunch, M. E. (Eds.): *Graduate Training in Aging within the Social Sciences*. Ann Arbor, Michigan, University of Michigan Press, 1967.

Kreps, J. M.: *Lifetime Allocation of Work and Income: Essays in the Economics of Aging*. Durham, North Carolina, Duke University Press, 1971, p. 138.

Lorge, I.: Capacities of older adults. In Donahue, W. T. (Ed.): *Education for Later Maturity: A Handbook*. New York, Whiteside & Morrow, 1955.

Maddox, G. L. and Bierman, E. L.: *Research and Demonstration*. Washington, D. C., White House Conference on Aging, 1971.

Meyer, G. (Ch.): *Toward a Brighter Future for the Elderly: The Report of the President's Task Force on Aging*. Washington, D. C., U. S. Government Printing Office, 1970.

Moore, J. L. and Birren, J. E.: Doctoral training in gerontology: an analysis of dissertations on problems of aging in institutions of higher learning in the United States, 1934-1969. *J Gerontol, 26*:249-257, 1971.

Oriol, W. E.: Congress, politics and the elderly. In Maddox, G. L. (Ed.): *The Future of Aging and the Aged*. Atlanta, Ga., Southern Newspaper Publishers Association Foundation, 1972.

Owens, W. A., Jr.: Age and mental abilities: A longitudinal study. *Genet Psychol Monogr, 48*:3-54, 1953.

———: Age and mental abilities: A second follow-up. *J Educ Psychol, 51*:311-325, 1966.

Peterson, W. A. and Peters, G. R. (Eds.): Perceptions of aging. *Gerontologist, 11*:59-108, 1971.

Rich, T. A. and Gilmore, A. S.: *Basic Concepts of Aging—A programmed manual*. Washington, D. C., U. S. Government Printing Office, 1969.

Riley, M. W., Johnson, M. E. and Foner, A.: *Aging and Society. III. A Sociology of Age Stratification*. New York, Russell Sage Foundation, 1971.

Schaie, K. E.: Reflections on papers by Looft, Peterson, and Sparks: Intervention towards an ageless society? In Baltes, P. B. (Ed.):

Strategies for psychological intervention in old age. *Gerontologist,* Vol. 13, No. 1, 1973.

Schultz, J. H.: The future economic circumstances of the aged: Simulation projection. *Yale Economic Essays,* 7:145-217, 1967.

Thomas, H.: Theory of aging and cognitive theory of personality. *Hum Dev, 13*:1-16, 1970.

Toffler, A.: *Future Shock.* New York, Random House, 1970.

U. S. Bureau of Census: *Census of Population,* Vol. 1, Part 1. Washington, D. C., U. S. Government Printing Office, 1960.

U.S.D.H.E.W., National Institute of Child Health and Human Development: *Final Report: A Survey of the Training Needs and Mechanisms in Gerontology.* St. Louis, Mo., Gerontological Society, 1968.

U.S.D.H.E.W. Office of the Secretary: *Annual Report,* Administration on Aging. Washington, D. C., U. S. Government Printing Office, 1969.

U.S.D.H.E.W. Office of Education: *Educational Research and Development in the United States.* Washington, D. C., U. S. Government Printing Office, 1969.

Woodruff, D. S.: Biofeedback—Implications for gerontology. Paper presented at the 24th Annual Meeting of the Gerontological Society, Houston, October, 1971.

———— and Birren, J. E.: Age changes and cohort differences in personality. *Dev Psychol, 6*:252-259, 1972.

Chapter XI

RELEVANCE OF RESEARCH TO WORK WITH THE AGED

Lissy F. Jarvik and Donna Cohen

The fact is that when I come to think it over, I find that there are four reasons for old age being thought unhappy: First, that it withdraws us from active employment; second, that it enfeebles the body; third, that it deprives us of nearly all physical pleasure; fourth, that it is the next step to death.

Cicero, *On Old Age*

RESEARCH HAS BEEN defined as "a style of thought which emphasizes the importance of reliable information as a basis for action, critical evaluation of alternative ideas, and concern about the consequences of applied knowledge." (1971 White House Conference on Aging, Research and Demonstration, Washington, D. C., March, 1971, p. 1). For lack of adequate research, professionals in the field of gerontology have had to contend too often with unreliable information as a basis for action. Personal convictions and unproven inferences, attractively packaged and subjected to salesmanship by special interest groups, have been substituted for critical evaluation of alternative ideas. Though concerned about the consequences of applied knowledge, professionals have had practically no guidance in assessing the relative worth of their varied activities designed to aid the aged, because research efforts in the field of gerontology have been woefully inadequate. Indeed, gerontology could profit as much as molecular biology and physics did by mapping out questions and systematically testing multiple hypotheses. (Platt, 1964).

Less than a fraction of one percent of the annual expenditure for various programs related to the health and welfare of older people has been appropriated for research. In industry, allocation of three to five percent of operating budgets to fundamental and applied research is common. As a result, research in gerontology has been very limited and much of our information stems from the efforts of investigators working in areas peripheral to gerontology who have been supported by their parent disciplines rather than by funds earmarked for research in aging.

Research efforts have been concentrated largely in psychology, biology, and sociology. Since sociological research will be discussed in other portions of this book, the present chapter will concern itself primarily with research in biology and psychology as such may be of interest to the professional in gerontology. To facilitate discussion, the mental and physical aspects of aging will be taken up separately. Even though the distinction is artificial, there is an advantage in the clarity provided by adopting the old-fashioned dichotomy.

RESEARCH FINDINGS—WHAT ARE THEY?

Mental Changes

Perhaps the most important changes which occur with advancing age are those affecting the thinking and feeling of older individuals. The reported intellectual and emotional changes are responsible to a certain extent for the general reluctance to employ the elderly. The stereotype of impaired intellectual functioning, memory loss, and poor judgement helps contribute to the negative attitude towards aging and older people.

The mental changes commonly believed to characterize the elderly fall into several categories: (1) There are intellectual changes in the sense that older people are no longer as "sharp" or "quick-witted" as they were in their youth. (2) The difficulty in learning new material, which seems to mount as age increases, is exemplified by the ease with which children acquire a new language, and the comparative ineptness of adults. (3) The memory loss which occurs with advancing age is notorious, the classical example being the older person who fails to recall in the evening what he ate for breakfast that morning. Whereas intellectual deficit in terms of new learning can be masked and compensated for without detriment to routine activities, the memory impairment, when it becomes severe enough, interferes with everyday functions. Forgetting the contents of a shopping list, misplacing important papers and other items, or, going beyond that, losing one's way, eventually become incompatible with independent existence. It is this third category of malignant debilities—memory loss—which brings so many elderly persons into institutional settings, often after their forgetfulness has resulted in accidents or near-accidents because of failure to turn off gas stoves, cooking with plasticware, or wandering off. (4) There are also the personality attributes usually ascribed to the aged—rigidity, reluctance to accept new ideas or try novel approaches to a problem, increasing dependence, and life style changes.

Finally, we have the mental disturbances—psychoneurosis, alcoholism, character disorders, functional disorders (especially depression), and the various brain syndromes. A person over the age of 65 years admitted to a mental hospital is most likely to have symptoms of a brain syndrome—exhibiting confusion; loss of orientation in time, place, and person; withdrawal and emotional outbreaks; and paranoid ideation. Senility, however, is not the equivalent of senescence; it refers to the slow or rapid decline of body and behavior in a disease process. A majority of the aged never show symptoms of senility. It is important to emphasize that aging is part of the developmental continuum and does not imply pathology. Indeed, many of the changes have been related to diseases which occur in the upper age groups, rather than to advancing age *per se*.

The mental disturbances affecting the aged represent a major responsibility that we have been neglecting as a society. Approximately five percent of the elderly are institutionalized and this is probably an indication of availability rather than need (Simon, 1971). Although we can expect a greater proportion of older people to need physical and mental health care, it is necessary to devise and implement alternatives to institutionalization.

At the moment, the older patient either receives no psychiatric care at all or is institutionalized, as shown by the epidemiological data of Kramer and his co-workers (1973). Their data further reveal that 15-25 percent of the older people living in the community have mild to severe psychiatric problems.

What, if anything, has research contributed to help us understand and deal with these numerous and far from simple problems? First, to the issue of intellectual decline.

Changes in Intellectual Performance with Advancing Age

The stereotype of increasing age being invariably associated with intellectual decline is gradually being refuted by results of longitudinal research. True, if we look at people of different ages, we find that, in general, the younger the age group, the higher tend to be the scores on intelligence tests. However, these differences appear to be due in large part to differences between the age groups (cohort differences) in educational background; access to information such as that provided by radio, television, and other channels of communication; and general living conditions. The importance of intergenerational differences in intelligence (Nesselroade, Schaie, and Baltes, 1972; Schaie, 1970; Schaie and Strother, 1968) and personality (Woodruff and Birren, 1973) far exceeds that of individual differences dependent upon ages. In longitudinal studies, where the same individuals are followed over a number of years, the general trend has been stability rather than decline in intellectual functioning, at least up to the age of 75 years, despite marked differences in testing methods and subjects (age, intelligence, education, and socioeconomic background).

In 1961 Kleemeier, in his presidential address to Division 20 of the American Psychological Association, reported his observations in Moosehaven (a retirement home) which led him to conclude that a drop in I.Q. signalled the "imminence of death." (Kleemeier, 1962). Much work has supported his observation. Cognitive decline on tests devoid of a speed component may be indicative of a disease process, and such a decline shows a positive relationship with mortality (Baltes, Schaie, and Nardi, 1971;

Jarvik, Kallmann, Falek, and Klaber, 1957; Riegel, 1969, Riegel and Riegel, 1971; Riegel, Riegel, and Meyer, 1967, 1968). Stability rather than decline has characterized the healthy, non-institutionalized groups examined by Eisdorfer (1963) and Granick and Birren (1969), extending the original findings of Bayley and Oden (1955) and Owens (1953), of gains rather than losses through the middle and late decades. For example, Granick and Birren retested 23 survivors in 1968 of 47 healthy men who in 1956 ranged in age from 65-92 years. Stability was observed on all test scores with no significant decline on any subtest of the Wechsler Adult Intelligence Scale (WAIS) or the Raven Progressive Matrices (RPM), which led them to support the statement that cognitive decline, in the absence of illness, is not a necessary concomitant of later maturity.

The longitudinal study of Eisdorfer and his colleagues at Duke University has thus far completed data analysis for the first 10-year period in which four examinations were given at two- to three-year intervals. Each evaluation consisted of physical, psychiatric, psychological, and sociological examinations. Of the original 224 subjects tested in the 60-79 age range, 98 completed all four exams. The results from the cognitive battery indicate that the overall intellectual level of the subjects was partially correlated with survival (Eisdorfer and Wilkie (1973). Wilkie and Eisdorfer (1971) also have shown a decline in I.Q. among hypertensives age 60-69, followed for 10 years, while mildly hypertensives and normotensives did not show a similar decline.

Our own group at the New York State Psychiatric Institute has been carrying out follow-up investigations on survivors of an original sample of 268 twin subjects over the age of 65 years. The test battery covered medical and social aspects, and the psychological instruments were limited to five subtests of the Wechsler-Bellevue, a Tapping Test, and the Vocabulary List I of the Stanford-Binet. Three tests—Vocabulary, Similarities, and Digit Symbol Substitution—when used to test "Critical Loss," emerged as potential discriminators of those people who would not survive for five years. As decline on timed motor tasks failed to distinguish survivors and decedents, it is probable that the usual decline in speed is a general concomitant of aging, while "Critical

Loss' correlates more specifically with brain changes indicative of impending mortality (Jarvik and Blum, 1971).

An interesting controversy surrounds the question of differential decline of intellectual functioning with different ability levels. Baltes, Schaie, and Nardi (1971) have explored age-related mortality in a seven-year longitudinal effort with 500 persons, age 21-70 years. The test battery included the Thurstone Primary Abilities Test (PMA), allowing the derivation of several second-order factors, and Schaie's Test of Behavioral Rigidity. Results indicated that those people who could be retested after seven years, on the average, scored higher on general intelligence, cognitive flexibility (reasoning), and visuomotor flexibility, than did those who could not be retested (usually because of illness or death). There was no significant interaction between age and sex with retest participation.

Most longitudinal studies span the middle and late decades of life. However, the Institute of Human Development studies tap the early years and include two projects—the Berkeley Growth Study and the Oakland Study. While they differ in the age of the subject at initial testing—the Berkeley testing began between 12 and 21 months and the Oakland Study began at 10½ years—both cover an adult age span of about 20 years. Those in the Berkeley Growth Study were administered the Wechsler-Bellevue at 16, 18, 21, and 26 years, and the WAIS at age 36 years. Eichorn (1973) reports that the overall trend is an increase in scores from 16-26 at a decelerating rate for the men, and a slight decline for the women after 26. Men made much greater gains on all subtests, but the women started at a higher level on all subtests except arithmetic, and yet showed a gain at least through 26 years. The result is approximately equal means for the two sexes at age 36 years. Since no tests of significance are available, the differences between the sexes cannot be evaluated at this time.

Until recently, most longitudinal studies were concerned with a description of intellectual performance over time. Lately, however, some investigators have been able to look at personality variables in relation to mental functions. Thus, Honzik and Macfarlane (1973) examined subjects from the Berkeley Growth Study (infancy-40 years) in an effort to determine what personality factors can predict adult changes in intellectual functioning. The individuals with high I.Q.'s exhibited a tendency to be self-critical, introspective, to cope adequately, and to manifest little interest in others. The role of these personality factors in accelerating or retarding cognitive decline with advancing age awaits further research.

Sex differences have been largely neglected. Among the few reports are those of a twenty-year follow-up of aging twins. (Blum, 1969; Blum, Jarvik and Clark, 1970; Blum, Fossage, and Jarvik, (1972). The initial mean scores for women on a large battery of tests were all higher than those for men, except on two subtests of the Wechsler-Bellevue (Digits Forward and Digits Backward). However, there was a statistically significant difference on only two subtests—Tapping and Digit-Symbol Substitution. When scores were examined on the twenty-year retest, women again scored higher on all subtests. This time, four tests showed statistically significant differences—Tapping, Digit Symbol Substitution, Vocabulary, and Similarities. When annual rates of decline were computed for the twenty-year follow-up, men declined more rapidly than women on all tests except Digits Backward (Blum, Fossage, and Jarvik, 1972).

As previously mentioned, sex differences were also noted by Honzik and Macfarlane in intellectual performance between childhood and adulthood (up to age 36 years). Most studies of intellectual functioning, even in young persons, assessed the performance of both sexes as a group, and did not show significant differences between men and women (Blum, Fossage, and Jarvik, 1972). Differences do emerge when specific abilities are examined. Men are superior in spatial and arithmetic abilities, whereas women are generally superior in tasks with a high verbal loading. There is some indication that these differences persist with the observation of a continued discrepancy in the later years of arithmetic (Doppelt and Wallace, 1955) and verbal skills. (Feingold, 1950; Schaie and Strother, 1968; Young, 1971).

Rhudick and Gordon (1973) examined 83 healthy white collar and semi-professional workers in New England, age 64-94 years, at different intervals, using a variety of tests (WAIS, Minnesota Multiphasic Personality Inventory—MMPI, the Cornell

Medical Index, and the Leary Interpersonal Checklist). Raw scores indicated a slight gain on verbal, performance, and total WAIS scores during an eight-year period. Forty-three subjects declined and forty improved; women were more likely to improve than men. When the decliners and improvers were compared on personality variables measured by the Leary Interpersonal Checklist and the MMPI, the decliners seemed to be experiencing interpersonal difficulties and perceived themselves as more paranoid, dependent, and more aware of body discomfort.

Finally, Schaie and Strother (1968) report cognitive and personality data on twenty-five men and twenty-five women, age 70-88 years, recruited from a population of retired university professors. The subjects were examined with a psychological battery, a social history questionnaire, and a medical examination. The psychological battery included the Thurstone Primary Mental Abilities Test, Wechsler Memory Scale, the Symbol-Gestalt Test, the Edwards Personality Preference Schedule, and a Test of Behavioral Rigidity. Their subjects functioned well above the level of the average seventeen-year-old on verbal and numerical tasks. Overall, there was a deficit in this exceptional group's ability to reproduce visual figures, and decrements were most obvious in functions requiring visuo-motor coordination and speed. A significant decrement was observed on space and reasoning scores. There was also a sex difference—men showed a greater decrement on verbal meaning and reasoning, but scored significantly higher on spatial orientation scores. No sex differences were found on Wechsler Memory Scale scores.

In summary, the major findings with regard to intellectual functioning in the aged are as follows:

1. In the absence of disease, particularly cardiovascular and cerebrovascular diseases, abilities are maintained into the eighth decade of life. On those tests not involving a speed component there may even be an increase in test scores during late adulthood and senescence. In that sense, the intellectual decline of the aged is a myth—unless, perhaps, we get into the uppermost age groups (the ninth decade of life and beyond). In the healthy person, then, such decline is *not* characteristic of aging. It behooves us, therefore, to attempt to detect, as early as possible,

signs of illness in aging individuals. We must do so not only to prevent the physical consequences of cardiovascular disease, but, more important, to try and prevent the cognitive deterioration which seems to ensue from interference with adequate blood supply. Indeed, the physical aspects can often be managed much more easily than can the intellectual decline resulting from a specific illness. Mental changes, moreover, may be exquisitely sensitive indicators of underlying cerebrovascular dysfunction (Wilkie and Eisdorfer, 1971), and monitoring of intellectual performance may provide us with a clue that a compromise of the circulation is occurring before any other changes have become apparent. In terms of practical applicability, therefore, periodic follow-up of the cognitive acumen is indicated.

2. On tasks involving a speeded motor component there seems to be a decline, at least for most people, as they grow older. This decline does *not* appear to be associated with disease and reflects the general slowing of the aged. Theoretically, there are two approaches to handling the gradual, general slowdown. One of them is to try and correct its antecedents, the second, to compensate for its defects. Unfortunately, we do not have sufficient knowledge as to the underlying conditions responsible for the gradual slowing, intellectually as well as physically, which occurs with advancing age. We do know, however, that it is possible to compensate for this general slowing. Thus, a number of learning experiments, by allowing sufficient time during phases of learning, have demonstrated that, when conditions are suitably adapted to the aging organism, more information than previously thought possible is acquired by aging persons.

In practical terms, then, work, recreational, and social situations can be so redesigned and restructured to de-emphasize the speed element and to make it possible for the elderly persons to effectively learn new material, and, under such circumstances, make contributions that may rival, in adequacy, those of many younger individuals. These considerations and others would be important in continuing work and education over the lifespan. Given that the older person seems to be mainly troubled by pacing in the acquisition of new learning, and, given the acceleration of events and information in our age, it will be important to explore ways of assisting the coping processes of the older person.

Changes in Learning Ability with Advancing Age

In the usual learning experiments, the elderly clearly display a deficit when compared to younger persons, making as many errors of commission as the younger cohort, but exceeding them in errors of omission (Arenberg, 1965, 1967a, 1967b; Canestrari, 1963; Eisdorfer, 1965). The general impairment observed is again most pronounced in terms of pacing; the older person needs time to respond.

There is an increasing literature to suggest that attempts to control interference generally result in improved learning scores. Some examples are: clearer instructions, adequate pacing, reinforcement of rapid responses (Hoyer, Labouvie, and Baltes, 1971), and pharmacologic manipulation of autonomic responses (Eisdorfer, in press; Eisdorfer, Nowlin, and Wilkie, 1971).

Information on the problem-solving abilities of older persons is scarce. According to Wetherick, "failure to solve problems by the old is not attributable to the fact that they are rigid and hold onto beliefs without evidence. Rather, it is the other way around; due to an inability to handle disconfirming information, some old people cannot modify previous beliefs and continue to behave as if the negative evidence does not exist (Arenberg, 1973, p. 93)." It is tempting to speculate that the exposure to new and repeated experiences with the passage of time would enable the older person to bring a better perspective to problem-solving than that of younger individuals. However, much work still needs to be done to explore changes in concept-formation, strategy behavior, and decision-making with aging. With increasing age there seems to be an impairment of both analysis and synthesis (obtaining information and processing information).

In evaluating the results of learning studies, the well-known decline in sensory and perceptual functioning has to be taken into account. There are the non-neural changes interfering with vision, hearing, taste, smell, and touch. Many of these can be offset, at least to some extent, by increasing the intensity of the stimulus, but in view of wide individual differences in the degree of debility ensuing from these changes, adequate allowance has to be made in each case. More important than the non-neural changes are the neural ones, and these seem to vary across modalities. Thus, the older person seems to acquire auditory stimuli with greater ease than visual material, so that in practical terms every attempt should be made to supplement visual with auditory stimuli. Since older persons also need more time to recover from input (Eisdorfer and Axelrod, 1964), a longer interval is required between stimuli than for younger persons. Moreover, with increasing age there seems to be increasing difficulty in handling irrelevant stimuli (Rabbitt, 1965). Therefore, the number of stimuli to be presented at any one time, as well as their complexity, should be limited.

Changes in Memory with Advancing Age

There is the stereotype of forgetfulness as characteristic of old age as absent-mindedness is of professors, and yet, there are numerous exceptions to both generalizations. It is conceptually useful to regard memory as a time-related coding and storage process, proceeding from the time of registration forward through immediate, short-term, intermediate, and long-term storage intervals. There seems to be general agreement regarding a decline in short-term memory with aging, but the result of investigations dealing with intermediate and long-term memory are conflicting in the healthy older person. Arenberg (1973) states that the immediate memory does *not* decline, if immediate memory is operationally defined by performance on digit span, letter span, or word span tests. However, if immediate memory has a lengthy span (for example, in lists longer than seven words) recall does decrease with increasing age.

If a two-storage memory model is adopted, as has been done by Craik (1968), then, it may be said that primary storage—in which memories are subject to rapid decay and interference—does not seem to differ between age groups. Specifically, registration into primary storage does not show a deficit, according to evidence derived from dichotic stimulation experiments. By contrast, secondary storage—where interference and decay may play a minor role—seems to deteriorate with aging due either to failure in registration (into the secondary storage) or to less effective search for material to be retrieved from secondary storage. The deterioration in secondary storage is explained by both the assumption that the elderly are more subject to decay and more susceptible to interference (Arenberg, 1973).

As is true of research in learning, so it is with regard to memory, that we are handicapped by ignorance concerning biological mechanisms which underlie the formation and retention of memory. Among the first tasks is the investigation of how information is acquired and registered; only thereafter can retention and retrieval of information be logically explored. It is for this reason that whatever work on memory has been done has been largely concerned with immediate and short-term memory. Even here, we are not certain of the roles played by (1) nucleic acids as either contributing indirectly to malfunctioning or directly to the coding and processing in learning and memory; (2) molecular coding in the DNA-RNA matrix; and (3) alterations of proteins and lipids, regardless of age.

Changes in Personality with Advancing Age

The area of personality changes associated with aging is a poorly developed one. While Riegel's review (1959) still remains a good summary of personality theories and aging, Neugarten (1973) has recently published an excellent assessment of our limited data and theories of personality change. She admirably supports the notion that the area of personality is not limited when the emphasis is shifted to the field of aging. Much work is necessary to evaluate the social, psychological and biological events contributing to development throughout the life cycle "to investigate whether or not there are orderly and irreversible changes related to age that are significant in accounting for differences between adults (Neugarten, 1973, p. 318)."

Chown (1968) has compiled a valuable review of personality assessment by inventories and questionnaires, by life styles and activity patterns, and by coping strategies. At a recent International Conference on Social Gerontology held in Washington, D.C. (December 1971), Chown cautioned that, if we consider various dimensions of personality, "the quality of the dimension may differ between youth and age." Those factors contributing to a certain personality dimension in a younger cohort may or may not be identical with those contributing to that same dimension in an older cohort. For example, the passive or aggressive behavior displayed in early adulthood may be precipitated by competition with siblings and peers as well as rebellion against a dependence on parents. Some of these same factors, as well as different ones, for example, reactions to developmental crises, may contribute to aggressiveness exhibited in later years.

Marked personality changes with aging have not been substantiated with data. Perhaps the most commonly reported finding is a slight increase in introversion (Heron and Chown, 1967; Sealy and Cattell, 1965), and this dimension has been assessed only by written inventories heavily weighted with social items (Chown, 1972).

Birren and Woodruff (1973) pointed out that the results of accumulating longitudinal studies of personality differ from cross-sectional studies. For example, where data from the latter suggest increasing conservatism with aging, the longitudinal studies by Nelson (1954) and Plant (1965) both refute that notion.

There are not sufficient data to determine whether, as is commonly believed, older people are more rigid and reluctant to undertake new experiences (attitudinal rigidity) than younger persons. However, there is a component of rigidity—behavioral rigidity—which has been assessed in a longitudinal study of intellectual and personality variables (Schaie and Strother, 1968); the results suggest a loss of flexibility in that component after middle adulthood.

Rigidity is neither a simple nor a single concept. Schaie defines three kinds of rigidity; Chown, six; and Baer, eleven (Chown, 1968). Although Schaie (1958), Chown (1960), and Riegel and Riegel (1960) all report an increase in rigidity with age it is difficult to relate this phenomenon to the dynamic situation of everyday life.

We can define learning as a process of building up a storehouse of concepts and skills to solve problems, and personality as a second construct modulating the ability to solve problems.

We need to look at these constructs and to describe the relevant variables—intelligence, learning, memory, and personality—as a control system operating to direct behavior.

There is a growing literature associating behavior patterns, in the middle and later years of life, with the occurrence of disease (e.g., cancer, cardiovascular diseases). Underlying this line of reasoning is the hypothesis that certain illnesses, such as coronary heart disease, are related to chronic biologic stress mediated by personality patterns. Friedman and his associates (Friedman, 1969; Friedman, Rosenman, Straus, Wurm, and Kositchek, 1968; Rosenman, 1968; Rosenman, Friedman, Straus, Jenkins, Zyzanski, and Wurm, 1970) have specified coronary-prone (Type A) and non-coronary prone (Type B) individuals, who display differential incidence of cardiovascular disease and differential mortality rates in prospective research studies. Pattern A behavior is designated: "A characteristic action-emotion complex which is exhibited by those individuals who are engaged in a relatively chronic struggle to obtain a number of poorly defined things from their environment in the shortest period of time, and if necessary, against the opposing efforts of other things or persons in this same environment. This struggle has been encouraged by the contemporary Western environment because, unlike any previously known milieu, it appears to offer certain rewards and opportunities to those who can think, perform, communicate, move, live, and even play more rapidly and aggressively than their fellow men (Friedman, 1969)."

If confirmed, this avenue of research opens the possibility of isolating behavioral predictors of disease as well as the probability of preventing the occurrence of disease by hopefully repatterning personality and modifying behavior.

Changes in Mental Health with Advancing Age

Eisdorfer (1972) recently summarized a valuable perspective on mental health in the aged at an International Conference on Social Gerontology. Changes in mobility, health, and work status in a Western technological era lead older people to a dependency that is not easily tolerated by the young nor by the rest of society. Older people, in fact, become alienated and actively segregated from the society when they are retired or ill, because there are no expectations for maintaining the usefulness and dignity of either the healthy or sick older person. It is quite clear that the aged are a high-risk group for behavioral change accompanying chronic illness and social deprivation. Retirement, with pensions and/or social security lower than work income, ultimately forces the person to lose status and become downwardly mobile, and this is viewed disdainfully by an achievement-oriented society. For example, Eisdorfer suggests that becoming poor is in some ways worse than always having been poor, because this can be interpreted as a deep personal failure, resulting in lowered feelings of self-worth.

In the area of mental health we know little regarding the environmental and biological influences of maladaptation, the etiology of various disorders, and life-cycle personality development in the social structure. Older people are, however, vulnerable to innumerable stresses—physico-chemical, psychological, and social. Lowenthal and her colleagues (1967), have indicated that the cumulative effects of stress may lead to a breakdown in persons where none would have been predicted. These stresses include those due to illness and declining physical capacity, isolation and loneliness, bereavement, socioeconomic loss, and developmental crises. Involuntary changes in living patterns, including moves from home to an institution, between institutions, and relocations in the community to meet the demands of urban renewal, may even precipitate death.

Bereavement has severe consequences for the older person. Grief is a normal reaction to the death of a spouse or other intimates, but it disrupts interpersonal relationships. Stein, Williams, and Prada (1951) found different grief reactions in older people; such grief reactions appeared mainly as somatic illness. A high percentage of widows and widowers seen by private physicians have somatic symptoms (Kübler-Ross, 1969), and the proportion of patients developing a mental disorder within six months of the death of a spouse is greater than would be expected by chance (Parker, 1964a, 1964b). The death rates among widows and widowers are also much higher than for married persons of the same age (Kraus and Lilienfeld, 1959). Birren (1964) comments on the possible impact of bereavement (pp. 236-237):

> The death rates in young widows from cardiovascular disease is especially interesting and important, for it suggests that the consequences of bereavement and widowhood are such as to impose, over time, a disease pattern on the individual that would otherwise be most uncommon in an age and sex group.

Any attempt to assess the frequency of mental illness is complex, both because of our lack of basic knowledge and because many of the data we have come from mental hospitals, which represents a small, biased sample population. Simon (1971) indicates that in 1969 there were 120,000 persons 65 years and over in a total U. S. mental hospital population of approximately 400,000. Accurate and complete data regarding the incidence and prevalence of mental disorders are simply not available, since many of the elderly do not obtain satisfactory health care. The older person in rural areas may not have the mobility nor the motivation to visit a community mental health center. Lowenthal and her associates (1967) have estimated that more than three million older people living in the community suffer from moderate to severe psychiatric impairment and, yet, they may function adequately.

Most of the aged never display indications of organic brain syndrome (OBS), more commonly referred to as senility, consisting of disorientation, confusion, and memory loss. The memory deficiency may be either benign or malignant (Kral, 1970), where benign indicates a mild memory loss with little, if any, impairment of social intelligence; and malignant memory loss suggests deterioration in the ability to adjust and probable death within a few years.

Physical health is perhaps the most critical factor in the consideration of mental health. Simon (1971) cites that up to eighty percent of all older persons in urban psychiatric wards have a physical illness of some kind. Community residents, by contrast, are physically healthier and function better than institutionalized persons despite similar psychiatric disturbances.

Among mental health problems of the elderly, suicide is prominent. Indeed, white, divorced men over the age of sixty, with a tendency towards alcoholism and depression, face the highest risk of suicide. Successful attempts are more common in older than younger age groups and the methods include hanging, shooting, and drowning—all violent ways.

Physical Changes

Decline in Functioning with Advancing Age

Enfeeblement is so characteristic that it is nearly synonymous with old age. Aside from such notable exceptions as Pablo Casals —who at the age of 96 still gave concerts and conducted summer festivals—and Pablo Picasso—who until his death at 89 maintained a level of productivity envied by many a younger person— older individuals are both weaker and slower than their younger cohorts. In general physiological capacities decrease linearly and death rates rise exponentially with increasing chronological age. However, it is important to consider that aging rates are not irreversibly fixed. Whether physical deterioration is a constant and inevitable concomitant of old age remains a moot question, but it is known that there are marked individual differences in the onset, degree, and rate of decline. If certain exogenous influences should turn out to be key determinants in the regulation of nervous, hormonal, and muscular activity, then it should be possible to modify life-styles during the earlier years so as to optimize functioning in the later years (Jarvik and Cohen, 1973). For example, DeVries' (1970) data suggest that exercise can compensate for some age changes, and DiCarlo's findings (1972) point to the importance of an active life style—including mental as well as physical pursuits—for the maintenance of functioning in old age.

Among attempts being made to find ways of diminishing or retarding age-associated declines is the exploitation of biofeedback techniques for manipulating physiological variables (heart rate, blood pressure, vasoconstriction, and electrical activity of the brain). Training old and young people to produce physiologic changes at will may not only yield valuable information on the relation between physiology and behavior, but also may offer means of controlling such undesirable somatic changes as hypertension. In aging research, exercise, genetics, nutrition, and other factors have been confounded (Thompson and Botwinick, 1965).

Changes in Bodily Systems with Advancing Age

Age-related changes may be due to selective changes in the genome (hereditary components) as well as to changes in cell responses to other environmental factors. It remains to be elucidated how exogenous and endogenous events affect homeostasis and effect the death of the organism. We can say little about biochemical changes in DNA, RNA, and proteins with aging, because the results so far reported are fragmentary and contradictory. Medvedev (1967) has emphasized that contradictions should be expected in living systems which contain numerous enzyme and structural protein systems, each liable to show many variations. Structural proteins—collagen and elastin—show definite changes with aging, while other proteins—enzymes, globulins, histones, and albumins—show no clear pattern of alteration. Ideally, we should chart a profile of changes across tissues. Bellamy (1969) is among those who have argued that each tissue may age differently and should be studied separately and systematically.

The gradual loss of non-dividing or slowly dividing cells, although unequal across tissues, is one of the most widely accepted age changes. This loss is most noticeable in the brain, skeletal muscle, and kidney, and is commonly assumed to be responsible for a decrease in muscular strength, altered homeostasis, and mental impairment. Other changes include a general decrease in organ weight, an increasing diversity of cell size and arrangement, and the intracellular accumulation of various substances, including age pigments. The latter have been interpreted as lesions or waste products which might interfere with cellular activity, but the evidence is still unconvincing.

There are changes in every organ system, from demineralization of the skeleton to a series of possible alterations of the respiratory, cardiovascular, nervous, integumental, gastrointestinal, excretory, and urogenital systems. For example, the most striking changes in the nervous system are neuronal atrophy, pigment accumulation, decreased brain weight, and possibly unequal neural loss accompanied by glial proliferation.

Increase in Susceptibility to Illness with Advancing Age

The increased susceptibility to illness of the aged is astounding. In the United States, eighty percent of persons over the age of 65 years have one or more serious diseases. They suffer from "the very chronic diseases upon which this nation has focused its attention in an attempt to abort or lessen their impact. 1971 White House Conference on Aging, Research and Demonstration, Washington, D. C., March 1971, p. 23)." The cooperative program to combat heart attacks and strokes reflects the vast toll taken by cardiovascular disease, particularly among the aged. Osteoporosis (thinning of the bones) is a major cause of morbidity among the aged—who does not know an elderly lady who, as a result of a fractured hip, has become immobilized and rapidly deteriorated not only physically but mentally? And cancer, the major health problem of our time, as witnessed by the special institute created in 1971, affects a disproportionate number of elderly. These are but a few of the many examples that could be cited illustrating how readily the elderly succumb to disease. Indeed, the old question as to whether there exists an aging process independent of increased susceptibility to illness is still unanswered.

Regardless of the ultimate answer to that question, we know that a series of events occur over time, any set of which may culminate in the enfeeblement and ultimate demise of the individual. Postulated causes of decompensation in the elderly include genetic direction, electrolyte imbalance, cardiovascular and pulmonary insufficiency, infection and malnutrition, to mention only a few.

Although among the aged the prevalence of chronic diseases is high, this does not imply that growing old inevitably implies ill health. The unfortunate statistic citing eighty percent of all Americans over 65 years as suffering from one or more chronic diseases is the result of numerous factors: inadequate nutrition, inability of many older people to pay for health care, poorly distributed health care and service facilities (including preventive medicine facilities, out-patient services, and long-term care in an institution), professional and societal attitudes towards geriatric illness and care, the difficulties of translating research data for professionals, and the lack of basic understanding of most diseases.

Genetic Aspects

Longevity and Intelligence

Three basic methods have been used to investigate the genetics of the lifespan: pedigrees (family histories), demographic surveys, and twin studies (Jarvik, 1971). Although pedigrees, being derived from retrospective data, are restricted in their usefulness, they can establish sex-linkage, pleiotropism (the role of a single gene in the expression of several traits), and the mode of inheritance of various characteristics. Both Cohen (1964) and Jarvik (1971) emphasized the limitations of this approach when attempting to parcel out the hereditary components of longevity and the higher mental processes, since both probably represent the effects of several genes. However, it was from data collected by the pedigree method that the initial hypothesis of the inheritance of longevity evolved.

Population surveys, based on actuarial and census methods, yield data on vital statistics, hospital admissions, and mortality rates. This avenue has provided the information on the differential survival rates between the sexes. Furthermore, in every species, the female, on the average outlives the male. It has been postulated that the second X chromosome, which the human female possesses and not the human male, may be critical in determining her lower mortality. Sex-linked diseases (hemophilia, for example) provide the model according to which the effects of detrimental genes found on one X chromosome are neutralized by the activity of "normal" genes on the other X chromosome, in women but not in men.

Lastly, comparisons of monozygotic (one-egg twins theoretically assess the effect of environmental variation on a constant genotype, and comparison of dizygotic twin studies provides clues to the genetic-environmental interplay. When studying the genetics of behavior, or any other variable, one needs to consider that genotypic differences express themselves in many alternative ways depending upon the environment.

The twin study approach has been used to evaluate the heredity of longevity and intelligence. The work of Kallmann and his colleagues (Jarvik, Falek, Kallmann, and Lorge, 1960; Kallmann, 1953) showed that the mean intra-pair differences between lifespans of the same sex dizygotic twin partners were greater than those between monozygotic twins. One-egg twins generally died within five years of each other, although, on occasion, fifteen or more years elapsed.

Only a single group of researchers has explored cognitive abilities in the later years (Jarvik, Falek, Kallmann, and Lorge, 1960; Jarvik and Blum, 1971; Jarvik, Blum, and Varma, 1971), and they reported that genetic factors in intellectual performance appears to be manifest into the seventh and eighth decades. As early as 1950, intellectual functioning of monozygotic twins was shown to be significantly more similar than dizygotic twins in a variety of tests (Feingold, 1950).

Pathology

Although the hereditary determinants have been demonstrated in cardiovascular disease, neoplasms, organic brain syndrome, and various mental disorders, the genetic mechanisms remain generally unknown (Jarvik, 1971). The genetic aspects of mental illnesses have been especially neglected. In the rare brain atrophies—Alzheimer's, Jacob-Creutzfeld, and Pick's Disease —the analysis of pedigrees has provided conflicting information regarding their heritability. Much work is needed to clarify the etiology of these disorders.

Work is also scant on the genetic dimension of senile dementia, so that only the most general statements can be made. Further, arteriosclerotic dementias are difficult to differentiate from senile dementia, and we lack adequate information about non-genetic as well as genetic factors in both types of conditions (Zerbin-Rudin, 1967). There are no studies with good comparisons of the clinical, pathological, and genetic characteristics of the study populations. (Zerbin-Rudin, 1967). A dominant gene or several genes are more likely than a single recessive mode of inheritance. Kallmann (1953) was perhaps the first to suggest the polygenic control of senile dementia: "It may therefore be assumed that the genetic components in the etiology of the senile psychosis consist of polygenically determined variations in basic personality traits, potentialities of emotional adjustment to senescent decrepitudes, and general biological survival values (longevity)." He also showed that one-egg co-twins have the highest risk for concordance; two-egg twins showed significantly smaller concordance of senile psychosis than the one-egg twins.

Cytogenetics

Recent data indicate that, at least in women, the loss of one or more chromosomes occurs in a significant number of the cells examined from blood cultures of old persons (Hamerton, Taylor, Angell, and McGuire, 1965; Jacobs, Brunton, Court-Brown, Doll, Goldstein, 1963; Jacobs, Brunton, and Court-Brown, 1964; Court-Brown, Buckton, Jacobs, Tough, Kuenssberg, and Knox, 1966; Sandberg, Cohen, Rim, and Levin, 1967; Jarvik and Kato, 1970). The characteristic number of chromosomes (diploid) in each cell in humans is 46 (including the sex chromosomes), and they are divided into seven groups. Females appear to lose chromosomes within any of these groups (Neurath, DeRemer, Bell, Jarvik, and Kato, 1970). It has been postulated, although not satisfactorily demonstrated, that the X chromosome is more often lost in women and the Y chromosome lost in men.

The significance of this chromosome loss for brain-behavior relationships remains to be determined, since the only cell system studied has been peripheral leukocytes. If we assume that *any* rapidly-dividing system, such as glia in the brain, also display aneuploidy (cells with other than the diploid number of chromosomes), we may postulate that such chromosome loss affects the homeostatic balance of neural-glial relationships. Every white blood cell examined in an elderly female does not display an abnormal karyotype, but occasionally as many as one-third of them have been found to have lost one or more chromosomes (hypodiploid cells).

Two laboratories have reported a significant correlation of

memory deficits and hypodiploidy (Bettner, Jarvik, and Blum, 1971; Jarvik, Altschuler, Kato, and Blumner, 1971; Jarvik and Kato, 1969; Nielsen, 1968, 1970). Memory has been assessed by the Graham-Kendall Memory-for-Designs Test, the Stroop Color Word Test, and the psychiatric diagnosis of organic brain syndrome or senile dementia. Further work is needed to confirm the chromosome findings and to determine the cumulative effects of aneuploidy on specific dimensions of memory and senile dementia. It is possible that the correlation with memory loss may prove nonspecific, and such hypodiploidy may emerge as predictive of the disease condition of senile mental deterioration.

The association between hypodiploidy and cognitive changes may be a significant approach to explore the changing biological substrate of mental deterioration and mortality. Since a decline on specific intelligence subtests has been shown to predict death, chromosome monitoring may prove useful in determining whether hypodiploidy precedes, accompanies or follows mental changes (Jarvik and Cohen, 1972).

RESEARCH FINDINGS—HOW CAN THEY BE APPLIED?

The bio-decremental model has lent a bias to psychobiological and sociological investigations that has practically excluded a view of aging as an adaptive process. Indeed, the declining strength, mobility, energy, and stress tolerance of the body is unmistakable; behavior slows, some aspects of cognition are modified; depressive disorders increase; and vascular, immune, and stochastic alterations affect the health of the organism. However, despite these observations, the aging individual can still think, walk, talk, eat, sleep, write, dream, and love.

To date, the overwhelming impression from a review of the literature is a paucity of unequivocal findings. The studies have been relatively few and the results far from definitive. The relevance of some of the data is readily apparent, as, for example, the observation that healthy older persons generally show little decline in intellectual functioning if given sufficient time to perform the task in question. The need for adequate time in learning a new task, or integrating previous information, or responding to an altered situation, is a key element, and when sufficient time is provided, the performance of the elderly can be enhanced measurably. It may even be brought to the level at which many young persons function.

In working with the older person, therefore, it is desirable to adjust the pace of requirements. Further, it is important to avoid presenting too many stimuli at one time; the elderly seem less tolerant than the young to an overload of stimuli (finding it more difficult to ignore irrelevant stimuli), and frequently are unable to respond under such conditions. These guidelines, derived from research on intellectual activities, learning and memory are generally accepted but are only rarely applied in everyday settings.

The most important issue to be drawn from a review of research done to date is that we need careful evaluation of professional activities directed toward the aged. Too many of them are undertaken without solid evidence that they are of benefit to the recipient. It behooves us, therefore, to combine with each new project, with each service rendered to the aging population, and with each new program started for the elderly, a research design adequate to evaluate the results. With an acceptable scientific research design, it should become possible not only to provide immediately a higher level of service, but also to contribute eventually to the acquisition of knowledge in an area where it is sorely needed.

The quality of the society we will have by the 21st Century, with a projected forty-eight million people over the age of 65, will depend heavily on the research process which provides a data base for our social system. Research can be viewed as a social process, as pointed out by Maddox (1972), and there are different factors which affect which issues will be pursued. Knowledge gaps exist across all disciplines and the pursuit of complex problems such as the organization of the nervous system, the effect of illness on behavior, the maintenance of intellectual functioning, intervention with age groups and socialization into new work and leisure roles in the next century, will generate new questions. Researchers in aging and development today argue about the priority of narrowing gaps in basic sciences, planning and organizing health and other service roles, devising new methodologies, training manpower, and effecting social change. Here, individual desires and institutional structures are key influential forces.

The socio-political elements in the society generally dictate whether such areas as education, employment, health, housing, income maintenance, or transportation will receive financial support. It is important to realize the transactional nature of research; it is dependent on the interactions between gaps in basic knowledge, the inadequacy of current methodologies, advancing technology, evaluation of programs, and the whims of the socio-political climate (Maddox, 1972).

Simone de Beauvoir queries in her book *La Viellesse:* "What should a society be so that in old age a man remains a man?" This remarkably insightful question addresses our very expectations and attitudes towards both the healthy and ill aging populations. It is a mandate to develop an understanding of aging, to fund projects where we can apply research findings, and to maintain the dignity of human life.

BIBLIOGRAPHY

Arenberg, D.: Changes in memory with age. In Eisdorfer, C., and Lawton, M. P. (Eds.): The psychology of adult development and aging. Washington, D.C. *American Psychological Association,* 1973.

————: Anticipation interval and age differences in verbal learning. *J Abnorm Psychol, 70:*419-425, 1965.

————: Age differences in retroaction. *J Gerontol, 22:*180-184, 1967.

————: Regression analysis of verbal learning on adult age at two anticipation intervals, *22:*411-414, 1967.

Baltes, P. B., Schaie, W. K., and Nardi, A. H.: Age and experimental mortality in a seven-year longitudinal study of cognitive behavior. *Dev Psychol, 5:*18-26, 1971.

Bayley, N. and Oden, M. H.: The maintenance of intellectual ability in gifted adults. *J Gerontol, 10:*91-107, 1955.

Bellamy, D.: Aging and endocrine responses to environmental factors: With particular reference to mammals. *Hormones and the Environment.* Cambridge, The University Press, 1970.

Bettner, L. G., Jarvik, L. F., and Blum, J. E.: Stroop color word test, non-psychotic organic brain syndrome and chromosome loss in aged twins. *J Gerontol, 26:*458-469, 1971.

Birren, J. E.: *The Psychology of Aging.* Englewood Cliffs, New Jersey, Prentice-Hall, 1964.

———— and Woodruff, D. S.: Academic and professional training in the psychology of aging. In Eisdorfer, C., and Lawton, M. (Eds.):

The psychology of adult development and aging. Washington, D.C. *American Psychological Association,* 1973.

Blum, J. E.: *Psychological Changes Between the Seventh and Ninth Decades of Life.* Doctoral Diss., St. Johns University, N. Y., 1969.

————, Jarvik, L., and Clark, E.: Rates of change on selective tests of intelligence: A longitudinal study of aging. *J of Geron, 25*: 171-176, 1970.

————, Fossage, J. L. and Jarvik, L. F.: Intellectual changes and sex differences in octogenarians: A twenty-year longitudinal study of aging twins. *Dev Psychol,* 1972.

Botwinick, J. and Thompson, L. W.: Individual differences in reaction time in relation to age. *J Genet Psychol, 112*:73-75, 1968.

Canestrari, R. E.: Paced and self-paced learning in young and elderly adults, *J Gerontol, 18*:165-168, 1963.

Chown, S. M.: A factor analysis of the Wesley rigidity inventory: Its relationship to age and nonverbal intelligence. *J Abnorm Soc Psychol, 61*:491-494, 1960.

————: Personality and Aging. In Schaie, K. W. (Ed.): *Theory and Methods of Research on Aging.* Morgantown, West Virginia, University Press, 1968.

————: In International research and education in social gerontology: goals and strategies, *Gerontologist, 12,* 1972.

Cohen, B. H.: Family patterns of mortality and lifespan. *Q Rev Biol, 39*:130-181, 1964.

Court-Brown, W. M., Buckton, K. E., Jacobs, P. A., Tough, I. M., Kuenssberg, E. V., and Knox, J. D. E.: *Chromosome Studies on Adults.* Cambridge, The University Press, 1966.

Craik, F. I. M.: Short-term memory and the aging process. In Talland, G. A. (Ed.): *Human Aging and Behavior.* New York, Academic Press, 1968.

Di Carlo, T. J.: *Recreation, Participation Patterns, and Successful Aging.* Doctoral Diss. Teachers College, Columbia University, 1971.

DeVries, H. A.: Physiological effects of an exercise training regimen upon men aged 52-88. *J Gerontol, 25*:325-336, 1970.

Doppelt, J. E. and Wallace, W. L.: Standardization of the Wechsler Adult Intelligence Scale for older persons. *J Abnorm Soc Psychol, 51*:312-330, 1955.

Eichorn, D. H.: The Institute of Human Development studies. In Jarvik, L. F., Eisdorfer, C. and Blum, J. E. (Eds.): *Intellectual Functioning in Adults: Some Psychological and Biological Influences.* New York, Springer Publishing Company, 1973.

Eisdorfer, C.: Autonomic changes in aging. Paper presented at the Aging and the Brain Symposium, Houson, Texas, October 1971.

————: Verbal learning and response time in the aged. *J Genet Psychol, 107*:15-22, 1965.

————: The WAIS performance of the aged: A retest evaluation. *J Gerontol, 18*:169-172, 1963.

————: In International research and education in social gerontology: Goals and Strategies, *Gerontologist, 12*, 1972.

———— and Axelrod, S.: Senescence and figural after-effects in two modalities: A correction. *J Genet Psychol, 104*:193-197, 1964.

————, Nowlin, J., and Wilkie, F.: Improvement of learning in the aged by modification of autonomic nervous system activity. *Science, 170*: 1327-1329, 1970.

———— and Wilkie, F.: The Duke longitudinal study. In Jarvik, L. F., Eisdorfer, C., and Blum, J. E. (Eds.): *Intellectual Functioning in Adults: Some Psychological and Biological Influences.* New York, Springer Publishing Company, 1973.

Feingold, L.: *A Psychometric Study of Senescent Twins.* Doctoral diss., Columbia Univ., 1950.

Friedman, M.: The general causes of coronary artery disease. In Friedman, M. (Ed.): *The Pathogenesis of Coronary Artery Disease.* New York, McGraw-Hill, 1969.

————, Rosenman, R. H., Straus, R., Wurm, M., and Kositchek, R.: The relationship of behavior pattern A to the state of the coronary vasculature: A study of 51 autopsy subjects. *Am J Med, 44*:525-537, 1968.

Granick, S. and Birren, J. E.: Cognitive functioning of survivors vs non-survivors: 12 year follow-up of healthy aged. Paper presented at the 8th International Congress of Gerontology, Washington, D. C., 1969.

Hamerton, J. L., Taylor, A. I., Angel, R., and McGuire, V. M.: Chromosome investigations of a small isolated human population. Chromosome abnormalities and distribution of chromosome counts according to age and sex among the population Tristan Da Cunhe, *Nature, 206*:1232-1234, 1965.

Heron, A. and Chown, S. M.: *Age and Function.* London, Churchill, 1967.

Honzik, M. P. and Macfarlane, J. W.: Personality development and intellectual functioning from 21 months to 40 years. In Jarvik, L. F., Eisdorfer, C. and Blum, J. E. (Eds.): *Intellectual Functioning In Adults: Some Psychological and Biological Influences.* New York, Springer Publishing Company, 1973.

Jacobs, P. A., Brunton, M., Court-Brown, W. M., Doll, R., and Goldstein, H.: Changes of human chromosomes count distribution with age: Evidence for a sex difference. *Nature, 197*:1080-1081; 1963.

Jacobs, P. A., Brunton, M., and Court-Brown, W. M.: Cytogenetic studies in leukocytes on the general population: Subjects of ages 65 years and more. *Ann Hum Genet, 27*:353-362, 1964.

Jarvik, L. F.: Genetic Aspects of Aging. In Rossman, I. (Ed.): *Clinical Geriatrics.* New York, J. P. Lippincott Company, 1970.

———, Altschuler, K. Z., Kato, T., and Blumner, B.: Organic brain syndrome and chromosome loss in aged twins. *Dis Nerv Sys, 32*:159-170, 1971.

——— and Blum, J. E.: Cognitive declines as predictors of mortality in twin pairs: A twenty-year longitudinal study of aging. In Palmore, E. and Jeffers, F. C. (Eds.): *Prediction of the Lifespan.* New York, D. C., Heath, 1971.

———, Blum, J. E., and Varma, A. O.: Genetic components and intellectual functioning during senescence: A twenty-year study of aging twins. *Behav Genet,* 1972.

——— and Cohen, D.: A biobehavioral approach to intellectual changes with aging. In Eisdorfer, C., and Lawton, M. P. (Eds.): The psychology of adult development and aging. Washington, D.C. *American Psychological Association,* 1973.

——— and Cohen, D.: Chromosome monitoring as a technique to detect subclinical mental changes in the aged. Paper presented at the 9th International Congress of Gerontology, Kiev, U.S.S.R., July 1972.

——— and Kato, T.: Chromosomes and mental changes in octogenarians: Preliminary findings. *Br J Psychiatry, 115*:1193-1194, 1969.

——— and Kato, T.: Chromosome examinations in aged twins. *Am J Hum Genet, 22*:562-573, 1970.

———, Falek, A., Kallmann, F. J., and Lorge, I.: Survival trends in a senescent twin population. *Am J Hum Genet, 12*:170-179, 1960.

———, Kallmann, F. J., Falek, A., and Klaber, M.: Changing intellectual functions in senescent twins. *Acta Gent Statistica Med, 7*:421-430, 1957.

Kallman, F. J.: *Heredity in Health and Mental Disorders.* New York, W. W. Norton, 1953.

Kleemeier, R. W.: Intellectual change in the senium. *Proceedings of the Social Statistics Section of the American Statistical Association,* 1962.

Kral, V. A.: Clinical contribution towards an understanding of memory function. *Dis Nerv Sys, 31*:23-29, 1970.

Kramer, M., Taube, C. A., and Redick, R. W.: Patterns of use of psychiatric facilities by the aged: Past, present, and future. In: Eisdorfer, C., and Lawton, M. P. (Eds.): The psychology of adult development and aging. Washington, D.C. *American Psychological Association,* 1973.

Kraus, A. A. and Lilienfeld, A. M.: Some epidemiologic aspects of the high mortality rate in the young widowed group. *J Chron Dis, 10*:207-215, 1959.

Kübler-Ross, E.: *On Death and Dying.* London, The Macmillan Company, 1969.

Lowenthal, M., Berkman, P., and associates: *Aging and Mental Disorder in San Francisco.* San Francisco, Josey-Bass, 1967.

Maddox, G.: In International research and education in social gerontology: Goals and strategies. *Gerontologist, 12,* 1972.

Medvedev, Z. A.: Molecular aspects of aging. *Symposium of the Society of Experimental Biology, 21*:1-28, 1967.

Nelson, E. N.: Persistence of attitudes of college students fourteen years later. *Psychol Monog, 68,* (2), 1954.

Nesselroade, J. R., Schaie, K. W., and Baltes P. B.: Ontogenetic and generational components of structural and quantitative change in adult cognitive behavior. *J Gerontol, 27*:222-228, 1972.

Neugarten, B.: Personality change in late life: A developmental perspective. In Eisdorfer, C., and Lawton, M. (Eds.): The psychology of adult development and aging. Washington, D.C. *American Psychological Association,* 1973.

Neurath, P., DeRemer, K., Bell, B., Jarvik, L. F., and Kato, T.: Chromosome loss compared with chromosome size, age, and sex of subjects. *Nature, 20*:379-382, 1970.

Nielsen, J.: Chromosomes in senile dementia. *Br J Psychiat, 114*:303-330, 1968.

————: Chromosomes in senile, presenile, and arteriosclerotic dementia. *J Gerontol, 25*:312-315, 1970.

Owens, W. A.: Age and mental abilities: A longitudinal study. *Genet Psychol Monogr, 48*:3-54, 1953.

Parker, C. M.: Effects of bereavement on physical and mental health: A study of the medical records of widows. *Br Med J,* 2:274-279, 1964a.

————: Recent bereavement as a cause of mental illness. *Br J Psychiat, 110*:198-204, 1964b.

Plant, W. T.: Personality changes associated with college attendance. *Hum Dev, 8*:142-151, 1965.

Platt, J. R.: Strong inference. *Science, 146*:347-353, 1964.

Rabbitt, P. M. A.: Age and discrimination between complex stimuli. In Welford, A. T. and Birren, J. E. (Eds.): *Behavior, Aging and the Nervous System.* Springfield, Illinois, Charles C Thomas, 1965.

Rhudick, J. and Gordon, P.: The New England agecenter study. In Jarvik, L. F., Eisdorfer, C., and Blum, J. E. (Eds.): *Intellectual Functioning in Adults: Some Psychological and Biological Influences.* New York, Springer Publishing Company, 1973.

Riegel, K. F.: Personality theory and aging. In Birren, J. E. (Ed.):

Handbook of Aging and the Individual. Chicago, University of Chicago Press, 1959.

————: Research designs in the study of aging and the prediction of retest resistance and death. Paper presented at the 8th International Congress of Gerontology, Washington, D. C., 1969.

———— and Riegel, R. M.: A study on changes of attitudes and interests during the later years of life. *Vita Humana, 3*:177-206, 1960.

———— and Riegel, R. M.: Development, drop, and death, Unpublished manuscript.

————, Riegel, R. M., and Meyer, G.: A study of the dropout rates in longitudinal research on aging, and the prediction of death. *J Pers Soc Psychol, 4*:343-348, 1967.

————, and Riegel, R. M., and Meyer, G.: The prediction of retest resisters in longitudinal research on aging. *J Gerontol, 23*:370-374, 1968.

Rosenman, R. H.: Prospective epidemiological recognition of the candidate for ischemic heart disease. *Psychother Psychosom, 16*:193-201, 1968.

————, Friedman, M. Straus, R., Jenkins, C. D., Zydanski, S., and Wurm, M.: Coronary heart disease in the Western Collaborative Group study: A follow-up experience of $4\frac{1}{2}$ years. *J Chron Dis, 23*: 173-190, 1970.

Sandberg, A. A., Cohen, M. M., Rim, A. A., and Levin, M. L.: Aneuploidy and age in a population survey. *Am J Hum Genet, 19*:633-643, 1967.

Schaie, K. W.: A reinterpretation of age-related changes in cognitive structure and functioning. In Goulet, L. R. and Baltes, P. (Eds.): *Life-Span Developmental Psychology.* New York, Academic Press, 1970.

———— and Strother, C. R.: Cognitive and personality variables in college graduates of advanced age. In Talland, G. A. (Ed.): *Human Aging and Behavior.* New York, Academic Press, 1968.

Sealy, A. P. and Cattell, R. B.: Standard trends in personality development in men and women of 16-70 years, determined by 16 PF measurements. Paper presented at the British Psychological Society Conference, 1965.

Simon, A.: Mental Health. Background paper for the White House Conference on Aging, March 1971.

Stein, K., Williams, G., and Prada, M.: Grief reactions in later life. *Am J Psychiat, 58*, 1951.

Wetherick, N. E.: Changing an established concept: A comparison of the ability of young, middle-aged, and old subjects. *Gerontologia, 11*:82-95, 1965.

Wilkie, F. and Eisdorfer, C.: Intelligence and blood pressure in the aged. *Science, 172*:959-962, 1971.

Woodruff, D. S. and Birren, J. E.: Age changes and cohort differences in personality. Unpublished manuscript, University of Southern California, 1971.

Young, M. L.: Age and sex differences in problem-solving. *J Gerontol, 26*:330-336, 1971.

Zerbin-Rudin, E.: Hirntrophische prozesse. In Becker, P. E. (Ed.): *Humangenetik,* Band v/2, 1967.

Chapter XII

THE REALITIES OF INTERDISCIPLINARY APPROACHES: CAN THE DISCIPLINES WORK TOGETHER TO HELP THE AGED?

Frances M. Carp

"INTERDISCIPLINARY" IS THE NEW sesame. It has supplanted "multi-disciplinary" to signify the intent to work together. Can interdisciplinarity be more than a pious hope or futile word-magic? The question is posed here in relation to helping old people, but it is not unique to the disciplines as they operate in the field of gerontology. This issue is relevant to a variety of fields and problem areas in which "interdisciplinary" is the vogue. Writing of the social sciences generally, Sherif and Sherif (1969) note that:

> The qualifying term—interdisciplinary—is fashionable these days. Talking about problems of interdisciplinary relationships is a mark of being one of the "in-crowd." In the current lingo, it is almost as prestigeful to use the term *interdisciplinary* as to speak of being *knowledgeable*. (p. 3).

The same authors conclude: "No one can deny that a bleak picture confronts the interdisciplinary efforts in some quarters today." (p. xi). Paradoxically, gerontology's short history may give it advantage in dealing with this pervasive problem if, in this instance, youth is associated with not being "set in its ways." Interdisciplinary approaches which help the aged may guide disciplines in ways to work together effectively, more generally.

An Overview

This chapter deals with "interdisciplinary" and another latter-day slogan, "research utilization," in terms of the social psychology of prejudice. Its stance is purposefully argumentative, an invitation to rebuttal. Debates over alternative interpretations might develop positive answers to the question posed in the title and might be, in themselves, one form of mutual enterprise.

The chapter first sketches a brief background for separations between and within disciplines. It then turns to one type of apartheid which is pervasive throughout gerontology and which greatly hampers efforts to help the elderly: the alienation between research and service. For purposes of discussion, the chapter selects the service-research dichotomy as a special case of the more general problem of failure to work together to benefit old people. This discussion is more critical of the research side. All blame does not rest there. However, self-evaluation, on the part of each group, may improve the quality of dialog by reducing the defensiveness which seems to stem from blame-avoidant or extra-punitive tendencies on both sides.

The chapter returns to the issue raised in its title by citing one example of successful interdisciplinary work. This proves the possibility of an affirmative answer. The question remains: why is this success story so unusual? The concluding section of the chapter is a plea for systematic research: identification and manipulation of variables which determine the effectiveness of efforts, on the part of people from different backgrounds, to help the elderly.

The Separation

As a point of departure, the question may be asked: why is this topic nominated for attention? How has cooperation come to be a matter of concern in gerontology and elsewhere? Why is there need for a special mechanism or exorcism to promote interaction? Why do disciplines and sub-disciplines not interact naturally and as a matter of course when their interests and competencies intersect? To gain perspective let us look back, first at the separateness between the traditional disciplines relevant to gerontology, then at the apartheid between research and service, whether from different disciplines or the same one.

Specialization among academic disciplines seems to have started from the purest of motives, largely out of a desire to concentrate on problems in order to deal with them effectively. As the body of knowledge expanded, mastery and scope became increasingly incompatible as reasonable enterprises for one individual. Mastery became the route of the "professional" and "scientists"; breadth, that of the "amateur" and "dilettante." The emotional flavors of the four words reveal contemporary attitudes toward the disciplinarian and the non-disciplinarian as problem-solvers. The generalist may be a delightful companion, but he is not taken seriously during working hours. In a discussion of the ethnocentricity of the scholar, Campbell (1969) points out that "the ego ideal of the scholar calls for competence, for complete knowledge of the field he claims as his." (p. 342).

While disciplinary training prepared specialists increasingly to "deal in depth" with problems, the problems with which they were competent became increasingly narrow in scope. Therefore, more and more of the issues generated within society came to exceed the areas of competency and interest of any one discipline. Most of the vital issues for old people today—whether service or research—extend into the domains of several of the traditional disciplines.

The Role of Training

As specialization proceeded, it was reflected in and assisted by educational philosophy and practice. A "disciplinary identity crisis" appeared in the normal development of the student. Educators intentionally precipitate "identification" with the discipline: the neophyte must learn to perceive himself as, and to "think like," a social worker, psychologist, or whatever. In discussing the ethnocentrism of disciplines, Campbell (1969) points out that the ego-ideal of the scholar as teacher has been to turn out " 'chips off the old block,' Ph.D.'s . . . the same . . . as he." (p. 343).

These efforts to evoke "commitment to the field" are generally successful. Ask the next ten people you meet in the course of your work: "What are you?" or even "Who are you?" Probably eight will respond with the names of the traditional disciplines in which they were trained.

The binding strength of this commitment is revealed in the resistance of persons trained in traditional disciplines against converting to interdisciplinary fields such as gerontology. For most persons doing research or performing services for the old, the primary identification remains with the discipline of training. As trainers, these persons suffer ambivalence in regard to students' commitment to gerontology. Staffs and faculties of interdisciplinary gerontological training programs appear, often, to be in the uncomfortable position of the much-lampooned parent who shrieks, "Do what I *say,* not what I *do!*"

Indoctrination begins early. Even undergraduate students, once they have made vocational choices, show the effects of disciplinary identification. Their perceptions of unknown persons tend to be biased. "Good guys" are likely to be perceived as members of the student's chosen discipline, "bad guys" as members of some other. One study (Carp and DeRath, 1959) used a Picture Test comprised of drawings of men's faces, eight sets of eight pictures each, which had been standardized, using other groups of subjects, along the dimension of like-dislike. Upper-division male college students were asked to assign each of the eight men on each page to a pre-determined list of occupations. Consistently, "disliked" men were assigned to occupations other than that to which the respondent's college preparation led, while "liked" pictures were most often identified as those of men in the occupation of the student's choice.

Similar results were obtained with the same Picture Test using religious affiliation (Flyer and Carp, 1959) and ethnic background (Carp, in press). In all three studies, "likable" men were perceived as belonging to the group with which the respondent identified himself, while "dislikable" men were perceived as "others." Results of the latter two studies, on religion and ethnicity, are readily discussed in the context of bias and prejudice. There is aversion to these terms in relation to interdisciplinary perceptions. Nevertheless, it appears to be true that by the time scientific or professional training is complete, disciplinary indoctrination has imbedded strong in-group feelings and a sense of mission, and probably, in counterpoint, some alienation from and denigration of those who have made different vocational choices.

To recapitulate the argument to this point: concern for depth and accuracy of understanding, confronted with expansion of knowledge, led to distribution of topics among disciplines. Each discipline was largely responsible for the selection and preparation of its oncoming members. Generally, the selection and training function were carried out in relative psychological seclusion, though campuses and buildings were shared. Identification with the mentors, their ways of thinking, and their value systems came to be essential components of disciplinary training.

Disciples polarize around different identification figures or schools of thought even within one discipline—a further splintering of knowledge, disagreement about what is important, mutual disparagement, and loss of communication. Fealty to one's group must sometimes be demonstrated by avoiding others. (There were only sympathetic nods around the lunch table when one faculty member spoke of feeling "betrayed" when he learned that one of "his students" had enrolled in a course with a faculty member in the same department who adhered to a different theoretical position. The student, wisely, had waited to commit this breach of faith until his degree was secure.)

Multidisciplinary Attempts

The "multidisciplinary" phase in service, research, and training evolved in recognition of the fact that the discipline-by-discipline approach was not paying off in problem-solving. Real issues like those concerning the well-being of old people tend to cut across disciplinary domains; no one type of specialist can solve them. Assigning to the task a selection of persons with the variety of knowledges and skills encompassed by the problem seemed an appropriate remedial action.

Unfortunately, it was no solution. Physical proximity and assignment to "terms" often had little effect. It was as if the members of each discipline or sub-discipline came encapsulated in an invisible, impermeable membrane within which they pursued their own course, little affected by the physical and organizational proximity of the disciplinary "others." Multidisciplinary congregations did not sufficiently *interact*.

Now, Interdisciplinarity

So the watchword became "interdisciplinary." Not uncommonly, in grant applications or elsewhere, use of "inter-" as distinct from "multi-" disciplinary is stressed and justified in a phrase referring to the intention for "real give-and-take." Does this change in phraseology represent or forecast a behavioral alteration?

Creating cooperative and fruitful efforts at problem-solving may depend less upon selection of the most accurate description of the desired relationship, or upon reiteration of the magic word, than upon gaining insight into the reasons why persons from different backgrounds do not always work well together to help the aged. Impediments must be identified before they can be removed or reduced. Facilitators must be sought and strengthened.

Each combination creates different constellations. Each situation which involves a convocation of persons from different backgrounds is in some sense unique. Coverage of interdisciplinary approaches would be book-length, at least. Therefore it is necessary to limit the scope. Anyway, consideration of interdisciplinary approaches in general may be premature. In the inital search for impediments and facilitators it seems wise to narrow the focus, avoiding useless generalities and exploring in detail the factors which influence cooperation in more specific situations. Subsequent search for common denominators among successes and failures in interaction may provide a comprehensive view.

One Critical Gap: Service-Research

The immediate issue is where to begin. In any consideration of working together to benefit old people, there comes to mind not only the problem of cooperation among various combinations of the traditional disciplines but also, and perhaps more sharply, that of interaction between research and service, whether nominally from different disciplines or the same one. In a very real sense, research and service training within one academic department constitute different disciplines. Indeed, the estrangement between the investigator and the practitioner who share one disciplinary label may be particularly difficult.

If any form of interdisciplinary effort is to help old people, it must solve the practitioner-investigator stand-off. Neither total interaction among investigators in all disciplines nor complete interaction among practitioners in all disciplines will solve the problem. Fruitful interaction must involve research and practitioner components of relevant nominal disciplines. The service-research relationship is a problem common to all interdisciplinary efforts to benefit the old. For this reason, it demands first attention.

The research-service dichotomy may be in some ways a paradigm of separation according to training. Understanding it may generalize to other situations of separateness. At least, the service-research dichotomy is the most common or pervasive type, occurring throughout the field of aging, regardless of the "mix" or singularity of titular disciplines. Throughout the range of knowledge relevant to the needs of old people, lack of effective research-service interaction blocks utilization of research findings to the benefit of persons, and cuts "the pursuit of knowledge" loose from the realities of those persons and the world in which they live Because of the central importance of the practitioner-investigator alienation, the chapter selects it as a focus. The following sections deal with the nature of this separation and with possibilities for its amelioration.

One Strategy

Old people will be best served by continuous interaction between research and practice, through which the results of investigations are applied promptly and relevantly in services, and the vital issues of being old in today's world are constant stimuli and guides to research. Few statements could be made with so little fear of disagreement. The desirability of such a state of affairs is hardly questioned, in either research or service community. The problem, then, does not lie in lack of statement of a common goal, but in inability to reach it or unwillingness to accept the trade-offs necessary to its attainment.

Of late, there is increasing concern with "research utilization." Funding agencies urge service programs to embody the latest research findings, and investigators to consider applications of their research. Service agencies, by and large, are ready to apply information—from any source—which seems useful, according to their own standards, for meeting their own goals. Some people who conduct research are interested in applications of their findings, and in making their studies more relevant to the well-being of old people. Yet the conundrum continues.

What starting point seems propitious for unravelling the complex problem of investigator-practitioner interaction? One place to begin is with the investigator whose research may be relevant to the well-being of old persons. This is an appropriate, if painful, starting point for this author; an inventory of ways in which practitioners fail to meet my needs would be much easier. Research findings, no matter what their potential usefulness to the quality of life in later years, remain impotent for old people unless they are incorporated into action programs. Meyer *et al.* (1967) remind us that "Application does not follow automatically from understanding the behavioral tasks of interpersonal helping. . . . Only knowledge having promise for the use in the *actions* of professional helpers in pursuit of their change objectives can be considered applicable." (p. 166).

Surveying the Market

What must the investigator do to facilitate use of his research? Like the would-be purveyor of any commodity, he is well advised to start with identification of the potential consumers of his findings; he must become aware of who and where they are. This initial step toward research utilization is no easy one for the typical investigator. In all probability his training has conditioned him automatically to react to other investigators as the market for his research output. Communicating through the professional-scientific media, with others similar to himself, was an important part of his education and is a central part of his work. His effectiveness at it largely determines the success of his career, including the ability to obtain funds to continue his investigations. On the job, through scientific journals, and at professional meetings he receives knowledge about the work of other investigators which stimulates him to formulate hypotheses for investigations, and receives feedback concerning the cogency and value of his efforts.

According to Campbell:

> The departmental grouping of communicators allows unstable language to drift into unintelligibility across departments. A basic law is that speakers of the same language, once isolated into separate communities, drift into local idiosyncrasies and eventually unintelligibility, once the discipline of common conversation is removed. This tendency produces departmental linguistic idiosyncrasy even for shared contents and referents. Furthermore, as Edmund Leach and others have noted, such idiosyncrasy may be exaggerated as an ingroup solidarity device. What is despised as jargon by the outgroup may be the shibboleth of adequate professional training by the ingroup. (p. 337).

The Prime Market

Other investigators in the same discipline are the target population, the primary users of research findings at present. As usual, the consumer has a significant influence upon the product. The questions an investigator poses for study, the techniques he applies to obtain and process data, and the form and forum in which he reports results are largely influenced by the expectations of his peers in the research community. Thus he works in a sort of isolation ward: information about "important issues" comes from his replicates, and his skill in perceiving the needs of this in-group and reporting his findings to it are the means to gain and maintain place in it.

Furthermore, the scientific community pays homage to a jealous god. It is said that, during the Dark Ages, if one wanted to know the normal number of teeth for a horse, proper procedure was to look into the writings of Aristotle; only a heretic would "look in the horse's mouth." Questions which had not occurred to that long-dead authority—an insatiable observer of the natural world—were thereby defined as irrelevant to "true knowledge." The parallel may be overdrawn, but the point is an important one. The behavioral sciences, in particular, out of an almost pathological need to be acknowledged "scientific," relegate their disciples to second-class citizenship with the epithet "applied."

For example, Riley (1967) comments:

> It is not surprising, then, that many sociologists have doubts and anxieties about entering careers in applied fields or working in nonacademic settings. Negative reactions of their academic colleagues, either actual or anticipated, may add to their hesitation and reluctance. They hear much advice against a career outside the mainstream of the discipline. (p. 794).

Passwords to the inner circle are "pure science," "basic research" and "theory oriented." In this intellectual climate the investigator is trained and works.

Textbooks define the aim of science as understanding, interpreting, predicting and perhaps controlling aspects of reality. Ideally, each research project is directed toward this goal, and theories synthesize knowledge and accelerate its extension by suggesting predictions which provide shortcuts—to knowledge about the real world. The pursuit of knowledge, under the sign of "science" or any other, lies across the hard ground of reality. Whenever the current "authority" (whether Aristotle's writings or "scientific purity") impedes interaction between the investigator and the real world, knowledge is improverished or distorted.

The scientist's goal is not "research" but knowledge, and not "theory development" but system and efficiency in the pursuit of knowledge. However, this is a perilous course. The investigator can never select a completely satisfactory sample or control all the variables. Even replication and multivariate analysis using latest-generation electronic data processing equipment do not guarantee that findings will "hold up" in the infinitely complex world of reality.

On this basic issue, the "applied person" is perhaps not only braver than the "pure scientists" but also more faithful to the essential scientific dictum. Some among them may one day be revered as the new experimentalists. But, at the moment, the indoctrination of his years in training and the rewards of his working years tend to shape the investigator's behavior toward "purity" and "theory" so consistently that these become functionally autonomous motives (Allport, 1937). In a discussion of the moral obligations of the scientists, Ross (1965) suggests, "It may be, on occasion, that one should resist the pressures of scientists and choose problems of some significance to society." (p. 431).

Conducting research relevant to real situations is hazardous: findings may be applied and found invalid or of little importance in the lives of old people. A correlation coefficient may be statistically significant, yet account for so little variance that it is useless for any practical application. It is perhaps safer to frame a study in terms of some theory or other. This is a stimulating intellectual game which pays off in publications and prestige, and provides access to the in-group. The game is played with others like oneself—familiar, predictable, safe.

Is it any wonder that the scientific community is the major "consumer" of its own products? Identification of potential users of research findings within this community is made easy by the structure of scientific-professional organizations and publications. Interaction and communication seem to be no problem: they are so prolific that most people find it difficult to keep up with publications and meetings even in a sub-field.

Potential Consumers

The problem of research utilization is not the investigator's inability to "sell" his product; it is the homogeneity of his market, the need to diversify. Who are *potential* users of research findings in gerontology? What are new markets with needs the investigator might fill—and which would reward his efforts? The possibilities vary, of course, depending upon topic and content, and must be treated categorically here.

THE ULTIMATE CONSUMER. The question regarding new market for research output usually evokes as answer some institution or set of *institutions,* public and private agencies whose clients include or are limited to the old. However, *older persons* are the intended major beneficiaries of research in gerontology and therefore its ultimate potential users. The danger exists that research, nominally oriented to improvement of the quality of life for old people, may be warped not only to the career needs of investigators, but also to the special interests of service and finding agencies, and commercial purveyors of products and services.

The research community may pay too little attention to the ways its findings influence the lives of people, reputedly the objects of its concern. Service agencies may take too much upon themselves concerning what is "good for" clients. Commercial enterprises are expected to act in self-interest.

Against the preoccupation of investigators, the paternalism of agencies, and the profit motive of the marketplace, old people present no effective defense, let alone a competitive advantage for benefits. They are underprivileged financially and tend to be demeaned and devalued overwise. (On these points there is interdisciplinary accord; the research community has documented them *ad nauseum,* and the service community agrees.)

Generally, the old have tended to accept the societal put-down and to see themselves, as others see them, rather worthless and impotent. There are stirrings of change. Rise in the self-esteem and self-confidence of old people, and their recognition of their power of concerted action, are nicely demonstrated by the extent and quality of their participation in the White House Conference of 1971 compared to that of 1961. Old people may band together to demand that research programs more effectively meet their needs.

At present, the old do not often feel they are beneficiaries of research. There is some evidence that they (and other segments of society) are beginning to react against exploitation by investigators. While research people continue to solicit their cooperation in securing data by referring to such goals as "improving the quality of life in the later years," people see little improvement in their situations as a result.

Recently, an interdisciplinary "emergency meeting" of investigators in one catchment area was called because residents were refusing to serve, unquestioningly, as subjects or respondents. They wanted to be paid for their time, and pointed out that investigators did not donate theirs. They wanted to know what good the studies would do, in specific terms. They wanted to know when and how they would learn of the results of the studies. The "emergency" was an increase in research costs; the outcome of the meeting, a "gentlemen's agreement" that no investigator would pay respondents until all voted to do so. One result may be that studies underestimate the independence of "most people."

THE MEDIATING CONSUMER. While it is valuable for the investigator concerned with utilization of his findings to remember that old persons are the "ultimate consumers" of his gerontological research, it is realistic for him to recognize that service agencies must normally be middlemen. Here again, the investigator needs old people to serve as subjects or respondents for a study; he usually locates them in the community through some sampling procedure. People who make use of community services are likely to differ from the general population. Unless his study is specifically service-related, the investigator will avoid selection of subjects through agencies. However, when he wants to report findings in such a way that they can benefit old people, dissemination to individual old persons is not practical.

Research utilization requires different channels than does data collection. The usual procedure for data collection is from individual, somehow representative, old people to a data bank. The most effective channel for research utilization seems to be from processed data through a service agency to individual old persons. Then, for the researcher interested in improving the lot of old people, the task of market identification is to locate a service agency to which his studies may be relevant.

Contact

This brings the investigator to the critical "first impression." Generically, the problem is interaction with people from different disciplines. In terms of the example selected for purposes of this discussion, the problematic interaction is between Service and Research. Perhaps it is useful at this point to remember that these are functions, not persons. Research and service roles can be performed by the same person at different times. Yet commonly there seems to be lack of understanding and sometimes downright ill will between persons "doing research" and those "doing service." Right from the start, each seems to expect the worst from the other.

INITIATIVE BY RESEARCH. Sometimes the contact is initiated by investigators. An example is provided by a recent research ultilization conference. Gerontological investigators had identified service organizations to which their research seemed relevant, and invited representatives to meet with them to see what existing research findings were applicable, to learn what information Service needed which Research might subsequently provide, and to improve communication. The conference seemed to deepen antagonisms rather than provide an exchange of ideas. Through the several days of meeting, research people became increasingly vehement that research *does* have useful findings—without producing these findings to the satisfaction of practitioners; while service people became more and more belligerent in demanding "*What* findings?" or went home.

Challenge and defense were the predominant forms of "interaction." Two general patterns emerged. In one, a research member would present his paper, as scheduled on the formal agenda. From the Research side, perfunctory applause—they had heard and read his paper. From the Service side, squirming, head shakes, groans, muttered comments of "Why don't you speak English?" or "That's completely impractical." Gans (1971) comments, "The high levels of generality at which much of academic social science operates . . . breeds conceptual abstractness which results in concepts that cannot be applied to the real-life situations in which the policy designer works." (p. 22).

An example of the second pattern of interaction: a representative of Service had taken seriously the instructions of conference planners to bring questions of importance to people in his field. He had gone to considerable trouble to collect letters from members of his organization, specifying questions they wanted to pose to Research Past for reporting in terms they could understand, and to Research Future as topics for study. At the first meeting he described what he had brought, held the collection of letters for people to see, opened his mouth to present the issues, and was immediately pinned to the wall with a barrage of questions—about how he makes executive decisions! At the end of the conference he was still waving the collection of questions he had been asked to bring, and still asking for a chance to report on them. Though he stayed to the end, he resolved never again to become involved with Researchers. His parting comment: "I'd like to invite a few of *you* to attend one of *our* meetings and let you see what it's like to be outnumbered like this." The research people left, reassuring each other, "But we *do* have important findings for those people." A typical example of "we" vs. "they" and, sadly, little progress toward benefiting old people. Who had time to think of *them?*

This is one way in which contact, of a sort, is made. Research takes the initiative, with the stated purpose of "helping" Service. Lady Bountiful is rarely welcome. In addition, the research community seems unaware that "useful to practitioners" is a meaningful label only when it is attached by practitioners. If research is to be applied to benefit the old, it must prove helpful to persons who provide services for the old. No amount of protestation will suffice; the research product, in the hands of the practitioner, must make *his* work easier or more successful—in *his* view.

Generally, Service has made hard, lonely decisions in which Research has not assisted. When Research initiates interaction for utilization of his findings, he may sound supercilious. ("I have some important data on that, but of course I would have to qualify it in a great many ways, because so many variables are involved. I'll try to remember to send you an article of mine.")

According to Luchterhand (1967):

> Administrators usually want firm, clear generalizations which can be applied with complete confidence to particular clients or situations. But research findings are stated in terms of probabilities which apply to specified populations only. This tends to alienate practitioners, who may think that findings which are so hedged about with restrictions are of doubtful worth, if not actually useless. (p. 516).

On the other hand, Service may be all too well aware that many variables are involved—he works with most of them every day. He perceives a put-down, an implication that Research feels "above" him. He writes off the reprint without seeing it, though he feels that he could understand the study if it were not in disciplinary jargon. Furthermore, he suspects that the report, if deciphered, would prove totally impractical, and that the jargon is in part an effort to screen its triviality. At any rate, the jargon puts him on the outside. Research has once more eluded the sharing of responsibility and, worse, has managed to imply that Research is somehow superior. Service is frustrated, baffled and offended.

The investigator who wants to see his findings used to benefit old people might be well advised to consider further the strategy of the marketplace. Having identified the potential consumer, the next step is to study that market, uncover the predominant motives and needs within it, and package his product so that it meets those needs and satisfies those motives. Only then will it begin to meet his needs. For example, Gans (1971) calls upon the investigator to provide "dynamic theories of the social process to the policy designer so that he can find footholds from which to intervene" and "initiate action" rather than to construct theories which emerge out of a detached perspective in which the researcher is an "outside observer who is examining a society in which he is not involved." (p. 20).

INITIATIVE BY SERVICE. Responding to an approach on the part of Service may be easier for the investigator. Such an approach indicates that the service person has a felt need and perceives Research as a possible satisfier of it. (It is always nice to be wanted!) It was my great good fortune to be the recipient of such an approach when Marie McGuire, at that time the Director of the San Antonio Housing Authority, recognized the opportunity for research in connection with the first high-rise public housing for the elderly, Victoria Plaza. Very often I have wondered why that interaction, extending over a period of years, was both professionally productive and personally satisfying, with a minimum of defensiveness and misunderstanding between two people so differently trained.[1]

The very difference was probably one great advantage: the lack of overlap in background and purpose provided no area for competition or defensiveness. Each of us had a need which the

[1] However, Mrs. McGuire comments: "You may know that I had difficulties with the staff. 'The investigators will upset the old people, the research people are not in the real world,' etc., etc. ran the comments. I was warned many times by competent staff of the evils that would be generated by the investigator's work." (Personal communication, June 30, 1972).

joint venture met. Marie recognized that this first project should be studied in order that later ones capitalize on its faults and advantages. Looking back, Mrs. McGuire assesses the situation: "My cooperation probably emanated from a realization that no one in the mid-fifties had firm answers. You may recall that [the architect] and I had traveled about and studied 23 developments for the eldery, having no basis for decision except our own reactions. Study was obviously indicated and I saw one of the values of Victoria Plaza as leading to a few valid conclusions in design and operation. That piece you supplied and I was frankly delighted."[2] I was looking for an opportunity to observe the effects of manipulating environmental variables upon old human organisms, in order to test some hypotheses derived from psychological theory.

THE MATCHMAKER FUNCTION. The Hogg Foundation was open-handed with money on both sides—for service personnel additional to those the Housing Authority could provide, and with funds for research. Competition for financial support was not a factor.

The initiative was with Mrs. McGuire. Except for her action, no investigator would have heard of Victoria Plaza until long after the possibility for an impact study had passed. Here again, the Hogg Foundation played a vital role, that of locator. Marie recognized the opportunity for research but, like most service people, she did not know how to make the appropriate contact. The Foundation located a person with suitable background and brought us together under favorable circumstances. Service and research interactions, and interdisciplinary efforts generally, might be improved by a "matchmaker" function, which funding agencies or the Gerontological Society might undertake.

It is time for scientific associations to design the means by which social problems which science can help are brought to the attention of scientists, and whatever in science is relevant to those problems is brought to the attention of the appropriate laymen. There are always scientific administrators and statesmen to do such work. If it is done well, it could be one of the

2 Personal correspondence, June 30, 1972.

most effective social acts ever performed by scientists as scientists. (Ross, 1965, p. 438).

Motivational Differences

Research is largely synonymous with evaluation in the experience of service personnel who have contact with investigators. Evaluation studies are less likely than other research to seem irrelevant to the work of practitioners. However, they may call into question the way that work is being performed. "At the outset, therefore, practitioners may feel threatened by the researcher and ambivalent about undertaking the research, since the researcher, whether he likes it or not, is in the position of possibly 'criticizing' the work of the practitioner." (Rodman and Kolodny, 1965, p. 95).

Furthermore, much of it is evaluation under coercion: the requirement was written into acceptance of funding for the program. Yet, if the evaluation is not favorable, refunding will be denied. Marie sought the Victoria Plaza study because she wanted it, not because it was required or even "the thing to do." This may well be another reason for the relative success of our interaction. In many instances in which, nominally, the approach is made by service to research people, the former have been coerced into a vulnerable position which makes them defensive against the investigators whom they are forced to invite to come criticize them.

Here is a crisis of opposing motivational pressures which makes it almost impossible for Service and Research to interact other than as wary opponents. In the usual situation to be evaluated, Service has made the best decisions possible, and *knows* that the program is doing good. The old people who make use of the facility will lose those benefits (and staff will lose status or jobs) unless the evaluation is favorable. It is imperative that the benefits be documented. Research charges in with the stated goal of "finding out" and considerable disdain for what it perceives as the motive to "prove that"; and with a background in the intellectual game of criticism. Evaluators give themselves and each other points for flaws discovered.

The questioning attitude of the researcher is likely to be irritating to the practitioner. This is not because the practitioner is naive or blind to inadequacies in practice. Often it is because the probing of the researcher, at least initially, is an extra burden to the already overworked practitioner. (Rodman and Kolodny, p. 96).

Also, as Rodman and Kolodny point out:

> Built into the researcher's function is the role of innovator. This is parallel to the situation in an industrial organization where the goals of the research and production departments may be at odds because the former has a vested interest in discovering inefficiency and in altering the production process, while the latter has a vested interest in resisting changes that would upset the department and possibly disclose its inefficiency. (1965, p. 97).

Insofar as the evaluator's primary audience remains the research community, and he must protect himself from attack in that quarter, variables selected for inclusion in the evaluation must be measurable, as objectively as possible. This need on the part of Research, an imperative through selection into the field and training in it, often leads to assessment in terms which seem irrelevant to Service. This impasse is the same in gerontology or preschool education. Teachers *know* the children benefit from the program, despite the lack of evidence from standardized test scores: the tests do not deal with the important types of learning. Researchers shake their heads over educators who cannot be "objective."

The same motivational difference appears in regard to programs for the elderly or for a new vaccine. In regard to the latter, medical research sees only one legitimate course of action: test its effectiveness by administering the vaccine to a random half of the people, a placebo to the remainder. Medical practitioners believe that if clinical experience indicates even some protection from the vaccine, it should be given to everyone. Riley comments in regard to sociology:

> Whereas the sociologist as scholar typically *studies* the behavior of people, the physician or social worker is committed to *helping* the patient or client. Consequently, when the sociologist's subjects and the doctor's patients or social workers's clients are one and the same, the potential for conflict of emphasis is obvious. (1962, p. 792).

Wherever they are located, and whatever the subject-matter of interest, people "doing research" and those "doing service" have antithetical value systems which collide inevitably in the context of evaluation studies. The goal of Service is to apply, immediately, all that is known which may help the client. The goal of Research is to identify and test independent variables. The investigator usually has the additional agenda of stating the problem and findings in such a way that the study can be published. Unless these requirements are met, the investigator will not remain in a position to do further research to benefit the old, or his own career. Similarly, the service person has his hidden agenda, "proof" that his program works, so that he can continue to provide the service and maintain his career. Can these conflicting self-serving interests be reconciled?

In some instances, financing presents an even more directly competitive element to the situation. Many agencies fund research, demonstration and evaluation, and service programs. At least in the eyes of applicants, there is direct competition for funds, which are always inadequate. Service considers research a "frill" when money is limited; research believes its way is most economical and efficient: to find out what is best, before investing money in services.

Different Views of Old People

An interesting sidelight on the difference in viewpoint between research and service people is the disparity between their views of the "ultimate user" of gerontological research and services. As one result of the difference in motivation regarding old people, and the selection of those with whom they come into contact, research and service people usually have very different concepts when they use the words "old people." Welfare staffs see the very poor; clinic staffs see the unwell and the emotionally disturbed or incompetent; senior centers see certain categories of the mobile old; managers of Leisure Worlds, quite another. Each tends, inevitably, to base his concept of old people on the type with whom he deals. The investigator, similarly, tends to conceive of the old in terms of "his sample." If that sample is well drawn, his conception may be applicable more broadly than that of the typical practitioner. Which concept is superior depends upon the purpose.

The point for this discussion is that here, as elsewhere, use of the same term may obscure the fundamental difference in concept. The group social workers in a residence for the elderly, the attendant in a nursing home, and the investigator working with a national sample do not mean the same thing by "old people." This is one more factor in making each group feel that the others do not know what they are talking about. The amazing thing is that they can attend a conference together for several days before discovering this discrepancy—and, at the next meeting, the time may be equally long to rediscovery.

No Common Forum

There are profound differences between research and service personnel in motivation, viewpoint and vocabulary. For the most part, their professional and scientific vocabularies are separate, and use of the same terms by no means insures a common referent. Lack of a common forum fosters the other separations. While the Victoria Plaza experience was satisfying to me, its utility was seriously limited because of inadequacies is reporting. I did not report it in architectural and social work journals. Architects do not normally see behavioral-science periodicals or book lists. Psychologists do not know the names of architectural journals, let alone how to write reports for them.

The manuscript of *Victoria Plaza* was reviewed by several members of the staffs of the housing facility and the senior center with which it shared space, and revised in light of their comments. Nevertheless, it has serious limitations in cross-disciplinary and research-service communication. Marie McGuire comments: "It is interesting that even though your book was plainly written, I had innumerable calls asking what it meant and how to apply the findings."[3] She recommends the creation of what is essentially a new discipline, that of "adapter" who would "translate the findings (leaving out all reference to types of tests, scales, etc. and reference to extant research on other variables) and prepare them for applicability to operation policy formulation." "Adap-

3 Personal communication, June 30, 1972.

ters" might be trained also to translate service problems for investigators.

Gerontological scientists and practitioners, and investigators from different disciplines, tend to publish in and read separate publication lists, and to attend different meetings. The Gerontological Society provides a common ground, though its meetings are to some extent sectional, and its two publications appeal to somewhat different audiences.

One hopeful sign in regard to a common written forum, shared by practitioners and investigators from several disciplines, is *The Gerontologist's* effort to present research findings in format and style interesting to those who might use them. Unfortunately, this reinforces in the minds of some members of the research community the view that research papers in *The Gerontologist* are rejects from *The Journal of Gerontology*. It is the old familiar mechanism: if "one of ours" becomes too much involved with "them," he is set aside and put down. That a "scientist" would choose a forum shared with "applied people" is unthinkable. (Similarly, "Whitey" cannot believe any human being would not prefer to be white.)

A Recommendation

Over and over, it seems possible to interpret the reactions which create and maintain the service-research alienation or other forms of interdisciplinary non-interaction in terms of the mechanisms of prejudice as an ego-defensive attitude. Mann (1969) emphasizes that "prejudice serves functions other than the psychodynamic resolution of unacceptable impulses and anxieties. Prejudice may be learned and reinforced as a by-product of identification and socialization into one's own group; many individuals learn to conform to and identify with their own groups completely, and at the same time learn to distruct others." (pp. 117-118). Gerontology will make a major contribution to knowledge and to the general welfare by finding ways to modify these forces. This understanding might generalize to management of their other manifestations.

If the investigator is seriously concerned with interdisciplinary or research-service interaction, why does he not approach it like a problem to be solved? One answer is provided by Smelser (1967) who feels that:

> A vague romanticism often seems to govern thinking about the means of attaining the end of unification. It appears to me that many of the numerous interdisciplinary arrangements of the past two decades—institutes, centers, regional study groups, seminars, conferences, and panels—have rested on the belief, even hope, that if only scholars from different specialities are placed in one another's presence, some process of integration will occur spontaneously. Unfortunately, the endeavors based on this hope are usually quite barren, yielding mainly general talk *about* integration rather than results *of integration*. (pp. 38-39).

Practitioners can be excused for haranguing the issues of research-utilization; investigators cannot. Instead of essays on the feasibility of interaction we should produce research into its determinants. The procedure can follow traditional lines:

A. *Statement of the Problem.* The feasibility of productive interaction can be documented by a single case. An instance of practitioner-investigator interaction has been presented. One of successful work by investigators from many disciplines is better known: that of the Research Training Grant Application Review Committee for the National Institute of Child Health and Human Development. The suggestions of constituting this committee, with members from all disciplines relevant to any possible application for a training program, met considerable opposition as unrealistic. Many people consider it impossible for investigators from such diverse fields to deliberate and make recommendations. The Committee now has several years of successful work behind it. Members from the various disciplines seem to identify themselves as "we" of the Committee while conducting its work. The research-training value of the applications, not the disciplines involved, is the question at issue in Committee deliberations. Interesting by-products are the ease of communication among members, and the appreciation of one discipline's contributions to gerontology, on the part of members from different disciplines.

The issue is not *whether* interdisciplinary approaches can help the aged, but why some are successful and others are not. The problem is: how can various traditional disciplines, including their service and research components, be assisted to work better together to help the aged?

B. *Review of the literature* and preparation of a background statement.

C. *Statement of hypotheses.* One might be: the task is to convert the different, unfamiliar, threatening "other" so that he becomes sufficiently familiar and nonthreatening to be perceived as similar, and therefore incorporable into the "we." This coalescence should be promoted by contact as peers, with common goals, in noncompetitive situations, which provide need-satisfaction for all.

Uliassi warns that "the communication that is required must be something more than a condensed and mechanical transmission of 'findings.' What is called for is something akin to a dialogue," and that:

> Even this may imply an overly rational model of communication. As we move from more technical areas to more complex problems of social and political analysis, prediction and prescription, research itself becomes more difficult, more infused with values, more tentative in its results. At the same time, the policy-makers to whom it is addressed are themselves men and women of flesh and blood who cannot be expected to respond to research, in all cases, with dispassionate intellectuality. It is remarkable, I think, how little attention has been paid to this aspect of the communication process. We would never expect to change attitudes, for example, without understanding something about the functions they serve in the psychic economy of an individual; and we rarely assume that they can be changed by the gentle persuasiveness of reason alone. Yet this is precisely what we do assume most of the time and almost casually when we talk about the communicating research that is relevant to policy matters. (1971, p. 333).

D. *Definition of independent and dependent variables, of manipulations and expected consequences.* Table XII-1 outlines a few of the variables which can be manipulated, in an effort to find the optimal combination of conditions for multidisciplinary interaction. Obviously, the list is far from complete, and is intended only to suggest what needs to be done. The list of major variables should be completed and sub-categories expanded. For

TABLE XII-1

VARIABLES WHICH MAY INFLUENCE THE QUALITY OF INTERACTION

I.   Mode of Interaction
   A Written
      1. Format
         a. Programmed text
         b. Case studies
         c. Reference tome
         d. Periodical
      2. Style
      3. Frequency
      4. Distribution, locus
   B. Face-to-face
      1. Agenda
         a. Format
         b. Content
      2. Number of participants
      3. Composition of dyad or group
      4. Leadership
         a. Assigned-emergent
         b. Style
         c. Duration
      5. Uniqueness-redundancy
      6. Timing
         a. Length of session
         b. Time between sessions
         c. Time of par
         d. Proximity to other meetings
      7. Location, context
II.   Content of Communication
III. Initiative for Contact
IV.   Matchmaker Role
V.   Adapter Function
VI.   Accountability for Outcomes

example, many descriptors of the dyad or group may be relevant; not only the usual demographic and background descriptors, but also motivational variables. Sherif and Sherif (1969) suggest it is important to

> look toward the people entrusted with actual conduct of inter-disciplinary ventures. Were they experts who have shown any conviction, not to mention commitment, to the advantages to be gained from such efforts? Or were they experts or technicians with visibility who were brought to lend prestige to the effort, or who happened to be in the right place at the right time, or who were seeking an avenue for academic advancement or funds? (pp. xi-xii).

In addition, a roster of moderator variables must be compiled.

No doubt, interactions will prove important, and "optimal conditions" will vary. For example, face-to-face contacts may prove generally more effective than written. However, this overall superiority may not hold for every situation. Modal advantage may vary with such factors as the age, level of training and experience of the persons involved, as well as the type of material to be presented.

Both "written" and "face-to-face" cover wide territories. Hours have been wasted arguing whether interaction would be better served by programmed texts, case studies, reference tomes, or a new journal. The relative effectiveness of these and other forms of written communication can and should be *tested*. This involves straightforward, if complex, research design. Similarly, face-to-face communication can be a number of things. In carefully designed studies, such characteristics as size of group, composition of group, leadership (assigned vs. emergent, continuous vs. shifting, Robert's Rules of Order vs. arbitrator, etc.), time in contact, redundancy of contact and time interval between sessions for redundant contacts; and agenda (prepared vs. open, formal vs. informal, Delphi vs. encounter group) must be systematically manipulated and the effects observed.

The Criterion Problem

Effects on what? One requirement of designing research is to specify dependent variables. Submitting the problem of disciplinary interaction to research analysis will require decisions regarding desired outcomes. As the independent variables are manipulated, what is to be observed, in order to judge which manipulations are most effective and beneficial?

As usual with behavioral science research, the "criterion problem" is a sticky one. According to the assignment for this chapter —and according to the verbiage of investigators and service people from any and all disciplines—the purpose of interaction, and therefore the ultimate criterion of its effectiveness, is to "help the aged." Development of measures for this criterion is an urgent need, and would itself provide the context for evaluating various approaches to interaction among investigators and service people from various disciplines.

The basic problem is that various nominal disciplines, and service and research, may not have common views of what is "good for old people" and the old may hold yet another view. This possibility is strongly suggested by consistent differences among members of these groups in regard to "adjustment" of old people to a new living situation. (Carp, 1966). Service, research and the old should develop—interactively or in parallel—indicators of well-being for old persons. If one set of indicators can represent the view of all groups, well and good; if views are indeed divergent, this fact should be recognized, and the indicators used in any program of research or service must be specifically stated. Common use of a term which means different things to different users can lead only to further confusion and misunderstanding.

Gans (1971) stresses that "policy-oriented research must also be particularly concerned with the values of all those participating in or affected by a specific policy, not only to discourage the policy designer from imposing his own or his sponsor's values on the beneficiaries of the policy, but also to make sure that the designed policy bears some relevance to the aspirations of those affected by it." (p. 31).

Here is perhaps the nub of the problem of interaction between research and service—each thinks he "knows best" what is "good for old people." Their views are similar in being paternalistic. Both probably are resented by the intended beneficiary, for exactly that reason. Research data which promise anonymity sometimes pick up reactions against what seems to old people a "mother knows best" view on the part of service staffs. Clients are dependent upon the services and tend to inhibit criticism in order not to jeopardize their availability.

Service personnel tend to perceive old people as "needing to be taken care of," and research investigators tend to react to them as sources of data. Both perceptions lead to treatment of the old as passive-dependent, even while everyone reiterates the importance of independence on the part of the old. There is no need to repeat here the documentation that old people are treated like other "inferior" minority groups in this society. (Rosow, 1962) There is a real possibility that members of this society who "do research" and "do service" are not immune from this bias. The specific form of the "put-down" by Service and by Research suggests that perceptions of old people are colored by the personal needs of the viewer. If this proves true, a more objective definition of "helping the aged" must serve as criterion.

BIBLIOGRAPHY

Allport, G. W.: *Personality: A Psychological Interpretation*. New York, Holt, 1937.

Campbell, D. T.: Ethnocentrism of disciplines and the Fish-Scale model of omniscience. In Sherif, M. and Sherif, C. W. (Eds.): *Interdisciplinary Relationships in the Social Sciences*. Chicago, Aldine Publishing Co., 1969.

Carp, F. M.: *A Future for the Aged: The Residents of Victoria Plaza*. Austin, University of Texas Press, 1966.

————: Perceptual Bias in Regard to Ethnicity, in press.

———— and DeRath, Gilbert: The picture-choice test as an indirect measure of attitudes. *J Appl Psychol, 43*:12-15, 1959.

Flyer, E. S. and Carp, F. M.: The picture test: rationale and one validation of the method. *J Appl Psychol, 46*:226-230, 1959.

Gans, H. J.: Social science for social policy. In Horowitz, I. L. (Ed.): *The Use and Abuse of Social Science*. New Brunswick, N. J., Transaction, Inc., 1971.

Luchterhand, E.: Research and the dilemmas in developing social programs. In Lazarsfeld, P. F., Sewell, W. H., and Wilensky, H. L. (Eds.): *The Uses of Sociology*. New York, Basic Books, Inc., 1967.

Mann, L.: *Social Psychology*. Sydney, Australia, John Wiley & Sons, Australasia Pty, Ltd., 1969.

Meyer, H. J., Litwak, E., Thomas E. J., and Vinter, R. D.: Social work and social welfare. In Lazarsfeld, P. F., Sewell, W. H. and Wilensky, H. L. (Eds.): *The Uses of Sociology*. New York, Basic Books, Inc., 1967.

Riley, J. W., Jr.: The sociologist in the nonacademic setting. In Lazarsfeld, P. F., Sewell, W. H. and Wilensky, H. L. (Eds.): *The Uses of Sociology*. New York, Basic Books, Inc., 1967.

Rodman, H. and Kolodny, R. L.: Organizational strains in the researcher-practitioner relationship. In Gouldner, A. W. and Miller, S. M. (Eds.): *Applied Sociology*. New York, Free Press, 1965.

Rosow, Irving: Old age: One moral dilemma of an affluent society. *Gerontologist, 2*: (4) 182-191, Dec. 1962.

Ross, R.: Moral obligations of the scientist. In Gouldner, A. W. and Miller, S. M. (Eds.): *Applied Sociology*. New York, Free Press, 1965.

Sherif, M. and Sherif, C. W.: *Interdisciplinary Relationships in the Social Sciences*. Chicago, Aldine Publishing Co., 1969.

Smelser, N. J.: *Sociology and the oher social sciences.* In Lazarsfeld, P. F., Sewell, W. H. and Wilensky, H. L. (Eds.): *The Uses of Sociology.* New York, Basic Books, Inc., 1967.

Uliassi, P. D.: The prince's counselors. In Horowitz, I. L. (Ed.): *The Use and Abuse of Social Science,* New Brunswick, N. J., Transaction, Inc., 1971.

SUBJECT INDEX

AUTHOR INDEX

369